The Language Lover's Guide to

# Learning Portuguese

Russell Walker & Rafael Tavares

# The Language Lover's Guide to Learning Portuguese

## First Edition

Published by Aberto Publishing
www.abertopublishing.co.uk

ISBN (Paperback):    978-0-9929592-0-3
ISBN (eBook):        978-0-9929592-1-0

A catalogue record for this book is available from the British Library.

The exercises in this book relate to fictional events and people and are provided purely in order to demonstrate particular grammatical features. The cartoons are also fictional and any resemblance to any actual person, living or dead, is purely coincidental.

www.learningportuguese.co.uk
www.learn-portuguese-with-rafa.com

Cover Design: Russell Walker
Cover Photo: Faro Archaeological Museum, Faro, Portugal – Russell Walker

Main Text: Russell Walker, edited by Rafael Tavares
Exercises: Rafael Tavares, edited by Russell Walker
Illustrations (Main Text): Russell Walker
Illustrations (Exercises): Rafael Tavares

Dedicated to my wife, Emily, and my daughter,
Rachael – the two most important people in my life;
and in memory of my mum, Pauline.

*– Russell.*

Dedicated to you, who is reading this work, and to all
my former, present, and future students and readers –
the ones who really challenge me and show a
passionate interest in learning this beautiful
language.

*– Rafael.*

# About the authors

***Rafael Tavares*** graduated from the University of
Aveiro, Portugal, and completed his post-graduation
at King's College London, UK. He is the author,
editor and publisher of the very popular website
www.learn-portuguese-with-rafa.com, and has
developed a Computer Assisted Language Learning
program – www.rafas-vocabulary-ticker.com. At the
time of writing, he is spending his time in both
Portugal and Brazil, heading to Mozambique and
East Timor as his next destination.

***Russell Walker*** has been studying the Portuguese
language since 2001 and helping others to learn
Portuguese since 2005. He runs the highly
successful website www.learningportuguese.co.uk,
has worked as a voluntary interpreter, and has
travelled the Portuguese-speaking world, visiting
Portugal, Madeira, Cape Verde, The Azores, and
Brazil. He lives in Peterborough, UK, with his wife,
daughter, and a pet gerbil.

# Table of Contents

# Introduction

This is not so much a language course in the traditional sense – it is more of a study companion, which attempts to explain the things that you need to know to be successful in learning Portuguese. We have used technical terms where we felt it was necessary or useful, but have always attempted to explain what they mean as understandably as possible, and have worked on the assumption that you know absolutely nothing about grammar already.

We have tried to make liberal use of the more common technical terms, because it is good not only to know what they mean, but also to become familiar with them. That way, you at least have a fighting chance when studying other reference works. We have also tried to avoid using terms that have not already been explained – so hopefully you should be able to read this through from beginning to end and gain a progressive understanding. There is also a glossary at the end for handy reference when you forget what a term means.

The main focus of this book is on European Portuguese, but Brazilian alternatives are also given. Where there is a difference between the two, the European usage is signified by 'PT' and the Brazilian by 'BR'.

At various places in the grammar section of the book, there are sets of exercises to help you consolidate what you have learned. These have been prepared by taking into account the kind of language structures needed for day-to-day circumstances, and are accompanied by English translations, so they will also help build your vocabulary.

We wish you all the best and much success in your efforts to learn the beautiful Portuguese language.

Rafael and Russell.

# Part 1 – Pronunciation

*"Then said they unto him, Say now Shibboleth: and he said Sibboleth: for he could not frame to pronounce it right. Then they took him, and slew him." – Judges 12:6*

Pronunciation is arguably the most important aspect of learning a language. Of course, you don't have to be able to pronounce everything perfectly to be understood, and it will take time to get used to the strange sounds that you have to produce.

However, it is well worth spending time on getting the pronunciation right early on, as it can be extremely difficult and frustrating to try to correct bad habits later. As Portuguese is written virtually phonetically, learning the pronunciation rules will also give you confidence to read aloud fluently – even if you don't fully understand what you are reading.

"Say now 'engarrafamento'!"

# 1. General

As a general guide, stress the penultimate (last-but-one) syllable except where there is an accent, or the word ends with a diphthong (that is, 2 vowels which are pronounced as a single syllable – explained in full later on), or if it ends with any of the following letters: i; l; r; z; im; um; ins; uns – in which case, the stress is on the last syllable.

The text under the Portuguese words that follow is a pronunciation guide, and represents an approximate phonetic equivalent of the word in English such as you might find in a phrase book (we decided not to use 'phonemes' – like a dictionary uses – because that just means you have even more stuff to learn. The pronunciation guide is based on a neutral London accent, but is also designed to be generally usable by a wide range of English and American accents).

Square brackets indicate an approximation of a sound – i.e. where it is not possible to spell the actual sound phonetically. Where you encounter these, try to merge the sound of the previous syllable with the sound given in brackets, and you should be close to the real sound. The letters 'zh' in the pronunciation guides indicate a soft 'j', which sounds like the 's' in 'measure'.

Practise saying the following words out loud, remembering to emphasise the penultimate (last-but-one) syllable except where there is an accent, or the word ends with: i; l; r; z; im; um; ins; or uns – in which case, the emphasis is on the last syllable. The syllable represented in italics is the one that should be stressed. Don't worry about what the words mean yet – just practise pronouncing them.[*]

| uma | animal | Timóteo | Garrafa | fazer | setenta | Abril |
|---|---|---|---|---|---|---|
| *oo*ma | anim*al* | Ti*mo*teoo | gar*rah*fa | faz*air* | se*ten*ta | Ab*reel* |

| olá | dedo | você | sinto | aqui | algum |
|---|---|---|---|---|---|
| oh*lah* | *de*doo | voss*eh* | *sin*too | ak*ee* | alg*oom* |

---

[*] If you visit the website, www.learningportuguese.co.uk, you can hear these words (and many of the ones that follow) being spoken by a native Portuguese.

# 2. Diacritics

Diacritical marks are extra symbols that are placed above or below a letter to modify the pronunciation or clarify the meaning of a word. Their usage in Portuguese will be described in more detail as we come across them later, but to give you an overview, here is a list of all of the diacritical marks that are used in written Portuguese:

| Table 2.1: Portuguese diacritical marks | |
| --- | --- |
| ~ | Tilde (or 'squiggle'). Used to denote a nasal sound. |
| ´ | Acute. Stress is placed on this syllable, and the vowel sound is open (more about this in a minute!). |
| ^ | Circumflex (or caret, or 'little hat'). Stress is placed on this syllable and the vowel sound is closed (also explained below). |
| ` | Grave (pronounced 'grahve' – rhymes with 'halve'). Usually denotes 2 words squashed into 1 with the loss of a letter (typically a + as = às), but does not really affect pronunciation. |
| .. | Diaeresis (or 'two little dots'). Also known as an umlaut, although technically that is wrong in this case (but the symbol is the same). Appears over a 'u' to denote that the preceding 'q' should be pronounced 'kw' instead of 'k', or that the preceding 'g' should be pronounced 'gw' instead of 'g' (see consonant pronunciation section). Never used in Portugal, and now officially removed from the language in Brazil (since the orthographic agreement went into effect in 2009), except for personal names and imported words and their derivations – still, it is sometimes used by Brazilians, so you need to be aware of it. |
| ، | Cedilla (or 'little 5'). Only appears on the letter 'c' to denote soft pronunciation – like an 's' rather than a 'k'. |

Acutes and circumflexes indicate that the syllable on which they appear should be stressed (grave, diaeresis and cedilla do not indicate stress, tilde only indicates stress in words ending with ã – which are always nasal).

# 3. Vowels

There are 4 defined 'qualities' of Portuguese vowels, known as open, closed, reduced, and nasal. These are not really hard-and-fast rules of pronunciation, more a categorisation of the ranges of sound that the vowels can represent. It is important to recognise these distinctions, because certain words rely on them to make their meaning clear. For example, the word 'jogo' can mean either 'game' or 'I play', depending on whether the pronunciation of the first 'o' is open or closed. The basic ranges of sounds for these vowel qualities are set out in the following table:

**Table 3.1: Portuguese vowel qualities**

| Vowel | Open Pronunciation | Closed Pronunciation | Reduced Pronunciation | Nasal Pronunciation |
|---|---|---|---|---|
| a | The range of sounds between the 'a' in 'father' to the 'a' in 'cat'. | The range from the 'a' in 'cat' to the 'a' in 'postman'. | The range from the 'a' in 'postman' to virtually silent. | Pronounced through the nose, similar to 'an' in 'angry'. |
| e | Ranging from the 'e' in 'chalet' to the 'e' in 'net'. | Ranging from the 'e' in 'net' to the first 'e' in 'people' (often pronounced as a sort of cross between the 'ea' of 'ear' and the 'ai' of 'air' – requires careful listening practice!). | From the first 'e' in 'people' to the 'e' in 'payment' through to virtually silent. | Similar to 'an' in 'angel', although keeping a hint of the open 'e' sound, and pronounced through the nose. Can also be pronounced like 'en' in 'engine' if there is a circumflex (^) over the 'e'. Note: the letters 'en' are *never* pronounced like the 'en' in 'rendez-vous'. |
| i | Like 'i' in 'simple', but with a very slightly longer sound (tending towards the 'ee' of 'free'). No distinction is made between open, closed, and reduced. Note: the letter 'i' is never pronounced like the 'i' in 'like'. | | | Similar to 'En' in 'England'. |

| Vowel | Open Pronunciation | Closed Pronunciation | Reduced Pronunciation | Nasal Pronunciation |
|---|---|---|---|---|
| **o** | like 'o' in 'hot'. | From the 'oa' in 'coal' to the 'o' in 'look'. | like 'o' in 'who', but a very weak sound, almost like the 'u' in 'rightful'. As with other reduced vowels, it can range to virtually silent. | similar to 'on' in 'long'. |
| **u** | Like the last 'u' in 'kung fu'. No distinction is made between open, closed, and reduced. | | | Similar to 'un' in 'lung', but more of an 'oo' than an 'uh'. |

Knowing when to use what type of vowel is to a large extent dependent on practice, but there are some rules that can help you. If a vowel has a circumflex over it (^), it must be pronounced using the closed quality. If it has an acute accent (slanting upwards like this: ´ ), you must use the open quality – usually the acute é is pronounced as more of an 'ay'.

A tilde (˜) over a vowel indicates a nasal pronunciation, as does the letter m or n following the vowel (note that an 'n' or 'm' can follow a vowel which has an acute or circumflex accent over it – in which case both the nasal and open or closed qualities should be evident in the way you pronounce it).

When a word ends with a vowel, or starts with an 'e', you would normally use the reduced quality unless there is an accent to indicate otherwise – however, an 'e' at the end of a word, followed by a vowel at the start of the next word, normally requires the 'e' to become more closed – like the 'e' in 'people' (this is for ease of articulation).

So bearing in mind these principles, the following is a rather rough guide to get you started on pronouncing Portuguese vowels. With listening practice, you will be able to hone your pronunciation skills and will hopefully improve naturally as time goes by.

### Table 3.2: Portuguese vowel pronunciation

| a | like 'a' in 'cat' except when on the stressed syllable, when it is more like the 'a' in 'father'. |
|---|---|
| â | like 'a' in 'cat'. |
| á | sometimes like the 'a' in 'cat', sometimes like the 'a' in 'father'. |
| ã | similar to 'an' in 'angry'. |
| e | like 'e' in 'net' except when used as a word on its own without an accent or at the end of a word which is followed by a word that starts with a vowel, when it is pronounced like 'e' in 'people', or if it is followed by another vowel (in the same word), when it is more like the 'e' in 'chalet' (more of an 'ay' than an 'e'). |
| ê | like 'e' in 'net', or a cross between the 'ea' of 'ear' and the 'ai' of 'air'. |
| êm | like a more nasal version of the 'en' in 'engine'. |
| é | like 'e' in 'net', or like the 'e' in 'chalet'. |
| ém | like 'an' in 'angel'. |
| em | like 'an' in 'angel'. |
| i | like 'i' in simple, but with a very slightly longer sound (tending towards the 'ee' of 'free'). |
| o | usually like 'o' in 'hot' when stressed, but when on its own or at the end of a word, it is like a weak version of the 'o' in 'who'. Use of the closed quality (like the 'oa' in 'coal') is often impossible to determine except by careful listening practice – unless of course the circumflex (^) is used. |
| ó | like 'o' in 'hot'. |
| ô | like 'oa' in 'coal'. |
| u | like the last 'u' in 'kung fu'. |

A weak sound, such as produced when pronouncing reduced Portuguese vowels 'a' and 'e' is indicated in the pronunciation guides below by using superscript type (i.e. small and high like this). Reduced 'o' is represented by the letter 'u' (or sometimes 'oo'), because the English pronunciation of a 'u' is very similar to the Portuguese reduced 'o', but remember to weaken the sound of the vowel slightly. When a word starts or ends with an unstressed 'e', the vowel is usually dropped almost completely, and this is indicated below by the vowel being crossed out.

Where letters are enclosed in square brackets [like this], the sound of those letters should be merged with the sound of the previous letter or syllable. This is in an effort to try to represent sounds that don't exist in normal English usage.

Vowels that are followed by m or n, or have a tilde (~) over them are pronounced nasally, and this is represented in the pronunciation guides by '[ng]'. European Portuguese tend to slur a lot, making the language sound 'slushy' – almost drunken! Brazilians are a lot crisper and clearer, and they never drop reduced vowels completely.

| falo | livro | vendedor | o | tenho | gostamos |
|------|-------|----------|---|-------|----------|
| *fah*lu | *li[ee]*vru | vende*dor* | oo | *te[ay]*nyu | gosht*am*ᵒᵒsh |
| open 'a', reduced 'o'. | reduced 'o'. | closed 'e', closed 'e', open 'o'. | reduced 'o'. | open and nasal 'e', reduced 'o'. | reduced 'o', open (and slightly nasal) 'a', reduced 'o'. |

| guerra | filha | casa | avó | avô | você |
|--------|-------|------|-----|-----|------|
| *gai*rra | *fil*ya | *kah*za | av*oh* | avo*[ah]* | vo*sseh* |
| reduced 'a'. | reduced 'a'. | open 'a', reduced 'a'. | reduced 'a', open 'o'. | reduced 'a', closed 'o'. | open 'o', closed 'e'. |

## Diphthongs

Any pair of vowels that is pronounced as a single syllable is a diphthong. Not all diphthongs have accents on them – so don't be fooled into thinking that accents have anything to do with whether a vowel is part of a diphthong. Where two vowels have one sound, they form a diphthong. That's it.

Note: In all the following examples, 'ow' should be pronounced as in 'cow', not as in 'throw'

| | |
|---|---|
| **ão** | ow[ng] |
| **au** | ow |
| **ao** | ow (there is no discernible difference between the pronunciation of 'au' and 'ao') |
| **õe** | oi[ng] |
| **oi** | oi |
| **ãe** | aye[ng] |
| **ai** | aye (note, 'ai' is not always a diphthong. It is not a diphthong if it appears before a 'z' at the end of a word, before an 'nh' anywhere in a word, or before 'l', 'r', 'm' or 'n' if the consonant does not start a new syllable – don't worry too much about that though, I'm just being pedantic!) |
| **ou** | 'o' like in 'hot', but a little bit more drawn out (tending towards the 'o' in 'flow'). Note: This is very often mispronounced by the English! The temptation is to pronounce it like 'oo' in 'food', but this is wrong! |
| **ei** | 'a' like in 'hay' |

The following two diphthongs are only used to affect the pronunciation of a preceding consonant 'g'; or 'q'. Where a different consonant precedes the vowel pair, or a diaeresis (2 little dots) is used over the 'u', they are not diphthongs – both vowels must be pronounced.

| | |
|---|---|
| **ui** | same as the pronunciation of the Portuguese vowel 'i' (only a diphthong when used straight after a 'g', or 'q') |
| **ue** | same as the pronunciation of the Portuguese vowel 'e' (only a diphthong when used straight after a 'g', or 'q') |

The 'u' must effectively be ignored when it comes between the 'g' or 'q' and the vowel 'e' or 'i' (e.g., G*u*erra, G*u*itarra, G*u*ilherme, G*u*ilhotina). More on this in the consonants section, coming up next.

Note: Technically 'eu' and 'iu' are regarded as diphthongs, but personally I prefer to think of them as 2 separate vowels because they sound more like 2 separate syllables to me – albeit they are slurred together (e.g. 'eu' is pronounced almost like 'ayu').

The following words include some vowel pairs which are not diphthongs – to give you practice in both.

| então | foi | mãe | mau | mão | Paulo | pai |
|---|---|---|---|---|---|---|
| ent*ow[ng]* | foy | my[ng] | mow | mow[ng] | *Pow*lu | pie |

| falei | outro | pois | apoio | cães | região | |
|---|---|---|---|---|---|---|
| fa*lay* | *oh*tru | poysh | a*poy*u | kai[ng]sh | rezhi*ow[ng]* | |

| ruim | rainha | raiz | confusões | | pouco |
|---|---|---|---|---|---|
| ru*im[ng]* | rai*ny*a | ra*eezj* | confuz*oy[ng]sh* | | *poh*ku |

The words 'rainha' and 'raiz' use the 'ai' pairing, but are not diphthongs (were you paying attention?). There are not many words like that, so I'm being a bit mean really by throwing those two in! Most of the time that you come across 'ai', it will be pronounced like the 'ie' in 'pie'.

The Portuguese language also contains a few triphthongs – three vowels pronounced as a single syllable. Usually this is in the form of 'uei' following a 'g' or 'q' (e.g. 'queijo'), where the sound is the same as the diphthong 'ei'.

# 4. Consonants

Mostly the same as English, but…

| c | Soft (like in 'lace') if followed by an 'e' or 'i', otherwise hard (as in 'cold'). The only exception is where a cedilla is used ('ç') – which forces it to be pronounced softly even though the letter following is not 'e' or 'i' (note, the cedilla must not be used if the following letter is either 'e' or 'i'). |
|---|---|

| causar | aceitável | acabar | nação | criança | cuidar | alcança |
|---|---|---|---|---|---|---|
| kow*zar* | asay*tah*vel | aka*bar* | nas*sow[ng]* | kri*an*sa | kwi*dar* | al*kan*sa |

| g | Soft if followed by an 'e' or an 'i' (the same as a soft 'j' – like the 's' in 'measure'), otherwise hard (as in 'gold'). If the 'g' is followed by the letters 'ui' or 'ue', the 'u' is only there to 'harden' what would otherwise be a soft 'g' – the 'u' is therefore silent (or rather, it joins with the 'e' or 'i' to form a diphthong). Occasionally (in Brazilian Portuguese), you might still find a 'u' with a diaeresis (ü) following a 'g' (or a 'q')*. This signifies that the 'u' is not silent. A natural consequence of placing a vowel after a pronounced 'u' is that the 'gu' sounds like 'gw'. |
|---|---|

| ganhar | guiando | guardar | agir | gelo | água |
|---|---|---|---|---|---|
| gan*yar* | gee*yan*du | gwar*dar* | a*zhir* | *zhe*lu | *ah*gwa |

| lingüística (BR) | guerra | fugir | gato |
|---|---|---|---|
| ling*wish*tica | *gair*ra | foo*zhir* | *gah*tu |

| h | Silent if at the start of a word; pronounced like a 'y' if it comes after an 'l' or 'n'. Can be used with 'c' to form 'ch' which is pronounced 'sh'. Never pronounced like the typical English usage! |
|---|---|

| tenho | chuva | há | houve | falha |
|---|---|---|---|---|
| te*[ay]ny*u | *shoo*va | a | *oh*ve | *fal*-ya |

---

* Under the new Portuguese spelling agreement the diaeresis (ü) must not be used anymore.

| **j** | Always soft – like the 's' in 'measure'. |
|---|---|

| jogar | jantar | lojas | julgar | queijo |
|---|---|---|---|---|
| zho*gar* | zhan*tar* | *lozh*ash | zhul*gar* | *kay*-zhoo |

| **m/n** | When at the end of a word, 'm' is pronounced nasally, almost like 'ng' or 'ny'. Rather than close the lips (like you would in English), try to kind of swallow the ending. When words that end with 'm' are made plural, the 'm' is replaced with an 'n' (e.g. 'jovem' becomes 'jovens') – but still with the same nasal quality. |
|---|---|

| sim | tem | fazem | bom | jovens | bens |
|---|---|---|---|---|---|
| sim[ng] | taym[ng] | *faz*aym[ng] | bom[ng] | *zho*vayn[g]sh | bayn[g]sh |

| uns | trabalham | vantagem | fim | matar | mora |
|---|---|---|---|---|---|
| un[g]sh | tra*baly*am[ng] | van*tazh*aym[ng] | fim[ng] | ma*tar* | *mor*a |

| alguns | viagens |
|---|---|
| al*gun[g]sh* | vee*yah*zhen[g]sh |

| **q** | Like in English, 'q' is always followed by 'u' in Portuguese. If an unaccented 'e' or 'i' follows the 'u' (which is quite common), pronounce like 'k', otherwise 'kw'. If the 'u' has a diaeresis accent (ü), the 'q' should be pronounced 'kw' despite the following 'e' or 'i'. This rule is not always followed by European Portuguese (as they never use a diaeresis, whereas Brazilians sometimes do, even though it is no longer officially part of the language). |
|---|---|

| quer | qual | porque | que | conseqüências (BR) | quem |
|---|---|---|---|---|---|
| kair | kwal | *por*ke | keh or ke | konse*kwens*iash | kaym[ng] |

| r | 'Rolled', or flicked off the tongue (except at the end of a word) – more vigorously for a double 'r'. This is particularly difficult to achieve when in full flow, but for most people will come with practice. Brazilians tend to pronounce it like a guttural 'h', which is a lot easier and an acceptable alternative if you really can't manage to rrrrrrrrrr. When a word ends with 'r', some European Portuguese speakers add an 'e' sound to the end. |
|---|---|

| respeito | terra | grupo | parar | engarrafamento |
|---|---|---|---|---|
| rresh*pay*tu | *terr*rrrrra | *grroop*u | par*rar* | engarrrrrafa*men*tu |

| s | Pronounced 'sh' or like a soft 'j' if it immediately precedes a consonant (even if the consonant is the start of the next word) or if used at the very end of a sentence (Brazilian pronunciation however, is just like an English 's' in these circumstances). When situated between 2 vowels (even if the following vowel is at the start of the next word), it is pronounced like a 'z'. At all other times, it is a simple 's' sound. |
|---|---|

| casa | Cascais | senhor | desde | espera | resmungar |
|---|---|---|---|---|---|
| *kah*za | Kash*kaish* | sen*yor* | *dezh*de | esh*per*ra | rrrezhmun*gar* |

| meus | esposa | lembrar-se | as outras pessoas | reveses |
|---|---|---|---|---|
| *may*oosh | esh*poza* | laym[ng]b*rar*se | az *oh*trash pess-*oh*-ash | rev*e*sezh |

| v | Should be pronounced like in English, but often mutates to a 'b' especially by the northern Portuguese. This is due to lazy articulation – much the same as many English will mutate 'th' to 'f' or 'v'. |
|---|---|

| x | There aren't really any rules governing the pronunciation of 'x'! Some of its forms: j; sh; ks; s; z. If in doubt, pronounce it like a slushy mixture of a soft 'j' and 'sh'. For the most part, you just have to learn by exposure. It normally takes the form that is easiest to articulate for the given word, so you can usually take a fairly good guess. |
|---|---|

| táxi | baixo | excelente | exemplo | conexão | próximo |
|---|---|---|---|---|---|
| *tax*i | *by*-shu | eshe*len*te | e*zem*plu | konek*sow[ng]* | *pross*imu |

| z | If at the end of a word (with no vowel following at the start of the next word), pronounce like a soft 'j'. Otherwise, like the English 'z'. |
|---|---|

| trazer | faz | eficaz | limpeza |
|---|---|---|---|
| tra*zair* | fa*zh* | efi*cazh* | lim*pe[ay]*za |

People from certain parts of Brazil have a habit of pronouncing the letters 'de' and 'di' as a hard 'j' (like the English 'j'), so they say things like 'Bom jia'. Similarly, they often pronounce the letters 'te' and 'ti' like the 'ch' in 'chair'.

# 5. Practise!

Here is a mixture of words without a pronunciation guide, for you to practise on:

| gostamos | falar | reunião | almoço | menino | querem | foi |
|----------|-------|---------|--------|--------|--------|-----|

| palavra | carro | regiões | quente | embora | porém | fez |
|---------|-------|---------|--------|--------|-------|-----|

| ganhar | secreção | hotel | resguardar | enquanto | sempre | qualidade |
|--------|----------|-------|------------|----------|--------|-----------|

| engarrafamento | excelentíssimo | perspectivo | perspicácia |
|----------------|----------------|-------------|-------------|

Some techniques:

Practise reading Portuguese books or web pages – and when you do so, try to read aloud if at all possible. Read slowly enough to be able to pronounce every word clearly – don't be tempted to rush, as clarity is more important, and your speed will naturally increase over time anyway. Also listen carefully to educated native Portuguese speakers whenever you get the opportunity. Note the inflection in their voice, their rhythm and intonation, and of course their pronunciation. Try to copy the accent by doing an impression of a native speaker whose voice you are familiar with. Imagine the sound of that person talking, and try to read in the way that he or she would.

As with any language, those who are familiar with it will tend to neglect the formal rules of pronunciation. Sometimes, modifications of pronunciation become common and are even adopted as the standard pronunciation. For example, it is quite common to hear Portuguese speakers say 'tá' instead of 'está' – the 'sh' sound gets lost completely. These variations and peculiarities will gradually become apparent as you hear more of the spoken language.

A lot of beginners worry that if their accent sounds too authentic, people will assume that they are fluent and fire a barrage of rapid Portuguese at them. Even if this does happen, try to view it as a compliment! As long as you know how to say 'I don't understand' ('não entendo'), it doesn't really matter if people mistake you for a native (which is unlikely anyway!) – it is much better to sound as authentic as you can, because this makes you much more understandable. Just think about how difficult it is for any of us to understand a foreign person who has a very strong accent! Your efforts to mimic the accent will be appreciated by those you talk to.

# Part 2 – First Conversations

*"Things should be made as simple as possible, but
not any simpler." – Albert Einstein*

Although this is not a traditional language course, it is worth introducing a few words
and phrases. The first words you are likely to need to use in Portuguese are simple
greetings and basic manners. Read through the word lists on the following pages, and
practise saying them aloud.

# 6. Basic Greetings

## Table 6.1: Basic Greetings

| English | Portuguese | Pronunciation/Notes |
|---|---|---|
| Hello | Olá | *Olah* – This is quite an informal greeting. |
| How are you? (formal) | Como está? Como vai? | *Komu eshta?* / *Komo vye?* – You often say things differently depending on whether you are speaking formally or informally. Speak formally to people you meet for the first time, people older than you, or as a general sign of respect. |
| How are you? (informal) | Como estás? | *Komu eshtazh?* – This is the informal variation, which is only used with people you know well, family members, children, or people significantly younger than yourself. |
| I'm OK, thank you. | Estou bem, obrigado/a | *Eshtoh baym[ng], Obrigahdu/a* – lit. 'I am well, thank you.' This is perhaps the most common response to the above question. For 'thank you', men say 'obrigado', women say 'obrigada' (regardless of whether the person they are talking to is male or female). More on this later. |
| I am fine | Estou ó[p]timo/a | *Eshtoh ohtimu/a* – note that the 'p' in 'óptimo' (fine) is virtually silent (the Brazilian spelling, without a 'p', was adopted in the Portuguese orthographic agreement, so technically it should be omitted when writing). Again, whether to use 'ótimo' or 'ótima' depends on your own gender. |
| Is everything OK? | Tudo bem? | *Toodu baym[ng]?* – lit. 'everything well?' Note: This is probably the most common greeting in Portuguese – it is used much more frequently than 'como está?' (this is true in Portugal, despite it being a Brazilian expression). |
| Yes (all is OK) | Tudo [bem] | *Toodu* – lit. 'everything [well].' The 'bem' is optional when replying to the above question. |

| English | Portuguese | Pronunciation/Notes |
|---------|------------|---------------------|
| Not too bad | Mais ou menos | *Myze* oh *men*ush – lit. 'more or less.' Use this response if you want to indicate that you are a little 'under the weather'. |
| Pleased to meet you | Prazer | Pra*zair* – lit. 'pleasure.' |
| Very pleased to meet you | Muito prazer | M[ng]*wee*[ng]tu Pra*zair* – lit. 'much pleasure.' The word 'muito' has a very nasal sound, which kind of breaks the rules of pronunciation! Sometimes it can sound more like 'moitu', depending on the accent of the speaker. |
| Good Morning | Bom dia | Bom[ng] *dee*ya – lit. 'Good day' – a slightly more formal greeting than Olá – generally used up until noon. |
| Good Afternoon | Boa tarde | *Bo*a *tar*de (after midday). |
| Good Evening / Good Night | Boa noite | *Bo*a *noit*e – note that the same word, noite, is used for both evening and night. Switch from saying 'boa tarde' to 'boa noite' around sunset. |
| Note: You can mix Olá with bom dia, boa tarde, or boa noite to make another fairly informal greeting (e.g. Olá, bom dia) |||
| Goodbye | Adeus | A*day*ush – lit. 'To God'. Note that you can use bom dia, boa tarde, and boa noite to say goodbye as well. |
| 'Seeya' | Tchau/Chau | Chow – this is a Brazilian expression (an orthographical adaptation of the Italian word 'ciao', probably introduced to Brazil by Italian immigrants), but is widely used by Portuguese as well (some people also spell it 'Xau'). |
| See you later (same day) | Até logo | A*tay log*u – lit. 'until straight away', which doesn't really make sense, but then neither do a lot of things in Portuguese! |
| See you later (another day) | Até amanhã | A*tay* aman[ng]*yah* – lit. 'until tomorrow' – used even if you won't actually see the person for a few days. |

| English | Portuguese | Pronunciation/Notes |
|---------|-----------|---------------------|
| See you soon | Até já | A*tay* zhah – lit. 'until already' – you get the idea! |
| See you next time | Até a próxima | A*tay* a *pross*ima. |
| Yes | Sim | Sim[ng]. |
| No | Não | Now[ng] – can also mean 'not' or 'don't'. |
| Please | Se faz favor | Se fazh fa*vor* – often shortened to 'faz favor'. |
| | Por favor | Por fa*vor* – another alternative. |
| Thank you | Obrigado | Obri*gah*du – only said by males.* |
| | Obrigada | Obri*gah*da – only said by females.* |
| Thank you very much | Muito obrigado/a | Moo*i[ng]t*oo Obri*gah*du/a. |

To say 'you're welcome' (as a response to 'thank you') in Portuguese is 'de nada' (literally, 'of nothing' – which doesn't seem to make sense, but there you go). In other circumstances (e.g. when someone arrives at your home), 'welcome' would be 'bem vindo/a' (or more formally to a large group 'boas vindas'). The verb 'to welcome' is 'acolher'.

---

* There is some debate about the correct usage of the words obrigado and obrigada. The usage indicated above is by far the most common way the words are used, that is, men always say obrigado and women always say obrigada. This usage implies that the word is being used as an adjective to describe the one speaking (literally meaning 'obliged' – I am obliged to you for the favour).

Technically, it can be argued that the word obrigado, when used on its own to say 'thank you', is an interjection, not an adjective (in the same way that the word 'hello' is an interjection). Under this school of thought, both men and women should say obrigado regardless of whether they are addressing a man or a woman. Whilst this is probably the 'correct' usage, it is hardly ever encountered. Of course, if you are male, it doesn't really matter as you would say obrigado anyway.

In some regions, particularly the Algarve, it is common for both men and women to use both obrigado and obrigada – switching between them depending on the gender of the person they are talking to. However, this usage does not seem to have any rational technical explanation! I would therefore recommend against that usage unless you happen to live in a region where the locals would be offended if you addressed them differently.

# 7. Introductions

| Table 7.1 Introductions | | |
|---|---|---|
| *English* | *Portuguese* | *Pronunciation/Notes* |
| My name is… | Chamo me… | *Sham*u-m^e… – lit. 'I call myself…' |
| | O meu nome é… | ^oo *may*u *nom*e eh – lit. 'the my name is…' |
| What is your name? | Como se chama? | *Kom*u s^e-*sham*a? – lit. 'How do you call yourself?' |
| | Qual é o seu nome? | Kwal eh ^oo *say*u *nom*e? – lit. 'What is the your name?' |
| This is… | Este é… | *Esht*^e eh… (when introducing a male). |
| | Esta é… | *Esh*ta eh… (when introducing a female). |
| my wife | a minha esposa | a *min*ya esh*poz*a – lit. 'the my spouse' |
| | a minha mulher | a *min*ya mul*yair* – lit. 'the my woman' – 'mulher' is usually used to refer to your own wife, whereas 'esposa' can be used for your own, or someone else's wife. |
| my husband | o meu marido | ^oo *may*u ma*ree*du – lit. 'the my husband' |
| my girlfriend | a minha namorada | a *min*ya namo*rah*da – lit. 'the my girlfriend' – when used by a male (or gay female) referring to his (or her) female partner. |
| | a minha amiga | a *min*ya a*mee*ga – lit. 'the my friend' – when used to refer to a female friend without necessarily implying a romantic relationship. |
| my boyfriend | o meu namorado | ^oo *may*u namo*rah*du – lit. 'the my boyfriend'. |
| a friend | um amigo | oom[ng] a*mee*gu – a male friend. |
| | uma amiga | oom[ng]a a*mee*ga – a female friend. |

| English | Portuguese | Pronunciation/Notes |
|---|---|---|
| Do you speak English? | Fala Inglês? | *Fah*la Ing*le[a]ysh*? – Although the 'ê' sometimes sounds more open ('ay'), the circumflex still denotes that it should be a closed pronunciation. Listen carefully to a native speaker – the sound is like a cross between the 'ea' of 'ear' and the 'ai' of 'air'. The same is true of the words 'Inglesa'; 'Português'; and 'Portuguesa'. |
| I am learning Portuguese | Eu estou a aprender Português | *Ay*$^{oo}$ esh*toh* a apren*der* Port$^{oo}$*ge[a]y*sh. |
| I am English | Sou Inglês | Soh Ing*le[a]ysh* – only said by males. |
| | Sou Inglesa | Soh Ing*le[a]yz*a – only said by females. |
| I am Portuguese | Sou Português | Soh Port$^{oo}$*ge[a]ysh* – only said by males. |
| | Sou Portuguesa | Soh Port$^{oo}$*ge[a]yz*a – only said by females. |
| I am from England | Sou da Inglaterra | Soh da Ingla*terr*a – lit. 'I am from the England.' |
| I am from The USA | Sou dos Estados Unidos | Soh dos ~~E~~*shta*hdos Oo*nee*dos – lit. 'I am from the States United.' |
| I am from Australia | Sou da Austrália | Soh da Aoosh*trah*leea – lit. 'I am from the Australia.' |
| I am from Portugal | Sou de Portugal | Soh de Port$^{oo}$*gal* – they don't say 'from *the* Portugal' (like they do with England), just 'from Portugal' (like we do). Most other countries of the world require 'from *the*' ('do' or 'da' depending on the gender of the country – see section on nouns below). |
| Where are you from? | De onde é? | Di-*yon*dee-yeh? |
| in England | na Inglaterra | na Ingla*terr*ra – lit. 'in the England' |
| in Portugal | em Portugal | aym[ng] Portu*gal*. |
| I am from London | Sou de Londres | Soh de *Lon*dr$^{e}$sh. |
| Sorry! | Desculpe! | Desh*cool*pe! |

| English | Portuguese | Pronunciation/Notes |
|---|---|---|
| I am sorry | Lamento | La*men*tu – lit. 'I lament' (use this to sympathise with someone who has had some bad news). |
| | Peço desculpas | *Pess*u Desh*culp*ªsh – lit. 'I ask for excuses'. |
| Excuse me | Com licença | Com[ng] li*sen*sa – lit. 'with permission'. This is often said as a parting formality – for example, as a polite way to end a telephone conversation, or to walk away from a group conversation. |
| I don't understand | não entendo/não percebo | now[ng] en*ten*du / now[ng] per*sseb*u – lit. 'not I understand'. |
| so then | então | en*tow[ng]* – lit. 'then', but used frequently in places where English would say 'so', or 'right then'. A useful word for linking to a new subject without appearing too abrupt. |
| you (formal singular) | você | vos*seh* – A formal way of addressing someone (in Brazil they use você informally as well). |
| | o senhor | ᵒᵒ sen*yor* – lit. 'the gentleman.' |
| | a senhora | a sen*yor*a – lit. 'the lady.'<br><br>Note, the Portuguese generally speak more formally than the English, so although referring to someone as 'the lady' or 'the gentleman' would sound rather pompous to us, it is quite common in Portuguese. Senhor/Senhora can also mean sir/madam, Mr/Mrs ('Miss' would be 'a menina', or 'Senhorita'), or Lord/Lady. |
| I | eu | *A*yu / Eh-oo |
| he | ele | *ehl*e – the first 'e' is very closed, almost like an English 'i', whereas the second 'e' is barely audible (so it sounds almost like you are saying 'ill'). |

| English | Portuguese | Pronunciation/Notes |
|---|---|---|
| she | ela | *ehl*a |
| What do you do? | O que é que faz? | Okee *eh* kuh fazh? – lit. 'What is it that you do?' |
| I am a lawyer | Sou advogado | Soh advo*gah*du |
| I am a student | Sou estudante | Soh eshtu*dant* |
| I am unemployed at the moment | Estou desempregado neste momento | Esh*toh* dezempre*gah*du *nesh*tuh mo*men*tu |

# Part 3 – Grammar

*"Nothing in life is to be feared, it is only to be understood." – Marie Curie*

We have some good news and some bad news. Let's get the bad news out of the way first: if you are really going to get to grips with a language beyond the basics, you need to understand at least some grammar. Sorry, but there it is. Some people protest that you can learn a language just by being exposed to it, without having to learn the rules. This may be true, but the likelihood is that you will not have sufficient exposure to make a difference unless you go and live in a country where the language is spoken. Unless you can do that, the only way you are really going to make progress is to study and understand the grammar of your own language, and see how this compares with the grammar of the language you are learning.

The good news is that grammar is not really that difficult. There are some big words to get your head around, and quite a few rules, but if you are willing to put some effort into thinking about their practical application, it does all make sense. You just need to be realistic: it takes a few *years* to get to grips with a language.

Many language courses assume you are already familiar with grammar in your own language. Reference books, whilst enumerating the rules, don't always explain what they mean. The result of this is that people tend to gloss over grammar when learning a new language, and this makes the whole process a lot more difficult. A little extra effort to learn about grammar early on will make life a lot easier later on. Although it might seem like a lot to remember, you will find that with practice it just becomes second-nature, and you won't even have to think about it.

OK, pep talk over.

# 8. Introduction

To understand the structure of language in general, it is necessary to be able to identify the different types of word that make up a sentence. Strictly speaking, sentences are made up of 'clauses', clauses are made up of 'phrases', and phrases are made up of words, but don't worry about this – for our purposes, we will ignore phrases and clauses, and just refer to words and sentences because this is more understandable to the average reader.

Despite receiving a normal secondary education, and perhaps even scoring high marks in English, many adults find it difficult to define adverbs, adjectives, prepositions, etc. Maybe they didn't teach us very well, maybe they did but we weren't paying attention, or maybe we just forgot.

In any case, let's assume that you, as a reader are completely unaware of the difference between nouns, verbs, adverbs, adjectives, pronouns, etc. Apologies if any of this sounds patronising, but if, like many of us, you didn't learn this stuff at school (or forgot), then this will all be uncharted territory…

*Time for a snooze?*

# 9. Nouns and Articles

A noun is an identifier, so just check whether the word identifies what something or someone is. The thing identified by a noun can be tangible – like 'chair', 'door', 'car', 'book'; or it can be abstract – like 'thought', 'desire', 'mystery', 'effort'.

Sometimes, an identifier can consist of more than one word (e.g. 'beer bottle', 'car door'), in which case the group of words that make up the identifier is known as a 'noun phrase'.

Nouns can always be preceded by the definite or indefinite article (i.e. the word 'the' or 'a(n)' or 'some'), so if it does not make sense to use 'the' or 'a' before the word, it is likely not a noun. For example, take the word 'went' – it does not make sense to say 'the went', so 'went' is not a noun. Whereas, 'the concept' does make sense, so 'concept' is a noun.

Proper nouns are similar in that they act as identifiers, it's just that they define a particular instance of a noun – i.e. names (e.g., Fred, Emily, Tuesday, London). Proper nouns always start with a capital letter in English so they are usually easy to identify.

In Portuguese, nouns are either masculine or feminine. Unless you have studied another language before, this may seem a little odd because in English we only apply gender to people or animals unless speaking rhetorically.

The distinction as to which nouns are masculine and which are feminine is fairly arbitrary, but as a general rule, if the word ends with 'a' or 'ção' (equivalent to the English ending 'tion') or 'ade' or 'gem', it is usually feminine, and if it ends with an 'o', or 'l', or 'r' or 'á' (a-acute), it is usually masculine. Other endings can be masculine or feminine, and you just have to learn them as you come across them.

So what? Well, definite and indefinite articles, as well as adjectives have to 'agree' with the noun to which they relate – both in terms of gender, and plurality. What does this mean in practice? There are 4 (count 'em!) Portuguese words for 'the'. The one you use depends on whether the noun is masculine or feminine, and whether you are referring to one or more than one item.

| Table 9.1: The Portuguese definite article | |
| --- | --- |
| *Portuguese* | *English* |
| o | the (masculine singular) |
| os | the (masculine plural) |
| a | the (feminine singular) |
| as | the (feminine plural) |

A similar rule applies to the indefinite article:

| Table 9.2: The Portuguese indefinite article | |
| --- | --- |
| *Portuguese* | *English* |
| um | a or an (masculine) |
| uns | some (masculine plural) |
| uma | a or an (feminine) |
| umas | some (feminine) |

Take for example, the word 'livro' which means 'book'. This is a masculine noun, so when referring to one particular book ('the book'), you would say 'o livro', whereas to refer to a few books ('some books'), you would say 'uns livros'. To say 'the houses', which is feminine, would be 'as casas'.

The best way to learn which nouns are masculine and which are feminine is to learn the word along with the definite or indefinite article. There's no time like the present, so here are some nouns for you to learn:

**Table 9.3: Examples of Portuguese nouns**

| Portuguese | English |
|---|---|
| o amor | the love |
| a árvore | the tree |
| o banho | the bath |
| a bebida | the drink |
| a caneta | the pen |
| o carro | the car |
| a casa | the house |
| a comida | the food |
| o computador | the computer |
| a cortina | the curtain |
| o escritório | the office |
| a explicação | the explanation |
| o fim | the end |
| a flor | the flower |
| o gato | the cat |
| a idéia | the idea |
| o início | the beginning |
| o livro | the book |
| o país | the country |
| o pensamento | the thought |
| os sentimentos | the feelings |
| a televisão | the television |

## Confusing Nouns

Although the vast majority of nouns that end with 'o' are masculine, and the vast majority that end with 'a' are feminine, there are some that don't follow that rule, so it is easy to get caught out and use the wrong gender for the definite or indefinite article (or for an adjective – more on those later).

Sometimes this is because the noun is shortened and the long version follows the normal pattern, other times, the noun follows its etymology (origin) or it is just being awkward for no good reason! Here are some of the 'gotchas':

| *Table 9.4: Confusing Portuguese nouns* | | |
|---|---|---|
| *Portuguese* | *English* | *Notes* |
| o cinema | the cinema | |
| o clima | the climate | |
| o dia | the day | |
| a foto | the photo | 'foto' is short for 'fotografia' |
| o mapa | the map | from the Greek |
| a moto | the motorbike | 'moto' is short for 'motocicleta' |
| o planeta | the planet | |
| o poema | the poem | from the Greek |
| o problema | the problem | from the Greek |
| o programa | the programme | from the Greek |
| o sistema | the system | from the Greek |
| o telefonema | the phone call | |
| o teorema | the theorem | |
| a tribo | the tribe | |

Another noun that can cause some confusion for a different reason is the Portuguese word for fruit, which can be either 'fruto' or 'fruta'. Edible fruits like apples and grapes are usually referred to as 'fruta'. When using the word in a more generic sense, to mean that something is the product of something else, the word 'fruto' is used instead (e.g., 'frutos do mar' means 'fruits of the sea', or seafood; 'o fruto do meu trabalho' is 'the fruit of my labour'). 'Fruto' can be used for edible fruit too, if the context also makes reference to the plant or tree that produced it, but when referring to fruit on its own, you use 'fruta'.

*O programa tem uma foto dum planeta*

## Exercise 1: Articles

## Exercício 1: Artigos

*Answers on page 288.*

### Artigos definidos (o, a, os, as) – Definite articles (the)

All objects in Portuguese have both gender and number, and when we speak, these two attributes need to be clearly defined. If you are unsure of whether a word is masculine or feminine, you can look it up in a Portuguese dictionary. The entry in the dictionary should be followed by an italic '*m*' or '*f*' for 'masculine' or 'feminine'. After you have looked up all the words below that you are unsure of, go back and complete the exercises and see how many you can remember (don't forget about plurality!).

**1.1.** Please identify the correct definite article (o, a, os, as) for the following nouns.

1. _____ carro
*(the car)*

2. _____ casa
*(the house)*

3. _____ telemóvel
*(the mobile phone)*

4. _____ mulher
*(the woman/wife)*

5. _____ amigo
*(the male friend)*

6. _____ irmã
*(the sister)*

7. _____ laranja
*(the orange)*

8. _____ maçã
*(the apple)*

9. _____ amendoím
*(the peanut)*

10. _____ garfo
*(the fork)*

11. _____ chuveiro
*(the shower)*

12. _____ pente
*(the comb)*

13. _____ copo
*(the glass)*

14. _____ homem
*(the man)*

15. _____ jogos
*(the games)*

16. _____ olhos
*(the eyes)*

17. _____ professora
*(the teacher)*

18. _____ impostos
*(the taxes)*

19. _____ calções
*(the shorts)*

20. _____ filhos
*(the children)*

21. _____ hotel
*(the hotel)*

22. _____ animal
*(the animal)*

23. _____ lei
*(the law)*

24. _____ marido
*(the husband)*

25. _____ panela
*(the saucepan)*

26. _____ consultor
*(the consultant)*

27. _____ confusão
*(the confusion)*

28. _____ janelas
*(the windows)*

29. _____ dinheiro
*(the money)*

30. _____ informação
*(the information)*

31. _____ sapatos
*(the shoes)*

32. _____ encomendas
*(the parcels)*

33. _____ campo
*(the countryside/field)*

34. _____ pasta
*(the briefcase)*

35. _____ saco
*(the bag)*

36. _____ livros
(the books)

37. _____estação
*(the station)*

38. _____ canetas
*(the pens)*

39. _____ bolo
*(the cake)*

*Artigos indefinidos (um, uma, uns, umas) – Indefinite articles (a, an, some)*

**1.2.** Like in exercise 1.1, please identify the correct indefinite article (um, uma, uns, umas) for the following words.

1. _____ senhor
*(a gentleman)*

2. _____ cultura
*(a cultura)*

3. _____ computador
*(a computer)*

4. _____ relógio
*(a watch)*

5. _____ óculos
*(some eyeglasses)*

6. _____ sapatos
*(some shoes)*

7. _____ saias
*(some skirts)*

8. _____ gavetas
*(some drawers)*

9. _____ malas
*(some suitcases)*

10. _____ gravata
*(a tie)*

11. _____ caixas
*(some boxes)*

12. _____ copos de vinho
*(some wine glasses)*

13. _____ famílias
(some families)

14. _____ canil
(a dog kennel)

15. _____ marcação
(an appointment)

16. _____ batatas fritas
(some French fries)

17. _____ email
(an email)

18. _____ lugar
(a place / a seat)

19. _____ notas
(some bank notes)

20. _____ troco
(some change)

21. _____ táxis
(some taxis)

22. _____ pastelaria
(a pastry shop)

23. _____ cidade
(a city)

24. _____ semanas
(some weeks)

25. _____ negócios
(some businesses)

26. _____ empresas
(some companies)

27. _____ sapataria
(a shoe shop)

28. _____ camisas
(some shirts)

29. _____ supermercado
(a supermarket)

30. _____ gorjeta
(a tip)

31. _____ barulhos
(some noises)

32. _____ bagagem
(some luggage)

33. _____ portas
(some doors)

34. _____ viagem
(a trip)

35. _____ casacos
(some coats)

36. _____ saladas
(some salads)

37. _____ morangos
(some strawberries)

38. _____ bananas
(some bananas)

39. _____ ligação
(a connection)

### Quando usar os artigos definidos – When to use definite articles

Definite articles must be used in most cases except:
- when you ask for someone by name or call their name to get their attention.
- when you are talking about a well-known person.
- when you are talking about something in general – e.g. I like wine (all types of wine) as opposed to I like the wine (that particular wine).
- with the months of the year and most city and town names.

**1.3.** Please choose which of the following expressions are correct:

1.3.1. O António é meu vizinho. *(Antonio is my neighbour.)*          ____

1.3.2. Eu gosto muito de figos. *(I like figs a lot.)*          ____

1.3.3. O Peter, venha cá por favor. *(Peter, come here please.)*          ____

1.3.4. O carro dele é muito rápido. *(His car is very fast.)*          ____

1.3.5. Comida está fria. *(The food is cold.)*          ____

1.3.6. O chá é bom. *(The tea is good.)*          ____

1.3.7. Ele detesta café. *(He hates the coffee.)*          ____

1.3.8. Lisboa é uma cidade antiga. *(Lisbon is an old city.)*          ____

1.3.9. No agosto eu vou à praia. *(In August I go to the beach.)*          ____

## *Nomes confusos – Confusing nouns*

There are some nouns in Portuguese which may be a bit confusing in terms of gender (see Table 9.4, above).

**1.4.** Please complete with the indefinite articles (um, uma, uns, umas) the following words to identify their gender.

1. _____ problema
*(a problem)*

2. _____ universidade
*(a university)*

3. _____ consideração
*(a consideration)*

4. _____ continuidade
*(a continuation)*

5. _____ poema
*(a poem)*

6. _____ programa de televisão
*(a TV programme)*

7. _____ lugar de estacionamento
*(a parking space)*

8. _____ papel
*(a [piece of] paper)*

9. _____ cidade
*(a city)*

10. _____ teorema
*(a theorem)*

11. _____ cinema
*(a cinema)*

12. _____ planetas
*(some planets)*

13. _____ fotos
*(some photos)*

14. _____ dia
*(a day)*

15. _____ juíz
*(a judge)*

16. _____ clima
*(a climate)*

17. _____ mapa
*(a map)*

18. _____ telefonemas
*(some phone calls)*

19. _____ fim de semana
*(a weekend)*

20. _____ imagem
*(a picture)*

21. _____ tribo
*(a tribe)*

22. _____ moto
*(a motorcycle)*

23. _____ internet rápida
*(a fast internet [connection])*

24. _____ países
*(some countries)*

# 10. Verbs

Verbs are often described as 'doing words', in that they signify some form of action. Although this is true, there are some verbs that do not relate to obvious actions – in particular, auxiliary verbs such as 'would' and 'can' which are explained in a little more detail later. A good starting point though is to ask yourself which word denotes an action or process being carried out.

One way to identify a word as a verb, is to ask yourself whether you can precede it with 'I', 'we', 'you', 'he', 'she', 'it', and 'they' to denote somebody performing the action. For example, with the word 'went', try saying: 'I went, we went, you went, he went, she went, it went, they went' – it all sounds OK, so 'went' is a verb. However, if you try to do the same thing with a word like 'concept', you end up with nonsense: 'I concept, we concept, you concept, he concepts, she concepts, it concepts, they concept' – it just doesn't work. Concept therefore is not a verb. By the way, this prefixing with 'I', 'we', 'you' etc. is called 'conjugating' the verb.

Depending on the 'tense' of the verb (explained later), you might find that you have to modify the word slightly before you can conjugate it. If you come across a word that you think is a verb, but you can't conjugate it, try to modify it in such a way as to denote that you were in the habit of performing the action yourself. For example, take the word 'doing'. 'I doing, we doing, you doing, they doing' does not make sense. However, to denote that I am accustomed to 'doing' something, I would say 'I do'.

We can see then, that all we have to do in this example, is modify the word slightly by dropping the 'ing', which gives us 'I do, we do, you do, they do.' Basically, we are checking whether the word belongs to a 'family' of words that can be conjugated – if so, it is probably a verb. As you become more familiar with different verb forms, you will find that you recognise the different words that belong to a particular verb's 'family'.

Very occasionally, you might find that a verb cannot be fully conjugated – for example: 'rain'. It does not really make sense to say 'I rain, you rain, we rain' etc, but 'rain' is still a verb, and it can be conjugated as 'it rains'. The reason the full conjugation does not make sense is that the verb has a very specific application, i.e. to the weather (so 'it [the weather] rains' is the only conjugation that fits) – it is an impersonal verb. Full conjugation of a word like this could be used as a literary mechanism, but it is not used in every day speech.

Sometimes, the same word can be classified as a noun or a verb, depending on the context. For example, in the sentence 'he wanted to photograph me', the word 'photograph' is acting as a verb. However, saying 'he wanted to take my photograph', changes the word 'photograph' into a noun. For this reason, be careful when identifying verbs that the meaning of the word when conjugated is consistent with the meaning of the word in the sentence in which you find it. It might be best to first try to identify whether the word is a noun, and only if it isn't, try conjugation to see if it is a verb.

Here are some more examples of words that can be nouns or verbs depending on the context: paint; love; telephone; record (note the shift in stress when pronouncing the noun form and the verb form of 'record'); book; being; filling; helping; and lots of other words that end with 'ing'.

There is a lot more to be said about verbs and we will delve deeply into them a little later.

| Table 10.1: Examples of Portuguese verbs | |
|---|---|
| Portuguese | English |
| amar | to love |
| caminhar | to walk |
| garantir | to guarantee |
| ir | to go |
| nevar | to snow |
| perder | to lose |
| saber | to know (to have knowledge) |
| conhecer | to know (to be acquainted with) |
| ter | to have |

# 11. Adjectives

To identify an adjective, just check whether the word gives you more information about a noun. Adjectives always relate to nouns (sometimes indirectly – via a pronoun; see pronoun section), and usually describe them in some way, or give the noun a certain extra quality – e.g. to denote size/colour/texture/etc. Some examples of adjectives: brown; soft; musical; large; expensive; happy.

For instance, when we compare these two sentences:

- 'I see a car over there' – 'Eu vejo um carro lá'
- 'I see a beautiful car over there' – 'Eu vejo um carro bonito lá'

The word 'beautiful' (bonito) gives you more information about the car (a noun), so that's an adjective.

In English, adjectives normally appear before the noun they describe (e.g., 'the **black** shoes', 'a **small** table'). In Portuguese however, (as with other Latin-based languages) the adjective usually appears after the noun (e.g., 'os sapatos **pretos**', 'uma mesa **pequena**'). This takes a bit of getting used to, but it is actually more logical, especially when using several adjectives in a row, because you know which noun is being described up-front, whereas in English you have to wait for the sentence to finish before you know what is being spoken about.

Adjectives usually have a gender, and this must 'agree' with the gender of the noun being described. So a small house is 'uma casa **pequena**' but a small book is 'um livro **pequeno**'. Most adjectives also have plural forms (e.g., algumas casas **pequenas**, alguns livros **pequenos**).

Some adjectives do not have gender, but still have a separate plural form (e.g., um teste **fácil**, alguns testes **fáceis**, uma tarefa **fácil**, algumas tarefas **fáceis**), and others are fixed, or 'invariable' and remain the same regardless of the gender or number of the noun (e.g., um teste **simples**, umas tarefas **simples**). See the table and exercises below for more examples of these different types of adjective.

## Table 11.1: Examples of Portuguese adjectives

| Portuguese | | English |
|---|---|---|
| **Masculine** | **Feminine** | |
| barulhento(s) | barulhenta(s) | noisy |
| cansado(s) | cansada(s) | tired |
| amarelo(s) | amarela(s) | yellow |
| congelado(s) | congelada(s) | frozen |
| morto(s) | morta(s) | dead |
| vivo(s) | viva(s) | alive |
| chato(s) | chata(s) | boring |
| rápido(s) | rápida(s) | fast |
| bonito(s) | bonita(s) | beautiful/pretty |
| feio(s) | feia(s) | ugly |
| assustador(es) | assustadora(s) | scary |
| preto(s) | preta(s) | black |
| fácil/fáceis | | easy |
| interessante(s) | | interesting |
| brilhante(s) | | brilliant/shiny |
| grande(s) | | big/large |
| suficiente(s) | | sufficient/enough |
| feliz(es) | | happy |
| cor-de-rosa | | pink |
| violeta | | violet/purple |
| cor-de-laranja | | orange |
| amarelo-ouro | | yellow gold |
| verde-garrafa | | bottle green |

# Exercise 2: Adjectives

# Exercício 2: Adjectivos

*Answers on page 290.*

As noted above, there are adjectives that agree with the noun they describe in both gender and number, those that only agree in number and there are invariable adjectives (which do not change at all in any circumstances).

***Adjectivos variáveis em género e número – Adjectives that are variable in both gender and number.***

**2.1.** Please choose from the adjectives given in Table 11.1, above, the one that best fits each sentence and adapt it in accordance with the gender and number of the words it describes.

2.1.1. Os meus vizinhos são muito _____.
*(My neighbours are very **noisy**.)*

2.1.2. Os lugares onde ele nos leva são _____.
*(The places where he takes us are **scary**.)*

2.1.3. Ela gosta de vestidos _____.
*(She likes **ugly** dresses.)*

2.1.4. Eu gosto de ter casas _____ à volta.
*(I like having **pretty** houses around.)*

2.1.5. Cristiano Ronaldo é um jogador _____.
*(Cristiano Ronaldo is a **fast** player.)*

2.1.6. O carro _____ é o meu preferido.
*(The **black** car is my favourite one.)*

2.1.7. Eu hoje só quero uma cerveja _____.
*(Today I only want a **small** beer.)*

2.1.8. As flores _____ são caras.
*(The **yellow** flowers are expensive.)*

2.1.9. Os programas _____ de televisão não são educativos.
*(**Boring** TV programmes are not educational.)*

2.1.10. Os alimentos _____ são uma alternativa.
*(**Frozen** foods are an alternative.)*

2.1.11. Ponha as flores _____ no lixo, se faz favor.
*(Put the **dead** flowers in the rubbish, please.)*

### *Adjectivos Variáveis em Número – Variable Adjectives in Number*

**2.2.** Please choose from the adjectives in Table 11.1, above, the one that best fits in each sentence and adapt it in accordance with number (singular or plural) from the words listed below.

2.2.1. Uma casa _____ tem mais espaço.
*(A **big** house has more room.)*

2.2.2. Ele tem uma coisa _____ para me mostrar.
*(He has an **interesting** thing to show me.)*

2.2.3. Eu podia ver as pratas _____ da janela do quarto.
*(I could see the **shiny** silver from the bedroom window.)*

2.2.4. Eu acho que temos cerveja _____ para todos.
*(I think we have **enough** beer for everyone.)*

2.2.5. Podemos ver que eles são um casal _____.
*(We can see that they are a **happy** couple.)*

### *Adjectivos Invariáveis – Invariable Adjectives*

**2.3.** Complete the following sentences with the best invariable adjective from those provided in Table 11.1.

2.3.1. Não quero comprar um relógio caro, mas tem de ser _____.
*(I don't want to buy an expensive watch, but it has to be **yellow gold**.)*

2.3.2. Quase todas as meninas gostam muito de roupa _____.
*(Almost all little girls like **pink** clothing a lot.)*

2.3.3. No outono a maioria das flores silvestres ficam _____.
*(In autumn most of the wild flowers become **purple**.)*

2.3.4. A mesa de bilhar é _____.
*(The billiard table is **bottle green**.)*

2.3.5. Adoro ver o pôr do sol e o céu _____.
*(I love watching the sunset and the **orange** sky.)*

# 12. Adverbs

The concept of adverbs is very similar to that of adjectives – i.e. they are words that give more information about another word. As the term implies, adverbs are generally used to give extra information about a verb – usually to describe the action – e.g. to denote speed/sound/strength/etc.

Virtually all words that end with 'ly' in English are adverbs (the equivalent ending in Portuguese is 'mente' – e.g. profundamente = deeply).

However, although generally used to describe a verb, adverbs can also be used to describe other word types such as adjectives (although they are never used to describe a noun directly). For example: 'The physically, mentally, and emotionally exhausted girl arrived home.' – the adverbs in this sentence are 'physically', 'mentally', and 'emotionally', which in this case are being used to describe the adjective 'exhausted' (which in turn describes the noun 'girl').

Basically then, to identify a word as an adverb, check whether the word describes something. If it does, but does not relate directly to a noun, it is probably an adverb. Some words can be either an adjective or an adverb depending on the context. For example, the word 'fast' when used in the context of 'a fast car' is an adjective (describing the car, which is a noun), but when you say 'the car was going fast' it is an adverb (describing the action – 'going' – which is a verb).

We will look at some examples of adverbs in the exercises that follow.

## Exercise 3: Adverbs
## Exercício 3: Advérbios

*Answers on page 290.*

Whereas an adjective gives a specific quality to a noun, an adverb in turn, gives a certain quality to a verb and can also give quality to an adjective. Most Portuguese adverbs are easily guessable form their English form, but some are less obvious.

Adjectives ending in **-o** (masculine singular) change to the feminine singular before adding the suffix **-mente**, e.g. lento → lenta → lentamente (slow → slowly).

Usually adverbs are placed before the adjective or after the verb they give a quality to, e.g. 'Ele apareceu *rapidamente*' (He turned up *quickly*), 'O exercício é **aparentemente** difícil.' (The exercise is **apparently** difficult.). Another good tip is that many English words ending with '...ly' end in '...mente' in Portuguese.

**3.1.** Let's check out the following exercises in which you need to fill in the missing adverbs or adjectives as per the example:

> **Example: aparente → aparentemente** *(apparent → apparently)*

    3.1.1.  básico        → _____  *(basic → basically)*

    3.1.2.  _____ → rapidamente  *(rapid → rapidly)*

    3.1.3.  histórico     → _____  *(historic → historically)*

    3.1.4.  _____ → automaticamente  *(automatic → automatically)*

    3.1.5.  _____ → calmamente  *(calm → calmly)*

    3.1.6.  raro         → _____  *(rare → rarely)*

3.1.7.  profundo          →  _____  *(profund/deep →*
                                            *profoundly/deeply)*

3.1.8.  _____  →  atenciosamente  *(attentive → attentively)*

3.1.9.  imediato          →  _____  *(immediate → immediately)*

3.1.10. breve             →  _____  *(brief → briefly)*

3.1.11. _____  →  frequentemente  *(frequent → frequently)*

3.1.12. natural           →  _____  *(natural → naturally)*

3.1.13. _____  →  honestamente  *(honest → honestly)*

3.1.14. _____  →  inocentemente  *(naïve → naïvely)*

3.1.15. normal            →  _____  *(normal → normally)*

There are Portuguese adverbs (the most often used ones) which are completely
different from English (see also www.learn-portuguese-with-
rafa.com/portuguese-vocabulary.html#adverbs).

**3.2.** From the adverbs listed in Table 12.1, choose the one that best fits each sentence
(to make it a little harder, the adverb is not shown in the English translation).[*]

| *Table 12.1: Examples of Portuguese adverbs* | |
|---|---|
| *Portuguese* | *English* |
| bastante | enough/quite |
| bem | well |
| cuidadosamente | carefully |

* Some of these exercises have more than one possible answer – pick the one you think fits best.

| Portuguese | English |
|---|---|
| felizmente | happily / fortunately |
| raramente | seldom |
| juntos | together |
| profundamente | deeply |
| provavelmente | probably |
| hoje | today |
| amanhã | tomorrow |
| aqui | here |

3.2.1 Eu estou _____ feliz com os resultados do exame.
   *(I'm        happy with the exam results.)*

3.2..2 Nós trabalhámos _____ a semana passada.
   *(We worked        last week.)*

3.2.3. Eles não têm boas condições de trabalho _____.
   *(They don't have good working conditions        .)*

3.2.4. _____ tu precisas de ir ao dentista.
   *(        you need to go to the dentist.)*

3.2.5. Nós _____ vemos os nossos vizinhos por aqui.
   *(We        see our old neighbours around.)*

3.2.6. Apesar do tempo, você veio trabalhar _____.
   *(Despite the weather, you came to work        .)*

3.2.7. Eles conseguem melhores resultados a trabalhar _____.
   *(They can achieve better results by working        .)*

# 13. Pronouns

Pronouns are a kind of shortcut – language would be rather tedious without them. They are used in place of nouns or proper nouns – usually to avoid repetition. Often, a reference is made to a noun or proper noun directly, and then subsequent references to the person or thing are made using a pronoun. Examples of pronouns: him; her; it; his; their; you; them; me.

For example, to say 'Johnny tried to put the frog in Johnny's pocket, but the frog jumped out' does not flow very well, so we use pronouns like this: 'Johnny tried to put the frog in **his** pocket, but **it** jumped out'.

We will take a closer look at pronouns in Portuguese later, but for now it is enough to know basically what they are.

# 14. Suffixes, Contractions, and Conjunctions

Before we dive into prepositions and verbs, let's deal with some fiddly bits of the Portuguese language.

## Diminutive

Pick a noun, any noun. Want to make it smaller and cuter? Just add a diminutive suffix! Diminutives are nouns with a cute little tail. Typically, you just replace the final vowel ('a' or 'o') with either 'inho' or 'inha' (depending on the noun's gender) to denote a smaller size, or to make it sound more affectionate. So while 'uma caneta' is a pen, 'uma canetinha' is a cute ickle pen.

If the noun has the stress on the last syllable instead of the penultimate (e.g. because it ends with the letter 'r' or has a diacritic), the ending becomes 'zinho'. So a small computer ('computador') would be 'um computadorzinho'.

You can even make proper nouns diminutive, for example, 'Joãozinho' for 'little Johnny'. It also works with interjections ('tchauzino!' – an affectionate goodbye), and some adjectives and adverbs (e.g. 'bonitinha' – 'little beauty', or 'cutie').

## Augmentative

The opposite is also true – you can make something bigger and better by adding an augmentative suffix. The masculine version is 'ão' (or 'zão' for words with emphasis on the final syllable), and the feminine version is 'ona' (or 'zona').

So, 'uma mesa' becomes 'uma mesona' if it is really big. 'Um livrão' would be a very large book, or a book with great content. Again, it can be used with proper nouns ('Joãozão' would be 'big John'), and some adjectives and adverbs ('grandona' – not just big, but huge).

## Contractions

Whereas in English we quite often use an apostrophe to denote a shortened form of a word, or two words joined together (like 'wouldn't' and 'I'll'), this almost never happens in Portuguese. A rare example of this phenomenon still in use has its roots in the old Portuguese: 'd'agua' ('of water'), as in 'uma garrafa d'agua' ('a bottle of water'). Still, some words are joined together into a shortened form (but without the apostrophe).

The word 'em', which can mean 'in', 'on', or 'at', depending on the context, can be merged with the definite or indefinite article to form a single word. Just prefix the definite or indefinite article with the letter 'n', for example: em + a = na ('in the', 'on the', or 'at the'); em + uma = numa ('in a' or 'on a'). So to say 'I live in a house', instead of translating in full: 'Eu moro **em uma** casa', you can just say 'Moro **numa** casa.'

Please note that in Portuguese the contraction of prepositions (words like 'in', 'on', 'by', and 'for' – we will discuss them in more detail in the next chapter) with indefinite articles ('um', 'uma', 'uns', 'umas') is optional, but with definite articles ('o', 'a', 'os', 'as') it becomes compulsory.

The word 'de' ('of', or 'from') can be merged with the definite article to form 'do' and 'da' ('of the' or 'from the'). It can also merge with 'um' or 'uma' to make 'dum' and 'duma' ('of a'), and with 'este', 'esta', 'esse', and 'essa' to make 'deste', 'desse', etc. ('of this' or 'of these').

'Por' can also be merged with the definite article to make 'pelo' and 'pela' ('by the'), and 'a' ('to') can be treated the same way (a + a = à). All of these also have plural forms. Some pronouns are also contractions (e.g. 'dele'), but we will be looking into those a bit later.

### Table 14.1: Examples of contractions in Portuguese (preposition + article)

| Separate | Contraction | Translation |
|---|---|---|
| em + o | no | in the (masculine singular) |
| em + a | na | in the (feminine singular) |
| em + os | nos | in the (masculine plural) |
| em + as | nas | in the (feminine plural) |
| em + um | num | in a (masculine) |
| em + umas | numas | in some (feminine) |
| por + o | pelo | by the (masculine singular) |
| por + as | pelas | by the (feminine plural) |
| a + o | ao | to the (masculine singular) |
| a + os | aos | to the (masculine plural) |

| Separate | Contraction | Translation |
|----------|-------------|-------------|
| a + a | à | to the (feminine singular) |
| a + as | às | to the (feminine plural) |
| de + os | dos | of the (masculine plural) |
| de + a | da | of the (feminine singular) |
| de + uma | duma | of a (feminine singular) |
| de + este | deste | of this (masculine singular) |
| de + essas | dessas | of those (feminine plural) |

… and so on.

## Conjunctions

Conjunctions are 'joining words' that link two thoughts together in a sentence. They are typically a single word like 'and', 'but', 'however', and 'therefore', but they can be compound phrases such as 'as well as' and 'in order that'. Here are some of the most commonly used conjunctions in Portuguese:

### Table 14.2: Examples of Portuguese conjunctions

| Portuguese | English |
|------------|---------|
| e | and |
| que | that |
| do que | than |
| mas | but |
| ou | or |
| como | as |
| se | if |
| quando | when |
| porque | because |
| por causa de | because of |
| enquanto | while |

| Portuguese | English |
| --- | --- |
| onde | where |
| depois | after |
| assim | so/thus |
| porém | though/although |
| por isso/portanto | therefore |
| visto que | since |
| até | until |
| antes | before |
| senão | unless |
| logo que | as soon as |
| no entanto | however |

## Exercise 4: Diminutives and Augmentatives

## Exercício 4: Diminutivos e Aumentativos

*Answers on page 291.*

Diminutives and augmentatives are constantly used in Portuguese, so it's good practice to start getting used to them.

**4.1.** Please fill the gaps with the diminutives of the given noun in each sentence.

    4.1.1. O meu _____ (gato) é muito calmo.
       *(My **kitten** is very calm.)*

    4.1.2. Eles têm uma _____ (casa) muito bonita.
       *(They have a beautiful **cute little house**.)*

    4.1.3. Que _____ (tempo) gostoso nós temos hoje na praia.
       *(What **wonderful weather** we have at the beach today.)*

    4.1.4. Oh, que cachorro lindo. Ele é _____ (novo), não é?
       *(Oh, what a pretty dog. He is **very young**, isn't he?)*

    4.1.5. Este ano só tivemos problemas. Que _____ (ano) terrível.
       *(This year we only had problems. What a **terrible year**.)*

    4.1.6. Esta noite vou preparar um _____ (jantar) delicioso para as visitas.
       *(Tonight I'm going to prepare a **delicious dinner** for our guests.)*

**4.2.** Please fill the gaps with the augmentatives of the given noun in each sentence.

    4.2.1. Há um _____ (carro) à nossa porta.
       *(There is a **great car** outside our door.)*

    4.2.2.　O Ronaldo acabou de marcar um _____ (golo).
       *(Ronaldo has just scored a **magnificent goal**.)*

4.2.3.  O nosso _____ (chefe) é muito generoso.
*(Our **great boss** is very generous.)*

4.2.4.  Eu tenho um _____ (sofá) na minha sala.
*(I have a **huge sofa** in my lounge.)*

4.2.5.  Ele serviram um _____ (jantar) na boda de casamento
deles.
*(They served a **sophisticated dinner** at their wedding reception.)*

# Exercise 5: Conjunctions
# Exercício 5: Conjunções

*Answers on page 292.*

**5.1.** Please fill in the sentences below with the correct conjunction.

5.1.1. Eu como frutas _____ legumes porque são muito bons para a minha saúde.
*(I eat fruits **and** vegetables because they are good for my health.)*

5.1.2. _____ que a ciência provou que fumar provoca cancro, não fumo mais.
*(**Since** science has proved that smoking causes cancer, I don't smoke any more.)*

5.1.3. Eu gosto do Vinho do Porto _____ infelizmente hoje tenho que conduzir.
*(I like Port Wine **but** unfortunately today I have to drive.)*

5.1.4. Eu acho _____ não vou poder ir à festa hoje.
*(I think **that** I won't be able to go to the party today.)*

5.1.5. Eu vou dar um chocolate ao Pedro _____ ele comer a comida toda.
*(I'll give Pedro a chocolate **if** he eats all the food.)*

5.1.6. Eu tenho de preparar o jantar _____ eu chegue a casa.
*(I have to prepare dinner **as soon as** I get home.)*

5.1.7. Vocês querem o café com _____ sem açúcar?
*(Guys, would you like your coffee with **or** without sugar?)*

5.1.8. A Índia tem mais habitantes _____ Portugal.
*(India has more inhabitants **than** Portugal.)*

5.1.9. Nós hoje não podemos sair _____ chuva.
*(Today we cannot go out **because of the** rain.)*

5.1.10. Ela vai preparar o jantar _____ ele põe a mesa.
*(She is going to prepare dinner **while** he sets the table.)*

# 15. Prepositions

Prepositions are small words or phrases that usually follow a verb, relate to a noun and indicate the position of the noun in space or time. Prepositions can consist of a single word, in which case they are 'simple', or more than one word, in which case they are 'complex'. Here are some examples:

| Table 15.1: Portuguese prepositions | |
|---|---|
| *Portuguese* | *English* |
| a | at / in / on |
| a / para | to |
| acima de | above |
| antes de / perante | before |
| após / depois de | after |
| até | until |
| com | with |
| como | as |
| de / desde | from |
| diante de / perante | in front of |
| em | in |
| em / sobre | on |
| entre | between |
| para / por | for |
| perto de | near |
| por | by |
| sob | under |
| sobre | about |

Correct use of prepositions is just one of those things you have to learn through experience. There are places where prepositions are required in Portuguese where they wouldn't be in English, and vice-versa. As you begin to become familiar with whole phrases, you will get a feel for how prepositions work in Portuguese, and will begin to use them correctly almost sub-consciously.

To get you started though, here are some examples of phrases which require a preposition in Portuguese that is different to that used (if any) in English:

| *Table 15.2: Examples of prepositions in English and Portuguese* | | |
|---|---|---|
| *Portuguese* | *English* | *Literal Translation* |
| Eles estão **em** casa | They are **at** home | They are **in** house |
| Precisamos **de** ajuda | We need help | We need **of** help |
| Ela voltou **para** casa | She returned home | She returned **to** house |
| Eu gosto **de** vinho | I like wine | I like **of** wine |
| Tenho **de** suportar isso | I have **to** put up **with** this | I have **of** support this |
| Tenho **que** suportar isso | | I have **that** support this |

Puritans of English grammar sometimes say that a sentence should not end with a preposition, because this was the case with Latin. These days though, it is generally accepted that this rule does not apply to English, because to follow it requires some verbal gymnastics – for example, whereas we find it quite natural to say 'he knew what I was talking about' (which ends with a preposition), if you wanted to phrase that without ending with a preposition, you end up with 'he knew about what I was talking'.

Sir Winston Churchill is often credited with saying "to say that a sentence should not end with a preposition is blatant pedantry, up with which I shall not put!" – as an ironic example of how ridiculous this rule is when applied to English.

However, as Portuguese is much more closely related to Latin than English, I'm afraid this rule *does* apply to Portuguese. This means learning the gymnastics of rewording your sentences so that they do not end with a preposition. Sorry about that.

Although incorrect use of prepositions will make you sound 'foreign' to a Portuguese speaker, you will still generally be understood, so don't worry if you make mistakes. In any case, we have plenty of exercises here to help you get to grips with them!

## Exercise 6: Prepositions
## Exercício 6: Preposições

*Answers on page 292.*

Prepositions are small linking words. They can be of different types, such as prepositions of movement, of place, etc.

### *'a' and 'para'*

In Portuguese the difference between 'a' and 'para' might be very subtle: 'a' gives you the idea that you go somewhere for a short time, whereas 'para' gives you the idea of long term.

To better understand these two prepositions imagine 'para' as a one-way ticket and 'a' as a return ticket (more like to 'pop in' for a short time).

**6.1.** Please find the correct preposition '**a**' or '**para**' with the article that best suits each sentence:

Note: Some of these involve contractions – e.g. when the preposition '**a**' is followed by the definite article '**o**', they are joined together to form '**ao**'. Choose whether the correct preposition is '**a**' or '**para**', and if appropriate, use contractions to join the preposition to the article.

6.1.1. Ela vai viver _____ Los Angeles.
*(She's going **to** Los Angeles to live.)*

6.1.2. Porquê não vamos _____ cinema hoje?
*(Why don't we go **to the** cinema today?)*

6.1.3. Depois do trabalho eu vou _____ casa.
*(After work I'm going home [lit. **to** house].)*

6.1.4. Eu preciso de ir _____ supermercado comprar fruta.
*(I need to go **to the** supermarket to buy some fruit.)*

6.1.5. O Manuel vai voltar _____ França na semana que vem.
*(Manuel is going back **to** France next week.)*

6.1.6. Ela vai _____ casa buscar o guarda-chuva e já volta.
*(She's going home [lit. **to** house] to pick up her umbrella and she'll be right back.)*

6.1.7. Eles querem ir _____ praia hoje.
*(They want to go **to the** beach today.)*

6.1.8. Hoje à tarde elas vão _____ uma festa.
*(This afternoon they are going **to** a party.)*

6.1.9. Eu quero ir viver _____ o México.
*(I want to go and live in [lit. **to**] Mexico.)*

6.1.10. O pai dela vai _____ Rio de Janeiro a negócios.
*(Her father is going **to** Rio de Janeiro on business.)*

### *'por' and 'para'*

In Portuguese it's very easy to confuse the use of 'por' and 'para' – '**por**' is often translated as 'by', 'for', 'through', 'via', and you look backward as the reason why, whereas '**para**' gives you the idea of an aim looking forward, which is normally equivalent to 'to', 'for', 'towards' and 'in order to'.

**6.2** Please complete each sentence with either '**para**' or '**por**', again, using contractions where appropriate.

6.2.1. Eu vou _____ hotel agora. Estou cansado.
*(I'm going **to the** hotel now. I'm tired.)*

6.2.2. Eu vou visitar o Victor, mas tenho de ir _____ centro da cidade.
*(I'm going to visit Victor, but I need to go **through the** the city centre.)*

6.2.3. O trânsito _____ ponte é intenso.
*(The traffic **through the** bridge is intense.)*

6.2.4. _____ mim vocês podem avançar com a obra.
*(**For** me, you can go ahead with the work.)*

6.2.5. Quando eles viajam, eles vão sempre _____ autoestrada.
*(When they travel, they always go **by the** motorway.)*

6.2.6. Como se vai _____ museu?
*(How do you go **to the** museum?)*

6.2.7. Eu gosto de passear _____ rio.
*(I like to walk **by the** river.)*

6.2.8. Preciso de passar _____ hotel.
*(I need to stop **by the** hotel.)*

6.2.9. Na viagem do Brasil à Tailândia, eles passam _____ Paris.
*(On their journey from Brazil to Thailand, they pass **through** Paris.)*

6.2.10. Hoje em dia as pessoas aceitam ser exploradas _____ governos.
*(Nowadays people accept being exploited **by the** governments.)*

### 'em' and 'de'

While 'em' in Portuguese means 'in', 'on', 'at' in English, 'de' means 'of', 'from', or 'by' when it refers to a means of transport (e.g. 'Eu vou **de** carro' – 'I'll go **by** car).

**6.3.** Please fill in the spaces in the sentences below with either '**de**' or '**em**' (or the appropriate contraction).

6.3.1. A gente vai _____ avião.
*(We are going **by plane**.)*

6.3.2. Eu gosto de viajar _____ elético em Lisboa.
*(I like to travel **by tram** in Lisbon.)*

6.3.3. Eu sou _____ Irlanda.
*(I am **from** Ireland.)*

6.3.4. Estou _____ autocarro agora.
*(I'm **on the** bus right now.)*

6.3.5. Ela está _____ escritório às segundas e quartas feiras.
  (*She is **in the** office on Mondays and Wednesdays.*)

6.3.6. Eles vão _____ carro do Artur, e elas vão _____
táxi.
  (*They [the guys] go **in** Artur's car and they [the ladies] go **by** táxi.*)

6.3.7. _____ domingo ele volta para casa.
  (***On** Sunday he comes back home.*)

6.3.8. Eles querem saber _____ onde elas são.
  (*They want to know where they are **from**.*)

6.3.9. Eu tenho aulas _____ três às quatro horas.
  (*I have classes **from** three to four o'clock.*)

6.3.10. Eles não querem trabalhar _____ segunda a sexta.
  (*They don't want to work **from** Monday to Friday.*)

## *Locuções Prepositivas – Prepositional Phrases*

In Portuguese, some prepositions are made up of more than one word, especially when they refer to where objects or people are.

**6.4.** Please fill in the sentences below, by using the prepositional phrases presented in Table 15.3 with contractions if applicable.

| *Table 15.3: Portuguese prepositional phrases* | |
| --- | --- |
| *Portuguese* | *English* |
| em frente de | in front of / opposite |
| atrás de | behind |
| dentro de | inside [of] |
| debaixo de | underneath |
| ao lado de | beside |
| fora de | outside |

| Portuguese | English |
|---|---|
| à direita de | on the right of |
| à esquerda de | on the left of |
| em cima de | on top of |
| por cima de | above |
| entre | between |

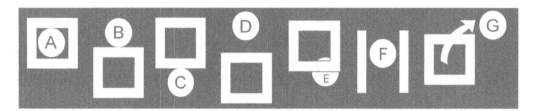

6.4.1. A bola **A** está _____ caixa.

6.4.2. A bola **B** está _____ caixa.

6.4.3. A bola **C** está _____ caixa.

6.4.4. A bola **D** está _____ caixa.

6.4.5. A bola **E** está _____ caixa.

6.4.6. A bola **F** está _____ as caixas.

6.4.7. A bola **G** está a ir para _____ caixa.
        *('está a ir para' = it's going to...)*

# 16. Verbs: The Infinitive

Let's get back onto verbs. The basic form of the verb is known as the 'infinitive', and is always preceded by the word 'to' in English (e.g., 'to read', 'to be', 'to love'). To find the infinitive then, try to convert the verb to a form which makes sense with the word 'to' in front of it. In the example on page 51, we found that 'went' is a verb, but 'to went' does not make sense! We have to convert 'went' to 'go', so the infinitive form of the verb is 'to go'.

The infinitive is the form of the verb that you will find defined in a dictionary. Usually, any other forms of a verb listed in a dictionary will point you to the entry for the infinitive. So another possible way of determining what the infinitive form of a verb is, would be to think of the form that you would use if you wanted to make a general dictionary definition for the verb.

Very occasionally, you might find that a verb does not have an infinitive form – an example of this in English is the word 'can'. The nearest you can find to an infinitive for this example is something like 'to be able to'. In this case, it is because 'can' is only ever used as an auxiliary verb, i.e. in conjunction with another verb (auxiliary verbs are explained more fully later). As with all exceptions, you just have to try to remember them as you come across them, but don't worry too much about this one!

After a while, you will find that it is quite easy to identify verbs, and that the infinitive form is obvious to you, so you will not need to keep conjugating words in your mind, or going through all of these rules. All you need is practice! So it would be good to pick up any piece of English literature and try to identify the verbs and infinitives in it. If you understand the way the English verbs work, you'll understand the way Portuguese verbs work as well.

Although strictly speaking, the infinitive always includes the word 'to', the verb form itself can be referred to as the infinitive even without the word 'to'. So it is correct to say that 'think' is the infinitive, as well as to say 'to think' is the infinitive. Normally you would only omit the word 'to' where the verb is being used in a compound form, that is, in conjunction with auxiliary verbs. Don't worry about this – it will all become clearer later. I hope.

Note: When using the infinitive form of an English verb, if you insert an extra word between the word 'to' and the verb, it is known as a split infinitive (e.g. 'to boldly go' – the word 'boldly' splits up the infinitive form of the verb 'to go').

## Exercise 7: Infinitive – Regular Verbs
## Exercício 7: Infinitivo – Verbos Regulares

*Answers on page 294.*

Before you can use Portuguese verbs correctly, you need to identify their meaning. With the help of a dictionary (if necessary), please write in front of each verb its meaning in English and vice-versa, as per the example provided. The verbs marked with an asterisk (*) are irregular.

**7.1.** Verb meaning from Portuguese to English:

| | | | |
|---|---|---|---|
| 1. ser * | _____ | 2. estar * | _____ |
| 3. fazer* | _____ | 4. trabalhar | _____ |
| 5. falar | _____ | 6. organizar | _____ |
| 7. escrever | _____ | 8. ler* | _____ |
| 9. responder | _____ | 10. ter* | _____ |
| 11. sair* | _____ | 12. querer* | _____ |
| 13. ir* | _____ | 14. trazer* | _____ |
| 15. provar | _____ | 16. continuar | _____ |
| 17. garantir | _____ | 18. assistir | _____ |
| 19. haver* | _____ | 20. poder* | _____ |
| 21. ligar | _____ | 22. dormir | _____ |

23. ganhar    _____    24. ver*    _____

25. vir*    _____    26. soltar    _____

27. comprar    _____    28. vender    _____

29. envolver    _____    30. lembrar-se    _____

**7.2.** Verb meaning from English to Portuguese:

1. to eat    _____    2. to drink    _____

3. to manifest    _____    4. to dine    _____

5. to fall asleep    _____    6. to watch*    _____

7. to want*    _____    8. to know [people/places]    _____

9. to give*    _____    10. to say*    _____

11. to call    _____    12. to meet up with    _____

13. to cook    _____    14. to have breakfast    _____

15. to go*    _____    16. to study    _____

17. to rest    _____    18. to have lunch    _____

19. to put*    _____    20. to type    _____

21. to switch on    _____    22. to warm up    _____

23. to clean _____ 24. to tidy _____

25. to memorise _____ 26. to prepare _____

27. to die _____ 28. to water _____

29. to book _____ 30. to sit _____

# 17. Verb Conjugation

Verbs form the backbone of any language, as they are the means by which we can describe things that have happened, are happening, would happen and will happen. As such, they are also the most complicated type of word, and can take on many different forms for different purposes. By modifying the infinitive form of a verb, we derive further words that retain the basic meaning of the infinitive, but identify:

 i) the person or thing performing the action, and
 ii) the time or conditions under which it is performed.

Verb conjugation is concerned with the first of these aspects – i.e. who or what performs the action (the second aspect is the 'tense' of the verb, which is addressed later – for now, we will stick with the present tense). The word 'conjugation' just means 'joining together', and in this context refers to the construction of verb forms by joining different endings to the 'stem' of a verb. This will become clearer as you start to look at the sample conjugations below.

In English, we tend to use nouns and pronouns to explicitly identify who or what performs an action – for example, '**I** read'; '**you** go'; '**John** does' etc. Our verb forms do not change as much as those in Portuguese, where the verb form itself implies who or what is performing the action (thus sometimes eliminating the need for nouns and pronouns where they would be used in English).

The majority of verbs in any language will follow a set of rules regarding the form used in any given situation. These are referred to as regular or 'weak' verbs. Irregular (or 'strong') verbs are those that do not follow the usual rules, and these have to be learned individually. Unfortunately, the most commonly used verbs in any language are usually also the irregular ones – they tend to become corrupted over the years due to being used so often – so it does require a bit of effort in learning irregulars before you can construct meaningful sentences.

The following is a sample conjugation of the English regular verb: 'to work'.

***English: to work***

| | |
|---|---|
| I work | we work |
| you work | you work |
| he/she/it works | they work |

Note that the only time the word 'work' is changed, is when we say 'he', 'she', or 'it' work**s** – where we add an 's' on the end.

Also, in the above conjugations, the words are presented in 2 columns. The first represents singular forms, and the second is for plural forms. So, the plural of 'I work' is 'we work', the plural of 'he', 'she' or 'it works' is 'they work', and the plural of 'you work' remains the same (in English we no longer differentiate between 'you' singular and 'you' plural – in old English, the plural pronoun was 'ye').

The 'I' and 'we' forms are referred to as the 'first person' (because they refer to the speaker), 'you' is the 'second person' (because it refers to the person being spoken to), and 'he/she/it/they' are the 'third person' (because they relate to a third party who is not being addressed – the person or thing we are speaking about). So, 'we work' can be referred to as 'the first person plural form from the verb to work'.

In Portuguese, we find that every form of the verb is different. The Portuguese equivalent of 'to work' is 'trabalhar', and it is conjugated like this:

### Portuguese: trabalhar

| | |
|---|---|
| trabalho | trabalhamos |
| trabalhas | trabalhais* |
| trabalha | trabalham |

Even though in Portuguese the verb form changes for each 'person', and in English it changes for the third person singular only, there are some letters which are always there – for example, in Portuguese, all of the forms of 'trabalhar' start with the letters '**trabalh**'. This portion of the word is known as the 'stem' – and for regular verbs, it remains the same regardless of the conjugation or tense. With irregular verbs however, the stem can change (in which case they are referred to as 'radical-changing' or 'stem-changing' verbs – we will deal with those later).

Almost all infinitives in Portuguese end with either 'ar', 'er', or 'ir' – even for irregular verbs. The most common ending is 'ar', and the least common is 'ir'. These different types of verb are categorised: 'ar' verbs are referred to as 'the first conjugation', 'er' verbs are 'the second conjugation', and 'ir' verbs are the 'third conjugation'.

---

* The 2nd person plural form is not used in modern Portuguese, but can be found in older writings. More about this later.

A handful of verbs have an infinitive ending with 'or' (e.g., pôr, compor), but these are so rare that they do not qualify for a category of their own. They have evolved from 2$^{nd}$ conjugation verbs ('pôr' used to be 'pôer') so they are still classed as belonging to the 2$^{nd}$ conjugation.

We will cover the personal pronouns that can accompany these verbs in more detail later, but here are the basic pronouns that you might need to use with verb conjugations:

| *English* | *Portuguese* |
|---|---|
| I | eu |
| we | nós |
| you | tu |
| you (plural) | vós (obsolete) |
| he/she | ele/ela |
| they | eles/elas |

So to put them in context:

### Portuguese: trabalhar

| | |
|---|---|
| eu trabalho | nós trabalhamos |
| tu trabalhas | vós trabalhais |
| ele trabalha | eles trabalham |

## First Conjugation Verbs

To help you consolidate this, here is another conjugation of a verb – given in both English and Portuguese. The Portuguese verb 'pensar' means 'to think', and because it ends with 'ar', it is a first conjugation verb.

### English: to think

| | |
|---|---|
| I think | we think |
| you think | you think |
| he/she/it/thinks | they think |

### Portuguese: pensar

| | |
|---|---|
| penso | pensamos |
| pensas | pensais |
| pensa | pensam |

Note that the endings of the conjugations are the same as the previous example. The Portuguese verbs trabalhar and pensar are both regular verbs of the first conjugation (i.e. they are regular, and end in 'ar'), so the endings attached to the stem (in the case of pensar, the stem is 'pens') are the same. All regular verbs that end in 'ar' will follow exactly the same pattern. The stem is always the infinitive minus the last 2 letters (well, nearly always – we'll deal with the exceptions later), and the endings will always be as above.

## Second and Third Conjugation Verbs

Now we are going to look at the second and third conjugations (i.e. verbs that end in 'er' and 'ir'). The principle is the same as for first conjugation ('ar') verbs – the pattern for each is the same for all regular verbs of the same conjugation. Take a few minutes (or hours!) trying to memorise the endings for each type of verb.

*The second conjugation regular verb: comer (to eat).*

| | |
|---|---|
| como | comemos |
| comes | comeis |
| come | comem |

*The second conjugation regular verb: escrever (to write).*

| | |
|---|---|
| escrevo | escrevemos |
| escreves | escreveis |
| escreve | escrevem |

*The third conjugation regular verb: garantir (to guarantee).*

| | |
|---|---|
| garanto | garantimos |
| garantes | garantis |
| garante | garantem |

*The third conjugation regular verb: assistir (to attend; to watch [BR]).*

| | |
|---|---|
| assisto | assistimos |
| assistes | assistis |
| assiste | assistem |

## Usage of different 'Persons'

The second person singular form (you) in Portuguese is only used informally – i.e. with people you know very well: family members, children, those of the same age as you (when you are young), or those considerably younger than yourself. To express a verb in the second person singular form formally, you actually use the *third* person singular form of the verb. When you think about it, this makes sense, because as you have already seen, the polite Portuguese word for 'you' is the equivalent of saying 'the lady' or 'the gentleman' – so you are actually using the third person anyway (for example, to politely say 'you work', you are effectively saying 'the lady/gentleman work**s**' – so the verb 'to work' is expressed in the third person singular form 'works').

As has already been mentioned, the English language no longer differentiates between singular and plural forms of the second person ('you…'). Portuguese is similar, in that the second person plural form is very rarely used nowadays. Instead of this, the third person plural is usually used – so to say that 'you (plural) do something' is effectively the same as saying 'they do something'. You might occasionally find the old second person plural form in literature, so is worth knowing about, but it is rare to hear it in spoken Portuguese.

In many cases, it is obvious from the verb ending who is performing the action, so it is sometimes unnecessary to use the equivalent of the pronouns 'I', 'we', or 'you'. To say 'I work', you can just say one word in Portuguese: 'trabalho'. Likewise, to say 'we work', you just need one word: 'trabalhamos'. However, if you want to emphasise who is doing the work, you do need to use the pronoun. For example, to say '*I* work, but *he* doesn't work' in Portuguese (with the emphasis on 'I' and 'he'), it is necessary to use the Portuguese equivalents of the pronouns 'I' and 'he' ('eu' and 'ele') – 'Eu trabalho mas ele não trabalha'.

If you prefer, it will not sound wrong if you use pronouns all of the time, like we do in English – you just need to be aware that it is not always necessary, so that you can identify and understand what others say and the way they say it.

## Exercise 8: Regular Verbs
## Exercício 8: Verbos Regulares

*Answers on page 295.*

As you know, all Portuguese verbs can be grouped into 3 categories: verbs ending in 'ar' (first conjugation), 'er' (second conjugation), and 'ir' (third conjugation). Then, you also have verbs which follow a regular pattern (called regular verbs) and those which don't (called irregular verbs). For now, we will stick with regular verbs in the present tense (so the following exercises follow the same patterns that you have already learned in this chapter).

**8.1.** Please fill in the gaps using the present tense of the verbs (in brackets). This time only regular verbs ending in 'ar' will be used (i.e. first conjugation regular verbs).

    8.1.1. Em Portugal o comércio _____ (começar) às nove horas da manhã.
        *(In Portugal, commerce **starts up** at nine o'clock in the morning.)*

    8.1.2. Eu _____ (apanhar) o comboio das dez horas todos os dias.
        *(I **catch** the ten o'clock train every day.)*

    8.1.3. A Paula só _____ (trabalhar) quatro horas por semana.
        *(Paula only **works** four hours a week.)*

    8.1.4. Nós raramente _____ (almoçar) em casa durante a semana.
        *(We rarely **have lunch** at home during the week.)*

    8.1.5. Ela _____ (tocar) piano muito bem.
        *(She **plays** piano very well [tocar = to play instruments].)*

    8.1.6. Eles _____ (jogar) futebol todos os fins de semana.
        *(They **play** football every weekend [jogar = to play sports].)*

    8.1.7. O telefone nunca _____ (tocar) à noite porque eu desligo a ficha.
        *(The telephone never **rings** at night because I disconnect the plug [tocar = to ring].)*

8.1.8. O senhor _____ (pagar) a conta?
*(Sir, do you **pay** the bill?)*

8.1.9. Vocês _____ (tomar) o café com ou sem açúcar?
*(Guys, do you **take** your coffee with or without sugar?)*

8.1.10. O Ivo e a Inês _____ (estudar) português.
*(Ivo and Inês **study** Portuguese.)*

**8.2.** Now, let's check out how well you know your regular second conjugation ('er') verbs in Portuguese. Please fill in the gaps with the given second conjugation verbs in the present tense only.

8.2.1. Ao almoço e ao jantar nós _____ (beber) um copo de vinho.
*(At lunch and dinner we **drink** a glass of wine.)*

8.2.2. Normalmente eu _____ (resolver) todos os problemas do meu departamento.
*(Normally I **solve** all the problems in my department.)*

8.2.3. O John e a Joanna _____ (aprender) português na internet.
*(John and Joanna **learn** Portuguese on the Internet.)*

8.2.4. Eu já não _____ (escrever) cartas, eu envio e-mails.
*(I don't **write** letters anymore, I send emails.)*

8.2.5. A senhora, onde _____ (viver)?
*(Madam, where do you **live**?)*

8.2.6. Eu _____ (viver) e trabalho em Maputo, em Moçambique.
*(I **live** and work in Maputo, in Mozambique.)*

8.2.7. Na tua cidade _____ (chover) muito?
*(In your city does it **rain** a lot?)*

8.2.8. Eu _____ (atender) o telefone quando ele toca.
*(I **pick up** the phone when it rings [atender o telefone = to pick up the phone].)*

8.2.9. Nós _____ (correr) todas as manhãs durante 30 minutos.
*(We **run** every morning for 30 minutes.)*

8.2.10. Eu _____ (responder) aos meus e-mails logo que eles chegam.
*(I **answer** my emails as soon as they arrive.)*

**8.3.** Now that you have successfully learned the first two conjugations, let's check your performance with the present tense of third conjugation ('ir') verbs.

8.3.1 Ele _____ (despir) o casaco quando chega a casa.
*(He **takes** his jacket **off** when he gets home.)*

8.3.2. Eu _____ (abrir) a porta para si, minha senhora.
*(I'll **open** the door for you, madam.)*

8.3.3. Eles _____ (dividir) o bolo em fatias na festa.
*(They **divide** the cake in slices at the party.)*

8.3.4. Ao fim de semana nós _____ (preferir) ficar em casa.
*(On weekends we **prefer** to stay at home.)*

8.3.5. O comboio _____ (partir) às vinte horas e trinta minutos.
*(The train **departs** at 8:30pm.)*

8.3.6. Elas não _____ (conseguir) ter concentração com barulho de fundo.
*(They don't **manage** to concentrate with background noise.)*

8.3.7. A gente _____ (servir) o jantar entre as 6.30h e as 10.00h da noite.
*(One **serves** dinner between 6:30 and 10:00 in the evening.)*

8.3.8. Normalmente tu _____ (dormir) bem à noite?
*(Do you normally **sleep** well at night?)*

8.3.9. Nós _____ (subir) a montanha com muito esforço.
*(We **climb** the mountain with much effort.)*

8.3.10. Há dois aviões para Luanda. Um _____ (partir) às 11hrs e o outro às 17hrs.
*(There are two flights to Luanda. One **departs** at eleven o'clock and the other one at 5pm.)*

## Exercise 9: Verbs with Prepositions

## Exercício 9: Verbos com Preposições

*Answers on page 296.*

We looked at prepositions in chapter 15 – small words that are usually associated with a verb and used to refer to the position of a noun in space or time. Now that we have become familiar with conjugating verbs, we can combine this with using prepositions for the next exercise.

Some Portuguese prepositions when put together with certain verbs change the original meaning of the verb.

**9.1.** Let's have a look at some very useful verbs with prepositions below and use the right verb with its preposition and article to complete each sentence (with or without contractions).

| *Table 17.1: Portuguese verbs with prepositions* | |
|---|---|
| *Portuguese* | *English* |
| gostar de | to like |
| acabar por | to end up |
| acabar de | to have just [done something] |
| começar a | to start [doing something] |
| entrar em | to enter / to get in |
| sonhar com | to dream of |
| sair de | to leave [from] / to exit [from] |
| pensar em | to think of |
| apaixonar-se por | to fall in love with |
| ir ter com | to go and meet up with |
| vir ter com | to come and meet up with |

9.1.1. Todas as noites eu _____ um mundo mais humano e justo.
*(Every night I **dream of** a more humane and just world.)*

9.1.2. Ele é um escravo do trabalho. Ele sempre _____ escritório tarde.
*(He's a work slave. He always **leaves the** office late.)*

9.1.3. Ela _____ comer uma sobremesa depois do almoço.
*(She **likes** to have a dessert after lunch.)*

9.1.4. Normalmente nós _____ preparar o jantar às 18.00hrs.
*(Usually, we **start to** prepare dinner at 6pm.)*

9.1.5. O clube _____ campeonato de futebol este ano.
*(The [football] club **enters** the Football Championship this year.)*

9.1.6. Senhor Jonas, o senhor _____ a sua esposa ao café?
*(Mr. Jonas, are you **going to meet up with** your wife at the café?)*

9.1.7. Ele vai _____ desistir da ideia.
*(He will **end up** giving up the idea.)*

9.1.8. Eu _____ ir ao teatro logo à noite.
*(I'm **thinking of** going to the theatre tonight.)*

9.1.9. Nós _____ falar com o Diretor.
*(We **have just** spoken with the Director.)*

9.1.10. Eles conhecem-se e ela _____ ele imediatamente.
*(They meet each other and she **falls in love with** him straight away.)*

9.1.11. Eles _____ a Maria aqui ao bar.
*(They'll **come and meet up with** Maria here at the bar.)*

# 18. Verb Tenses

Although I get tense when my wife is in a mood, the words 'tense' and 'mood' have a somewhat different meaning when applied to language!

*I get 'tense' when my wife is in a 'mood'*

The tense of a verb is a means of identifying the time at which the verb was, is, would, or will be carried out (the word 'tense' is derived from the Latin 'tempus', meaning 'time'). Tense can also be used to convey the idea of what might, could, should, or would happen, or have happened.

There are many different tenses that can be applied to verbs, and in Portuguese each tense has its own set of verb conjugations. English verbs are easier to learn, because we tend not to change the conjugations so much. This means that there are fewer words to memorise – we often rely on auxiliary verbs to form the different tenses.

## *Moods*

As well as being divided into tenses, verbs are split into more generalised categories according to the type of tense. These categories are called 'moods'.

The most common mood is known as the **indicative**. This just means that the verb indicates a fact; the verb is being used in such a way as to give certainty to the action. For example, 'I will walk home' – there is no uncertainty as to what is going to happen. 'I walk home every day' is also in the indicative mood because it's a fact.

The **conditional** mood requires that some condition be met for the action to become certain. In English, this is achieved using the auxiliary verb 'would'. So 'I would walk home' is in the conditional mood, and so is 'I would have walked home'.

Other tenses that carry some degree of uncertainty fall under the **subjunctive** mood. An example of this mood is 'If I were to walk home...'. The subjunctive mood is not used as often as the others, so it is better to concentrate your efforts on tenses in the other moods first. However, the subjunctive is used consistently by Portuguese speakers, so you will have to at least understand it when you hear it, and eventually take the plunge and try to learn the conjugations (you will be perfectly well understood if you use indicative tenses where you should use subjunctives, but you will sound foreign to a native).

Then there is the **imperative** mood, which relates to commands or requests (e.g., 'keep off the grass', 'leave me alone', 'follow the signs').

We have already met the **infinitive**, and this is also a 'mood'. There are actually two tenses that belong to the infinitive mood. The most common one is the one that you have already learned about, and is generally just referred to as 'the infinitive', but to be more technical, it is actually 'the impersonal infinitive.' The other infinitive is 'the personal infinitive' which does not really exist in English, but does in Portuguese (more on that later).

Sometimes, different tenses belonging to different moods can have the same name. Where this is the case, the tense is identified by the name and the mood together. So the present subjunctive is a different tense to the present indicative – both dealing with the present, but one that carries a degree of uncertainty (subjunctive), and one that is definite (indicative). If a tense that can be used in more than one mood is referred to without specifying the mood, the more commonly used tense is assumed (this usually means the indicative mood).

# 19. Irregular Verbs

You can't run away from them forever I'm afraid. Those horrible words that refuse to conform to any rules just have to be learned the hard way. We are going to take a look at a few irregular verbs – the most common ones – as this will greatly increase your ability to express yourself with a limited vocabulary. There are more examples of irregular verbs (fully conjugated in all the tenses) in the reference section at the back of the book.

### To Be Or ... To Be?

Just to make a difficult situation worse, one of the most common verbs: 'to be' is not only irregular in Portuguese (and in English for that matter), it is also translated into 2 different Portuguese verbs, depending on the context.

*"Ser or Estar? That is the question!"*

The slightly more common version is **ser**. This is used with reference to defining characteristics, or permanent states. For example, to be male or female is a defining characteristic, so you would use the appropriate conjugation of the verb 'ser' to say 'I am male' or 'they are female'.

For non-defining characteristics, or temporary states, you use the word **estar**. So you would have to use this word to say something like 'I am tired', or 'she is late'.

The most important question to remember when trying to decide whether to use ser or estar is this: 'Is what I am talking about a defining characteristic (ser) or not (estar)?' It is best not just to ask yourself 'is what I am talking about temporary or permanent?' – because although often used as a rule of thumb, this does not always work!

For example, when talking about your occupation, you might want to say something like 'I am a secretary'. Being a secretary, whilst not necessarily a permanent state, *is* a defining characteristic – something that could be used to identify you as a particular individual. So in this case, you would use 'ser'. Likewise, to say 'I will be the chairman of the meeting' – you are not going to be the chairman of that meeting for the rest of your life, but being the chairman is something that will identify you, so again, ser would be used. You will get some practice on this soon…

Here is the full conjugation in the present tense of both ser and estar:

### *The second conjugation irregular verb: ser (to be – characteristic)*

| | |
|---|---|
| sou | somos |
| és | sois |
| é | são |

### *The first conjugation irregular verb: estar (to be – non-characteristic)*

| | |
|---|---|
| estou | estamos |
| estás | estais |
| está | estão |

And just for comparison, the same irregular verb in the present tense in English (to be):

| | |
|---|---|
| I am | we are |
| you are | you are |
| he/she/it is | they are |

Here are a few more examples…

- 'Portuguese **is** a very easy language to learn.' – 'O português **é** uma língua muito fácil de aprender.' – in this case, 'easy' (fácil) is a word that defines Portuguese, so you would use **ser**.
- 'He **is** asleep.' – 'Ele **está** a dormir.' (PT) / 'Ele **está** dormindo.' (BR) – You could not really say that a person can be identified by whether or not they are asleep! So in this case, you would use **estar**.
- 'I am going **to be** honest.' – 'vou **ser** honesto.' – A defining characteristic, so you would use **ser**.

A very useful irregular verb is 'to go'. You will find out why this verb is particularly useful shortly. Here is the Portuguese conjugation of this verb in the present tense:

### *The third conjugation irregular verb: ir (to go)*

| | |
|---|---|
| vou | vamos |
| vais | ides |
| vai | vão |

Here is another common irregular: 'to have'.

### *The second conjugation irregular verb: ter (to have)*

| | |
|---|---|
| tenho | temos |
| tens | tendes |
| tem | têm |

This verb, 'ter', can also be used to mean 'must' – in a similar way to the English verb 'to have'. For example, we might say something like 'I have to eat', meaning 'I must eat'. In Portuguese, you would use 'ter' like this: 'Eu tenho de comer'. Note that the verb 'eat' is given in the infinitive, and the word 'de' is used between the two verbs (so literally, it is 'I have of to eat'). Instead of 'de', the word 'que' is sometimes used, so 'eu tenho que comer' means exactly the same thing.

Another very useful irregular verb is 'to do' – which in Portuguese (and other European languages) is actually the same as 'to make' – so Portuguese speakers learning English have the same trouble with our two verbs 'to make' and 'to do' as we have with their 'ser' and 'estar'!

### *The second conjugation irregular verb: fazer (to do; to make)*

| | |
|---|---|
| faço | fazemos |
| fazes | fazeis |
| faz | fazem |

Just one more! A bit of an odd one, this – 'haver'. Oh, and, er, before I explain what it means, I have a bit of a confession to make. I lied. You remember earlier on I mentioned that there were 2 different Portuguese words for 'to be'? Well, that's not entirely true. There are 3 (well, maybe 4 if you include 'ficar', but don't worry about that).

### *The second conjugation irregular verb: haver (to be [impersonal]; to have [auxiliary])*

| hei  | havemos |
|------|---------|
| hás  | haveis  |
| há   | hão     |

'Impersonal' means that it does not relate to any grammatical 'person' (we covered grammatical 'persons' on page 86). When 'haver' *is* used with a grammatical person, it means 'to have' (and is a posh version of the verb 'ter', used mainly in writing rather than in speech, and it is only used as an auxiliary verb – i.e. when saying one *has* to do something). The third person singular form ('há') can be translated as 'there is' or 'there are'.

'Há' is a useful word to know, although it seems a little awkward to use because it sounds similar to 'a' meaning 'the' (feminine singular), and the same as 'a' meaning 'to'; and 'à' meaning 'to the' (feminine singular) – not to mention 'a' meaning 'her' or 'it' (feminine) (which we haven't discussed yet). Don't let that put you off though – whenever you want to say 'there is' or 'there are', use 'há' – it will usually be clear what you mean from the context anyway. *

All right, that's enough for now! Before you start practising these new verbs, let me tell you why **ir** (to go) is such a useful one to remember. So far, we have been concentrating on verbs in the present tense, to talk about things that are happening now. We will soon be looking at how to express verbs to indicate actions in the past or future, but a nice little shortcut to be able to talk about the future is to prefix the verb you want to use with the appropriate conjugation of **ir**.

Let's say for example, that you wanted to construct a sentence like this: 'I will work here.' This is the future tense, which in English is quite simple – just prefix the verb with 'will' – but in Portuguese requires learning a whole new set of conjugations. Instead of learning the future tense, you can just rephrase your sentence like this: 'I am going to work here.' ('Eu vou trabalhar aqui').

So first of all, just take the appropriate conjugation of 'ir' – in this case, 'vou' ('I go', or 'I am going to') – and append the infinitive of the verb you want to express, so for our example you can say: 'vou trabalhar aqui'.

---

* In Brazilian Portuguese, the word 'tem' ('one has') is frequently used instead of 'há' to express the idea of 'There is / There are'.

Other examples: 'vou pensar' means 'I am going to think', 'vamos comer' means 'we are going to eat' etc. Very handy.

The only two exceptions are when the infinitive is also 'to go' ('ir') or 'to come' ('vir') – in which case, the infinitive must be omitted to avoid redundancy. For example, 'I am going to go to the shops' is 'vou às lojas', **not** 'vou **ir** às lojas', and 'they are going to come home now' is 'eles **vêm** para casa agora', **not** 'eles vão **vir** para casa agora'.

## Exercise 10: Irregular Verbs – Ser or Estar (*To Be*)
## Exercício 10: Verbos Irregulares – *Ser* ou *Estar*

*Answers on page 297.*

We know that sometimes we might feel confused over whether to use 'ser' or 'estar'. OK, not anymore!

**Ser is used with defining characteristics or permanent conditions** such as:

- nationalities → Nós **somo**s Mexicanos. *(We **are** Mexicans.)*
- origin → Eu **sou** de Lisboa. *(I **am** from Lisbon.)*
- professions or job tittles → Eles **são** os diretores. *(They **are** the directors.)*
- marital status → Ele **é** casado. *(He **is** married.)*
- possession → A bola **é** minha. *(The ball **is** mine.)*
- time, such as hours, dates, weekdays → **São** três horas. *(**It's** three o'clock.)*
- location of something unmovable → A loja **é** alí. *(The shop **is** over here.)*
- material things are made of → A porta **é** de vidro. *(The door **is** made of glass.)*

**Estar is used with temporary or changeable states** such as:

- location of something movable → Eu **estou** em Londres. *(I **am** in London.)*
- weather and temperature → Hoje **está** sol. *(Today **is** sunny.)*
- greetings → Como **está**? *(How **are** you?)*
- feelings → Eles **estão** com frio. *(They **are** cold.)*
- surprise → Tu agora **estás** tão magra! *(You **are** so slim now!)*

**10.1.** Fill in the gaps with either 'ser' or 'estar' in the present tense.

10.1.1. Onde _____ o dicionário?
*(Where **is** the dictionary?)*

10.1.2. _____ sete horas. O filme vai começar.
*(It's seven o'clock [lit. '**they are** seven hours']. The movie is going to start.)*

10.1.3. A Maria _____ do Canadá.
*(Maria **is** from Canada.)*

10.1.4. Tel Aviv _____ em Israel.
*(Tel Aviv **is** in Israel.)*

10.1.5. O café _____ muito quente.
*(The coffee **is** very hot.)*

10.1.6. O Carlos não pode ir tabalhar hoje. Ele _____ muito doente.
*(Carlos cannot go to work today. He **is** very ill.)*

10.1.7. Amanhã _____ sexta-feira ou sábado?
*(**Is** tomorrow Friday or Saturday?)*

10.1.8. Ela _____ loira e de olhos azuis.
*(She **is** blonde and blue-eyed.)*

10.1.9. Meu deus! Os pneus do carro _____ carecas!
*(My god! The car tires **are** worn out!)*

10.1.10. Este carro _____ cem por cento elétrico.
*(This car **is** one hundred percent electric.)*

10.1.11. Os carros _____ no estacionamento.
*(The cars **are** in the car park.)*

10.1.12. O Paulo _____ alto e forte.
*(Paulo **is** tall and strong.)*

10.1.13. Hoje o dia não _____ bonito.
*(Today **is** not a beautiful day.)*

10.1.14. O Alexios _____ grego.
*(Alexios **is** Greek.)*

10.1.15. Onde é que vocês _____ agora?
*(Where **are** you now guys?)*

10.1.16. A Maria e a Joana _____ simpáticas.
*(Maria and Joana **are** nice people.)*

10.1.17. _____ nós que pagamos o jantar.
*(We **are** the ones who will pay for dinner.)*

10.1.18. Eu e o Mário _____ um casal feliz.
*(Mário and I **are** a happy couple.)*

10.1.19. O senhor _____ sentado à mesa.
*(Sir, you **are** sitting at the table.)*

10.1.20. Eu _____ o pai do Francisco.
*(I **am** Francisco's father.)*

## Exercise 11: Irregular verbs

## Exercício 11: Verbos irregulares

*Answers on page 297.*

There are verbs that we use a lot and whose frequent use has made them become corrupted over time. These we call irregular verbs. There are many irregular verbs in Portuguese, but the most frequent ones are shown in Table 19.1:

| *Table 19.1: Common Portuguese Irregular Verbs* | |
| --- | --- |
| *Portuguese* | *English* |
| ser | to be (characteristic / unchanging) |
| estar | to be (non-characteristic / changeable) |
| ir | to go |
| ter | to have |
| dar | to give |
| ver | to see |
| fazer | to make / to do |
| vir | to come |
| pôr | to put / to place |
| poder | to be able to / can |
| trazer | to bring |
| sair | to go out |
| saber | to know (information, not people or places) |
| querer | to want |
| dizer | to say / to tell |
| haver | to have (auxiliary) / to be (impersonal) |

**11.1** Please study the verbs in the above table (you can look them up in the comprehensive verb tables at the end of the book), then fill in the gaps with these irregular verbs in the present tense.

11.1.1. Eu _____ (ser) o Carlos.
*(I **am** Carlos.)*

11.1.2. Eu _____ (ser) casado.
*(I **am** married.)*

11.1.3. Eu _____ (ter) 35 anos.
*(I am 35 years old [lit. I **have** 35 years].)*

11.1.4. Eu e a minha mulher Joana _____ (ter) dois filhos.
*(My wife and I **have** two children.)*

11.1.5. Agora, eu e a minha família _____ (estar) em Luanda, em Angola.
*(Now, my family and I **are** in Luanda, in Angola.)*

11.1.6. Normalmente aos fins de semana _____ (ir) viajar pelo país e conhecer outras cidades.
*(Normally at the weekends **we go** travelling through the country and we get to know other cities.)*

11.1.7. Os meus filhos _____ (sair) com os amigos que conhecem da Internet.
*(My children **go out** with their friends that they have met on the internet.)*

11.1.8. Eles também _____ (dizer) que é bom conhecer pessoas novas em diferentes partes do mundo.
*(They also **say** that it's good to know new people in different parts of the world.)*

11.1.9. Durante a semana eu _____ (poder) ir a casa e almoçar com a minha família.
*(During the week, **I can** go home and have lunch with my family.)*

11.1.10. A empresa onde eu trabalho _____ (dar) muitos benefícios aos funcionários.
*(The company I work for **gives** many benefits to its employees.)*

11.1.11. Quando acabo de trabalhar, eu passo pela escola e _____ (trazer) os meus filhos para casa.
*(When I finish work, I pass by the school and **I bring** my kids home.)*

11.1.12. Quando chegamos a casa, os meus filhos _____ (fazer) as tarefas da escola e depois brincam com os amigos e com o cachorro.
*(When we get home, my children **do** their homework and then play with their friends and the dog.)*

11.1.13. Sim, _____ (haver) um cachorro pequeno adotado por nós na nossa casa.
*(Yes, **there is** a puppy adopted by us in our home.)*

11.1.14. Normalmente, eu e a minha mulher _____ (vir) do trabalho cedo.
*(Normally, my wife and I [we] **come** from work early.)*

11.1.15. Quando chegamos a casa _____ (pôr) o trabalho de parte e conversamos uns com os outros de coisas agradáveis.
*(When we get home, **we put** work to one side and we talk with each other about pleasant subjects.)*

11.1.16. Normalmente passamos tempo de qualidade juntos e _____ (poder) dar apoio uns aos outros.
*(Normally we spend some quality time together and **we can** give support to each other.)*

11.1.17. Eu _____ (sair) da rotina quando chego a casa.
*(I **get out** of my routine when I get home.)*

11.1.18. Eu _____ (ver) alegria quando estou com a minha família.
*(I **see** happiness when I am with my family.)*

# 20. Radical-Changing Verbs

Occasionally, even a regular verb can be referred to as 'radical-changing' (radical-changing means that the stem is altered in some way – the word 'radical' comes from the Latin 'radicalis' meaning 'by the roots').

This happens when either:

i)   the spelling of the stem for one or more of the verb forms has to change in order to keep the pronunciation consistent, or

ii)  the spelling remains the same, but the pronunciation of the stem changes – the stressed vowel changes from a closed quality to an open quality.

The first type of radical-changing verb occurs as a result of the peculiarities of hard and soft pronunciation of the letters 'c', and 'g'. For example, the verb 'agradecer' – which means 'to thank' – requires a cedilla to be placed on the 'c' for the first person singular form – 'agradeço'. This is done in order to keep the pronunciation of the stem unaltered (in this case, to keep the 'c' soft). Similarly, the verb 'agir' – meaning 'to act' – requires the 'g' to be changed to a 'j' for the first person singular ('ajo') – again, to keep the pronunciation of the stem consistent.

It is not really worth going into detail about the second type of radical-changing verb, because there are no rules to tell you when this change in pronunciation should happen. However, you may notice in reference works that certain forms of regular verbs whose stems remain orthographically consistent (that's a posh way of saying 'are spelt the same') are marked as 'radical-changing', in which case you will know that you need to alter the vowel quality of the stressed syllable from closed to open when you pronounce the affected forms of such verbs. Just to confuse matters further, some regular verbs are radical-changing in European Portuguese pronunciation, but not in Brazilian! Aaarrgh!

Please don't spend your nights lying awake worrying about radical-changing verbs! The above explanation is just given for completeness, and for the benefit of those who want to understand the deeper implications of verb conjugation.

# 21. Auxiliary and Compound Verbs

Verb forms can be classified as either simple or compound. A simple verb form is made up of a single word, whereas compound forms require the addition of one or more other verbs to make the meaning clear. In a compound verb, any such 'extra' verbs are known as 'auxiliary'. Auxiliary verbs are also sometimes known as 'helper verbs' – because they help to provide another verb with a shade of meaning that it cannot represent using any of it's own (simple) forms.

In English, we use compound verbs a lot more than the Portuguese do. For example, when we use verbs negatively, we have to use the auxiliary verb 'do' (e.g., 'I **do** not think', 'they **do** not eat'). We have already seen how the verb 'to go' can be used as an auxiliary to refer to the future. Sometimes you can use several auxiliary verbs together to provide greater precision (a somewhat convoluted example: 'He would have had to have been going').

The verb that is being 'helped' by an auxiliary is used either in its infinitive form, or in a form known as a 'participle' – this is true in both English and Portuguese. A participle is a word derived from a verb that can also be used as an adjective. There are two types of participle, known as the present participle, and the past participle. Not surprisingly, present participles refer to an action or description that is current or ongoing, whereas past participles refer to completed actions or descriptions. There is no such thing as a 'future participle', because we can also use present and past participles to talk about the future. Try not to let that disturb you! We will come back to participles later.

# 22. Present Indicative and Present Continuous

We have been using verbs in the present tense so far. However, as there is more than one present tense, to be more accurate, we should use the correct technical term, which is the present indicative. Other present tenses include the present continuous and the present subjunctive – we will come onto subjunctive tenses later.

The present indicative is the basic present tense that we are already familiar with – it usually denotes that the action is something that the subject is in the habit of doing (we walk, they eat, I work, etc.). The conjugations given on pages 84 and 85 are all in the present indicative. Occasionally it can be used to describe a more immediate action (e.g. I understand), and this happens more often in Portuguese than in English. We tend to use the future tense for actions that will take place immediately whereas in Portuguese, immediate actions can use the present tense – eg. if the telephone rings, in English we might say 'I'll answer that' – which uses the future tense – but in Portuguese you could say 'I answer that', using the present indicative.

For more literal explanations of what is happening at the present moment, we usually employ what is known as a continuous (or progressive) tense, making use of a compound verb form. For example, to say 'I work here' implies that the person speaking is in the habit of working here. If we wanted to refer to what is happening at this very moment, we would say 'I **am working** here'. A literal translation of 'I am working here' would be 'eu estou a trabalhar aqui' in European Portuguese or the Brazilian equivalent: 'eu estou trabalhando aqui' – so whilst we are still referring to the present, these forms are not present indicative, but present continuous (or progressive).

### *Present Continuous of the regular verb trabalhar (to work) – PT*

| | |
|---|---|
| estou a trabalhar | estamos a trablahar |
| estás a trabalhar | estais a trabalhar |
| está a trabalhar | estão a trabalhar |

### *Present Continuous of the regular verb escrever (to write) – PT*

| | |
|---|---|
| estou a escrever | estamos a escrever |
| estás a escrever | estais a escrever |
| está a escrever | estão a escrever |

### *Present Continuous of the regular verb garantir (to guarantee) – PT*

| | |
|---|---|
| estou a garantir | estamos a garantir |
| estás a garantir | estais a garantir |
| está a garantir | estão a garantir |

Because the present continuous uses estar + a + the infinitive, the conjugations are the same for all verbs (regular and irregular). Brazilians use a slightly different form:

### *Present Continuous of the regular verb trabalhar (to work) – BR*

| | |
|---|---|
| estou trabalhando | estamos trabalhando |
| estás trabalhando | estais trabalhando |
| está trabalhando | estão trabalhando |

### *Present Continuous of the regular verb escrever (to write) – BR*

| | |
|---|---|
| estou escrevendo | estamos escrevendo |
| estás escrevendo | estais escrevendo |
| está escrevendo | estão escrevendo |

### *Present Continuous of the regular verb garantir (to guarantee) – BR*

| | |
|---|---|
| estou garantindo | estamos garantindo |
| estás garantindo | estais garantindo |
| está garantindo | estão garantindo |

As you can see, instead of the infinitive (e.g. 'trabalhar'), Brazilians use the gerund, or present participle ('trabalhando'). Don't worry about that too much right now, as we will be looking at the present participle in more detail later, but it is important to note that this verb tense is one of the main grammatical structures that differentiate European Portuguese from Brazilian Portuguese.

## Exercise 12: Present Continuous
## Exercício 12: Presente Contínuo

*Answers on page 298.*

**12.1.** Depending on the version of Portuguese you are mastering (European or Brazilian), please fill in the gaps with the present continuous of the given verbs.

12.1.1. Hoje está um tempo horrível e _____ (chover) constantemente.
*(Today's weather is horrible and **it's** constantly **raining**.)*

12.1.2. Eu estou _____ (tomar) um café agora.
*(I **am having** a coffee right now.)*

12.1.3. Manuel, o telefone _____ (tocar). Atenda por favor.
*(Manuel, the telephone **is ringing**. Pick it up please.)*

12.1.4. Eles _____ (ler) as notícias no jornal.
*(They **are reading** the news in the newspaper.)*

12.1.5. Nós _____ (ver) televisão.
*(We **are watching** TV.)*

12.1.6. Ó Maria e Joana, vocês _____ (fazer) os exercícios?
*(Hey, Maria and Joana, **are you doing** the exercises?)*

12.1.7. As crianças _____ (brincar) no parque.
*(The kids **are playing** in the park.)*

12.1.8. Eu não _____ (dizer) que isso está errado. Só precisa de ser revisto.
*(**I'm** not **saying** this is wrong. It just needs to be revised.)*

12.1.9. Eles _____ (apanhar Sol).
*(They **are sunbathing**.)*

12.1.10. A água _____ (ferver).
*(The water is **boiling**.)*

# 23. Preterite Indicative

Now we will take a look into the past. You might think that the past tense is called 'the past tense' – but I'm afraid you would be wrong. For some reason, grammarians (that's what you call the nutters who make this stuff up) have decided to call it 'the preterite' or 'preterite indicative', or if they're feeling kind, just 'the simple past'.

By the way, Americans sometimes spell this as 'preterit' without a final 'e' – this American spelling reflects the correct pronunciation: it should be pronounced 'pret-er-rit' not 'pret-er-right'. The word preterite is derived from the Latin 'praeteritum' meaning 'past' (grammarians just luuurve Latin).

The concept is very similar to using the present tense – you just have to learn the new tense conjugations. There are actually several ways to refer to something that happened in the past, each with varying shades of meaning, and the preterite represents just one of these ways. To give you an example of what I mean, take a look at the following sentences:

I walked home.
I was walking home.
I have walked home.
I had walked home.
I would have walked home.

Each of these sentences describes something involving the past, but they carry different shades of meaning by employing different tenses. The preterite is the simplest of these, that is, the first example above 'I walked home'. It refers to someone or something directly having done something (he ran, they ate, we went, etc.). For regular verbs, this means using a different set of endings on the stem of the infinitive. The following examples of regular Portuguese verbs illustrate the full conjugation of the preterite tense.

### Preterite indicative tense of the first conjugation regular verb: trabalhar (to work)

| | |
|---|---|
| trabalhei | trabalhámos (the acute á sounds a little more open than its present indicative equivalent) |
| trabalhaste | trabalhastes |
| trabalhou | trabalharam |

### *Preterite indicative tense of the first conjugation regular verb: pensar (to think)*

| | |
|---|---|
| pensei | pensámos |
| pensaste | pensastes |
| pensou | pensaram |

### *Preterite indicative tense of the second conjugation regular verb: comer (to eat)*

| | |
|---|---|
| comi | comemos (note: 1st person plural is exactly the same as in the present indicative) |
| comeste | comestes |
| comeu | comeram |

### *Preterite indicative tense of the second conjugation regular verb: escrever (to write)*

| | |
|---|---|
| escrevi | escrevemos |
| escreveste | escrevestes |
| escreveu | escreveram |

### *Preterite indicative tense of the third conjugation regular verb: garantir (to guarantee)*

| | |
|---|---|
| garanti | garantimos (again, no change from the present indicative) |
| garantiste | garantistes |
| garantiu | garantiram |

### *Preterite indicative tense of the third conjugation regular verb: assistir (to attend; to watch [BR])*

| | |
|---|---|
| assisti | assistimos |
| assististe | assististes |
| assistiu | assistiram |

Here are some examples of irregular preterites:

### *Preterite indicative tense of the irregular first conjugation verb: estar (to be)*

| | |
|---|---|
| estive | estivemos |
| estiveste | estivestes |
| esteve | estiveram |

*Preterite indicative tense of the irregular second conjugation verb: ser (to be)*

| | |
|---|---|
| fui | fomos |
| foste | fostes |
| foi | foram |

*Preterite indicative tense of the irregular third conjugation verb: ir (to go)*

| | |
|---|---|
| fui | fomos |
| foste | fostes |
| foi | foram |

No, it's not a misprint. The preterite forms of the verbs 'ser' and 'ir' are identical. So to say 'I was' ('eu fui'), is exactly the same as to say 'I went' ('eu fui'). Strange, but true. The good thing is that when you learn one verb, you are learning two verbs at the same time!

Interestingly, the preterite is used even for negative statements in Portuguese – we don't do this in English. For example, to put 'I thought' into the negative, we would say 'I did not think'. Because we use 'did' (an auxiliary verb), we have to change 'thought' to 'think' (the infinitive). Portuguese is a lot simpler. 'I did not think' would be translated 'não pensei' (lit. 'not I thought'), which is much more logical, and does not require you to change the verb form or use any auxiliary verbs. That's why you sometimes hear Portuguese people who are learning English say things like 'I didn't thought'.

## Exercise 13: Preterite Indicative

## Exercício 13: Pretérito Perfeito do Indicativo

*Answers on page 298.*

As we have seen, the Portuguese preterite ('eu tomei', for instance), refers to a one-off situation commonly equivalent to the English preterite ('I took') and typically requires an expression that defines where exactly in the time line the action happened such as 'ontem' (yesterday), 'na segunda-feira passada' (last Monday), 'ontem à noite' (last night), etc.

**13.1** Please observe Mário's timetable for last week, and write an account of his activity with the sentences given using the preterite of the given verbs in **bold**, as per the example.

|  | De manhã | À tarde | À noite |
|---|---|---|---|
| Sexta-feira | **acordar** às 8.00 horas. **levantar-se** às 8.15 horas. **tomar** o pequeno almoço (EU) / café da manhã (BR). **correr** às 10hrs. **responder** aos emails. | **marcar** duas reuniões. **ler** a correspondência . **escrever** o relatório. | **Jantar** com clientes. **dançar** na discoteca. **dormir** tarde. |
| Sábado | **levantar-se** tarde. **almoçar** com a namorada. | **visitar** um amigo. **lavar** o carro. **lanchar**. | **encontrar-se** com amigos no café. **assistir** a um concerto. |

acordar = *to wake up*
levantar-se = *to get up**
tomar o pequeno almoço = *to have breakfast (PT)*
tomar o café da manhã = *to have breakfast (BR)*
correr = *to run*
responder = *to reply / to answer*
marcar = *to schedule*
ler = *to read*
escrever = *to write*

jantar = *to have dinner / to dine*
dançar = *to dance*
dormir = *to sleep*
almoçar = *to have lunch / to lunch*
visitar = *to visit*
lavar = *to wash*
lanchar = *to snack*
encontrar-se com* = *to meet up with*
assistir = *to attend*

---

*Verbs that end with -se are reflexive, and we will cover them in more detail later. For the purposes of this exercise, you can treat them the same as other verbs, but just add the -se suffix (e.g. Ele levantou-se).

*Example:* Na sexta-feira de manhã da semana passada, o Mário **acordou** às 8 horas.

_____

_____

_____

_____

_____

_____

_____

No sábado, _____

_____

_____

_____

_____

_____

_____

# 24. Imperfect Indicative

Not too difficult eh? All right then, let's start to make things a little more interesting. Another tense that has to do with the past is the 'imperfect indicative'. Basically, this refers to an action that took place in the past, but was ongoing for a period of time and where the time of completion of the action is not specified. It is precisely because of this lack of a specified time that the tense is called 'imperfect'.

We don't really have a direct equivalent in English – we use the preterite, past continuous, or conditional instead (more on those further down). Here are some English equivalents of the imperfect indicative:

- I **was working** here in those days (past continuous) – Eu **trabalhava** aqui nessa altura (imperfect indicative).
- I **worked** here in those days (preterite) – Eu **trabalhava** aqui nessa altura (imperfect indicative).
- In those days, I **would work** here then go home (conditional) – Nessa altura, eu **trabalhava** aqui e depois ia para casa (imperfect indicative).

In English, it is typically the context that places the use of the verb in the imperfect – in the above examples, the use of 'in those days' indicates an ongoing action with no specific start or end. Without that context, we would not know that it was imperfect (relating to an ongoing past action without a specified completion event). In Portuguese, the verb ending directly implies the imperfect aspect, so you don't need the extra contextual information to know that the timing of the action that the verb relates to is not specific.

This tense is also used when you want to refer to something that used to happen. You can either use the appropriate conjugation of the verb in the imperfect indicative tense directly, or use the appropriate conjugation of the verb 'costumar' in the imperfect, followed by the infinitive of the verb you are referring to (so 'Eu costumava trabalhar aqui' and 'Eu trabalhava aqui' could both be used to mean 'I used to work here').

***Imperfect indicative tense of the first conjugation regular verb: trabalhar (to work)***

| | |
|---|---|
| trabalhava | trabalhávamos |
| trabalhavas | trabalháveis |
| trabalhava | trabalhavam |

*Imperfect indicative tense of the first conjugation regular verb: pensar (to think)*

| | |
|---|---|
| pensava | pensávamos |
| pensavas | pensáveis |
| pensava | pensavam |

*Imperfect indicative tense of the second conjugation regular verb: comer (to eat)*

| | |
|---|---|
| comia | comíamos |
| comias | comíeis |
| comia | comiam |

*Imperfect indicative tense of the second conjugation regular verb: escrever (to write).*

| | |
|---|---|
| escrevia | escrevíamos |
| escrevias | escrevíeis |
| escrevia | escreviam |

*Imperfect indicative tense of the third conjugation regular verb: garantir (to guarantee).*

| | |
|---|---|
| garantia | garantíamos |
| garantias | garantíeis |
| garantia | garantiam |

*Imperfect indicative tense of the third conjugation regular verb: assistir (to attend; to watch [BR])*

| | |
|---|---|
| assistia | assistíamos |
| assistias | assistíeis |
| assistia | assistiam |

Irregular imperfect indicatives…

*Imperfect indicative tense of the irregular first conjugation verb: estar (to be)*

| | |
|---|---|
| estava | estávamos |
| estavas | estáveis |
| estava | estavam |

***Imperfect indicative tense of the irregular second conjugation verb: ser (to be)***

| | |
|---|---|
| era | éramos |
| eras | éreis |
| era | eram |

***Imperfect indicative tense of the irregular third conjugation verb: ir (to go)***

| | |
|---|---|
| ia | íamos |
| ias | íeis |
| ia | iam |

So when you are talking about something that extended over an indefinite period of time – as opposed to an event or something that was accomplished – you use the imperfect indicative rather than the preterite.

## Foi or Era?

Note the difference between the words 'foi' (preterite) and 'era' (imperfect indicative) – and their equivalents for the other 'persons' of their respective tenses. This is often the source of confusion, because both words are usually translated as 'was' in English, and both come from the verb 'ser'. The rule is exactly the same as for the other verbs though – 'foi' is used for an event or accomplished action, and 'era' relates to an action or process which occurred over an indefinite period of time in the past. So...

A exposição **foi** boa     The exhibition was good (referring to a known time period)
**Era** um homem bom     He was a good man (over an unspecified period of time)

The verb 'foi' in the first sentence tells you that the exhibition had both a beginning and an end in the past, whereas 'era' defines neither the beginning nor the end of the action. That's why we call it imperfect – as it imperfectly defines when the action took place.

## Past Continuous

The imperfect indicative can be used to create the past continuous tense (the past equivalent of the present continuous we already looked at on page 108). As noted above, in English we often use the past continuous in places where the Portuguese would use the imperfect indicative (or sometimes the present perfect, discussed later), but the Portuguese still use the past continuous when they want to describe events that were ongoing in the past when something else happened (for example, 'I was working when the postman came.' – 'Eu estava a trabalhar quando o carteiro veio.' (PT) or 'Eu estava trabalhando quando o carteiro veio.' (BR).

The past continuous is formed by taking the imperfect indicative of the verb 'estar' and adding 'a' + infinitive (PT) or the present participle (BR) – in the same way that the present continuous is formed with the present indicative of 'estar'). For example, 'eu estava a trabalhar'. It can also be used in the subjunctive mood to convey uncertainty of action (present participles and the subjunctive mood are both covered in later chapters).

Here are the conjugations of the past continuous for regular verbs in European Portuguese (for Brazilian, just replace 'a trabalhar' with 'trabalh**ando**', 'a escrever' with 'escrev**endo**', 'a garantir' with 'garant**indo**' and so on.):

*Past Continuous of the first conjugation regular verb: trabalhar (to work)*

estava a trabalhar          estávamos a trabalhar
estavas a trabalhar        estáveis a trabalhar
estava a trabalhar          estavam a trabalhar

*Past Continuous of the first conjugation regular verb: pensar (to think)*

estava a pensar             estávamos a pensar
estavas a pensar           estáveis a pensar
estava a pensar             estavam a pensar

*Past Continuous of the second conjugation regular verb: comer (to eat)*

estava a comer              estávamos a comer
estavas a comer            estáveis a comer
estava a comer              estavam a comer

### *Past Continuous of the second conjugation regular verb: escrever (to write)*

| | |
|---|---|
| estava a escrever | estávamos a escrever |
| estavas a escrever | estáveis a escrever |
| estava a escrever | estavam a escrever |

### *Past Continuous of the third conjugation regular verb: garantir (to guarantee)*

| | |
|---|---|
| estava a garantir | estávamos a garantir |
| estavas a garantir | estáveis a garantir |
| estava a garantir | estavam a garantir |

### *Past Continuous of the third conjugation regular verb: assistir (to attend; to watch [BR])*

| | |
|---|---|
| estava a assistir | estávamos a assistir |
| estavas a assistir | estáveis a assistir |
| estava a assistir | estavam a assistir |

The irregulars follow exactly the same pattern – just append 'a' + infinitive to the imperfect indicative of 'estar'.

# Exercise 14: Imperfect Indicative
# Exercício 14: Imperfeito do Indicativo

*Answers on page 299.*

To sum up the rules, the imperfect is used in the following situations:

- When you <u>describe</u> a story. On these occasions you may use expressions like 'antigamente' (formerly), 'antes' (before), 'naquele tempo' (back then) and other similar expressions. e.g. 'antigamente eu **fazia** exercício duas vezes por semana.' (Formerly, **I used to do** exercise twice a week.)

- When you talk about <u>two actions in the past</u> where one is longer than the other. e.g. 'Eu **preparava** o jantar quando o telefone **tocou**.' (I was preparing dinner, when the phone rang). Here, 'preparava' is imperfect whereas 'tocou' is preterite (it is also possible to use the past continuous here in Portuguese, as we would in English, i.e. 'Eu estava a preparar o jantar quando o telefone tocou').

- When you want <u>to express an intention</u> in the past, e.g. 'Ontem eu **ia** visitar o Pedro, mas **acabei** por não ter tempo.' (Yesterday **I was going to** visit Pedro, but I **ended up** not having the time). Here, 'I was going' is imperfect and 'ended up' is preterite.

- When you <u>describe two long actions</u> that were occurring at the same time in the past. e.g. 'Enquanto eu **trabalhava** eles **aprendiam**.' (While I **was working**, they **were learning**).

- When you talk about <u>time, or age in the past</u>, e.g. 'Quando eu **tinha** 5 anos...' ('When I was 5... [lit. **had** 5 years]').

- As an alternative way to <u>express the conditional</u>, e.g. 'Eu **comprava** esse livro, mas não tenho dinheiro.' (I **would buy** that book, but I don't have the money).

**14.1.** Please fill in the gaps with the Imperfect Indicative of the given verbs:

14.1.1. Antigamente eu _____ (correr) 5 kms por dia.
   *(Formerly I **used to run** 5kms a day.)*

14.1.2. Ele _____ (levantar-se) sempre muito cedo.
   *(He always **used to get up** very early in the morning.)*

14.1.3. Depois, _____ (tomar) um duche bem quente antes de ir trabalhar.
   *(Then, he **used to take** a very hot shower before he went to work.)*

14.1.4. Quando eu _____ (ser) mais jovem, eu saia mais do que agora.

*(When I **was** younger, I used to go out more often than now.)*

14.1.5. Dantes, eu _____ (apanhar) sempre o comboio das sete horas.

*(Before, I always **used to take** the seven o'clock train.)*

14.1.6. Em criança, eu _____ (jogar) bem à bola.

*(In my childhood, I **played** ball very well.)*

14.1.7. Dantes eles _____ (ser) médicos de medicina geral, agora são especialistas.

*(Before they **were** general practitioners, now they are specialists.)*

14.1.8. Nós _____ (assistir) a todas as aulas sem exceção.

*(We **attended** all the classes without exception.)*

14.1.9. A casa _____ (ser) grande mas acolhedora.

*(The house **was** big but cozy.)*

14.1.10. Ela já _____ (estar) lá quando eu cheguei.

*(She **was** already there when I arrived.)*

## Exercise 15: Preterite or Imperfect Indicative?

## Exercício 15: Pretérito Perfeito ou Imperfeito do Indicativo?

*Answers on page 299.*

You may agree that sometimes it is quite difficult to figure out whether you should use the preterite or imperfect when you tell a story in the past. The distinction between them is a question of concept. If you understand the concept you are very likely to use these two tenses correctly.

**15.1.** Please fill in the gaps with either the preterite or imperfect of the given verbs. If you haven't learned the verbs by heart yet, you may want to make use of the verb reference tables at the end of the book.

15.1.1. Antigamente as pessoas _____ (ter) uma vida mais modesta.
 *(Formerly, people **used to have** a more modest life.)*

15.1.2. Quando nós _____ (sair) do cinema _____ (chover).
 *(When we **left** the cinema it **was raining**.)*

15.1.3. Quando eu _____ (ser) mais novo, eu _____ (falar) com toda a gente.
 *(When I **was** younger, I **used to chat** with everyone.)*

15.1.4. Eu _____ (ler) o meu livro quando a Ada e o John

_____ (bater) à porta.
 *(I **was reading** my book when Ada and John **knocked** on the door.)*

15.1.5. Eu não _____ (poder) ir com vocês ao jantar. Eu

_____ (estar) doente.
 *(I **wasn't able to / couldn't** go with you to the dinner. I **was** ill.)*

15.1.6. Ontem, às onze horas da noite eu ainda _____ (estar) no escritório.
 *(Yesterday at eleven o'clock in the evening I **was** still in the office.)*

15.1.7. Antes ele _____ (usar) óculos, mas agora não. Agora ele vê bem.

*(Before he **used to wear** eyeglasses, but not now. Now he sees well.)*

15.1.8. A exposição _____ (ser) boa, mas _____ (estar) lá muita gente.

*(The exhibition **was** good but there **were** too many people there.)*

15.1.9. Eu _____ (ir) visitar o Paulo, mas não sei se ele está em casa.

*(I **would go** and visit Paulo, but I don't know if he is at home.)*

15.1.10. Eu _____ (poder) conduzir mais depressa, mas é perigoso e ilegal.

*(I **could** drive faster, but it's dangerous and illegal.)*

# 25. Future Indicative

Let's switch to the future now. Again, there are various shades of future (I will go, I will have been, I might go, etc.), so there are various tenses that relate to the future. The simplest of these tenses is simply known as 'future' or 'future indicative' which is a fairly logical name really (the grammarians must have been having an 'off' day). In English, we achieve this tense by using the auxiliary verb 'will', or sometimes 'shall' (strictly speaking, in English, you are supposed to use 'shall' for the first person, and 'will' for the second and third person – unless you are trying to add emphasis, in which case you use them the opposite way round).

In Portuguese, the future tense is not used very often – they tend to use the appropriate conjugation of 'ir', followed by the infinitive of the verb (e.g. 'vou comer' instead of 'comerei'). You are more likely to come across the future indicative in writing than in speech. The true future indicative is a simple form, and is conjugated as follows:

*Future indicative tense of the first conjugation regular verb: trabalhar (to work)*

| | |
|---|---|
| trabalharei | trabalharemos |
| trabalharás | trabalhareis |
| trabalhará | trabalharão |

*Future indicative tense of the first conjugation regular verb: pensar (to think)*

| | |
|---|---|
| pensarei | pensaremos |
| pensarás | pensareis |
| pensará | pensarão |

*Future indicative tense of the second conjugation regular verb: comer (to eat)*

| | |
|---|---|
| comerei | comeremos |
| comerás | comereis |
| comerá | comerão |

*Future indicative tense of the second conjugation regular verb: escrever (to write)*

| | |
|---|---|
| escreverei | escreveremos |
| escreverás | escrevereis |
| escreverá | escreverão |

***Future indicative tense of the third conjugation regular verb: garantir (to guarantee)***

garantirei			garantiremos
garantirás			garantireis
garantirá			garantirão

***Future indicative tense of the third conjugation regular verb: assistir (to attend; to watch [BR])***

assistirei			assistiremos
assistirás			assistireis
assistirá			assistirão

Irregular verbs and the future indicative…

***Future indicative tense of the irregular first conjugation verb: estar (to be)***

estarei			estaremos
estarás			estareis
estará			estarão

***Future indicative tense of the irregular second conjugation verb: ser (to be)***

serei			seremos
serás			sereis
será			serão

***Future indicative tense of the irregular third conjugation verb: ir (to go)***

irei			iremos
irás			ireis
irá			irão

A helpful hint for remembering the future indicative forms, is that they all start with the full infinitive – not just the stem of it (although not all irregular verbs do so). Be careful though not to confuse the third person plural form of the future indicative with the preterite third person plural, as they both start with the full infinitive – e.g. 'assistirão' vs. 'assistiram' (in terms of pronunciation the former is stressed in the last syllable – assisti*rão*, and the later in the last-but-one syllable – assist*ira*m).

# Exercise 16: Future Indicative
# Exercício 16: Futuro do Indicativo

*Answers on page 300.*

As in English, you can also express the future in two different ways in Portuguese:

1. I am going to eat → Eu vou comer (compound: ir + verb)
2. I will eat → Eu comerei (simple: future indicative)

**16.1.** Politicians are experts in using the future when they express their promises during an election campaign. Please fill in the gaps in the future tense as per the example given.

> *Example:* Eu _____ serei _____ (ser) um bom líder político.
> *(I **will be** a good political leader.)*

> 16.1.1. Eu não _____ (subir) os impostos.
> *(I **won't raise** the taxes.)*

> 16.1.2. Eu também _____ (aumentar) as pensões.
> *(I'm also **going to raise** pensions.)*

> 16.1.3. _____ (haver) mais postos de trabalho.
> *(**There will be** more jobs.)*

> 16.1.4. Os medicamentos _____ (ser) mais baratos.
> *(Medicines **will be** cheaper.)*

> 16.1.5. A minha administração _____ (contratar) mais médicos, e mais ambulâncias.
> *(My administration **will contract** more doctors and more ambulances.)*

> 16.1.6. Os transportes públicos _____ (estar) mais baratos e acessíveis para todos.
> *(Public transport **will be** cheaper and more accessible for all.)*

> 16.1.7. Eu _____ (acabar) com a corrupção.
> *(I **will end** corruption.)*

16.1.8. Eu não _____ (deixar) as grandes empresas controlar o país.

*(I **won't let** the big corporations control the country.)*

16.1.9. Com a minha eleição, os deputados não _____ (ter) benefícios especias.

*(With my election, no Member of Parliament **will have** special benefits.)*

16.1.10. Todos os cidadãos _____ (ser) iguais perante a lei.

*(All citizens **will be** equal under the law.)*

# 26. Conditional

This is quite an easy one. Wherever you prefix an English verb with the word 'would', but without using the auxiliary verb 'have', you are using the conditional tense. Prefixing an English verb with the words 'would have' ('I would have walked home') is different – this would be the 'conditional perfect' tense (still in the conditional mood, but a different tense), so it is only if the verb concerned is immediately prefixed by 'would' in English.

Of course, the verb 'have' itself could be prefixed with the word 'would' ('They would have a pet cat, if…'), and this is conditional – it's only if 'have' is being used as an auxiliary verb that the tense would become the conditional perfect.

Examples of the conditional tense: 'I would go, but I'm busy'; 'He would walk home'; 'They would not believe me', 'I would have a burger if I wasn't on a diet.'

*Conditional tense of the first conjugation regular verb: trabalhar (to work)*

| | |
|---|---|
| trabalharia | trabalharíamos |
| trabalharias | trabalharíeis |
| trabalharia | trabalhariam |

*Conditional tense of the first conjugation regular verb: pensar (to think)*

| | |
|---|---|
| pensaria | pensaríamos |
| pensarias | pensaríeis |
| pensaria | pensariam |

*Conditional tense of the second conjugation regular verb: comer (to eat)*

| | |
|---|---|
| comeria | comeríamos |
| comerias | comeríeis |
| comeria | comeriam |

*Conditional tense of the second conjugation regular verb: escrever (to write)*

| | |
|---|---|
| escreveria | escreveríamos |
| escreverias | escreveríeis |
| escreveria | escreveriam |

### *Conditional tense of the third conjugation regular verb: garantir (to guarantee)*

| | |
|---|---|
| garantiria | garantiríamos |
| garantirias | garantiríeis |
| garantiria | garantiriam |

### *Conditional tense of the third conjugation regular verb: assistir (to attend; to watch [BR])*

| | |
|---|---|
| assistiria | assistiríamos |
| assistirias | assistiríeis |
| assistiria | assistiriam |

Irregular verbs in the conditional tense:

### *Conditional tense of the irregular first conjugation verb: estar (to be)*

| | |
|---|---|
| estaria | estaríamos |
| estarías | estaríeis |
| estaría | estariam |

### *Conditional tense of the irregular second conjugation verb: ser (to be)*

| | |
|---|---|
| seria | seríamos |
| serias | seríeis |
| seria | seriam |

### *Conditional tense of the irregular third conjugation verb: ir (to go)*

| | |
|---|---|
| iria | iríamos |
| irias | iríeis |
| iria | iriam |

## Exercise 17: Conditional

## Exercício 17: Condicional

*Answers on page 300.*

As we discussed before, you can use the Imperfect indicative to express the conditional, but that is a shortcut people use because there is also a proper conditional, and its endings are the same for all verbs. There are only 3 verbs that change their stem in the conditional mood (they are 'radical-changing'), and they are:

- Fazer → eu **far**ia (*not* fazeria) – I would do / I would make
- Trazer → eu **trar**ia (*not* trazeria) – I would bring
- Dizer → eu **dir**ia (*not* dizeria) – I would say

**17.1.** Please fill in the gaps with the verbs given in the Conditional.

17.1.1. Se eu não tivesse que trabalhar, eu _____ (fazer) uma viagem à volta do mundo.
*(If I didn't have to work, I **would do** a trip around the world.)*

17.1.2. Eu _____ (levar) a minha famíla comigo.
*(I **would take** my family with me.)*

17.1.3. Eles _____ (adorar) descobrir outros países e outras culturas.
*(They **would love** to discover other countries and other cultures.)*

17.1.4. Nós _____ (poder) provar outras comidas também.
*(We **could taste** other foods as well.)*

17.1.5. Nós _____ (beber) vinho e chá de várias origens.
*(We **would drink** wine and tea from different places.)*

17.1.6. E você, não _____ (fazer) o mesmo?
*(And you, **wouldn't** you **do** the same?)*

17.1.7. Você não _____ (dizer) a todos os seus amigos como é boa a aventura?
*(**Wouldn't** you **tell** all your friends how good the adventure is?)*

17.1.8. Você não lhes _____ (pedir) para viajarem consigo?
*(**Wouldn't** you **ask** them to travel with you?)*

17.1.9. No meu regresso, eu _____ (trazer) uma lembrança para todos os meus amigos também.
*(On my return, I **would bring** a souvenir for all my friends as well.)*

17.1.10. E depois de nós terminarmos a primeira viagem, _____ (começar) tudo de novo outra vez.
*(And after we had finished our first trip, we **would start** everything again.)*

# 27. Present and Past Participles

Participles are words that are formed from a verb, but that can be used as adjectives. They can also be used to form continuous and perfect tenses (we will come back to perfect tenses in a little while).

## The Present Participle

In English, all present participles end with 'ing' (and are also sometimes used as nouns, although this is not the case in Portuguese). For example:

- 'These are my painting gloves' – the present participle 'painting' is being used as an adjective (to describe the gloves).
- 'The painting is beautiful' – the present participle 'painting' is being used as a noun (a peculiarity of English).
- 'I had been painting for hours' – a compound form from the verb 'to paint' which uses two auxiliary verbs ('had' from 'to have', and 'been' from 'to be'), and the present participle 'painting' to form the past perfect continuous tense (this tense will also be covered later).

Interestingly, even irregular verbs in English all have an 'ing' form ('doing', 'being', 'going' etc.).

In European Portuguese, the present participle is made up of the word 'a' plus the infinitive form of the verb. So 'a trabalhar' means 'working', 'a escrever' means 'writing', and 'a discernir' means 'discerning'. This is true for both regular and irregular verbs.

In Brazilian Portuguese, the present participle always ends with the letters 'ndo'. First conjugation (ar) verbs have the ending 'ando', second conjugation (er) verbs have 'endo', and third conjugation (ir) verbs use 'indo'. So 'trabalhando' means 'working', 'escrevendo' means 'writing', and 'discernindo' means 'discerning'. As with English, even the irregular verbs follow the same pattern, which makes it nice and easy to form words like 'tendo' (having), 'fazendo' (making or doing), 'indo' (going) etc. The present participle is also known as the 'gerund' (pronounced 'jerund').

In Portuguese, the present participle is never used as an adjective – instead, they usually follow the noun with the words 'de' + the infinitive of the verb (e.g. 'luvas de pintar' – 'painting gloves', where 'pintar' is the infinitive 'to paint').

Also worthy of note, is that although in English we sometimes use the present participle as a noun, this is never done in Portuguese. So whereas we might refer to 'a painting', you would never refer to 'um pintando' – you would have to use the correct noun form, which is 'uma pintura'.*

Here are the Portuguese translations of the 3 examples given above (note that only one of them uses the present participle. This is because, as noted above, in Portuguese the present participle is only used as a verb (to form continuous tenses):

- 'Essas são as minhas luvas de pintar' – 'These are my **painting** gloves' – the preposition 'de' followed by the infinitive is used instead of the present participle.
- 'A pintura é bonita' – 'The **painting** is beautiful' – a separate noun form is used, again avoiding the present participle.
- 'Eu tinha estado **a pintar** durante horas.' (PT) or 'Eu tinha estado **pintando** durante horas.' (BR) – 'I had been **painting** for hours' – the present participle *is* used here (shown in bold) to create the compound verb form of the past perfect continuous tense.

## The Past Participle

The past participle can have irregular forms, and can easily be confused with the preterite. The principle is the same as for the present participle though – a past participle can be used as an adjective, but it refers to a past or completed action or description. When used as a verb (rather than as an adjective), it aways requires an auxiliary verb (usually either 'to have' or 'to be').

Unlike the present participle, which is not used adjectively in Portuguese, the past participle *is* used as an adjective in Portuguese – in the same way that it is used in English.

In English, past participles usually end in 'ed' and are also usually (but not always) spelt the same as the preterite forms. If you're not sure whether you are dealing with a preterite or a past participle, just remember that if used with an auxiliary verb, or as an adjective, it must be the past participle. For example:

---

* You can transform a verb into a noun in Portuguese by adding the determinate 'o' in front of the infinitive, e.g. 'O pintar é um passatempo muito bom'. – 'Painting is a very good hobby'. With this technique you can transform any verb into a noun (however, this does not involve using the present participle).

| Table 27.1: Comparison of preterite and past participle in English | |
|---|---|
| She **completed** the work. | Preterite. |
| She has **completed** the work. | Past participle (compound verb with the auxiliary 'has' from 'to have'). |
| The **completed** work. | Past participle used as an adjective. |
| I have **done** all that he asked of me. | Past participle (irregular). |
| I **did** all that he asked of me. | Preterite (irregular). |

Note: a common grammatical error in English (for verbs where the preterite and past participle are not the same) is to use the past participle without an auxiliary, or in a place where the preterite should be used (for example: 'I done my homework').

In Portuguese, regular past participles end in 'ado' for first conjugation verbs, and 'ido' for both second and third conjugation verbs ('er' verbs do not use 'edo' as you might expect). As this is completely different to the formation of the Portuguese preterite, the two are less likely to be confused in Portuguese than they are in English.

When used adjectively, to describe a feminine noun, 'ado' becomes 'ada', and 'ido' becomes 'ida', – e.g. 'Ela é a preferida'

Here are the translations of the above phrases in Portuguese (as you can see, the preterite and past participle are always different, unlike in English where this is only the case with irregular verbs):

| Table 27.2: Comparison of preterite and past participle in Portuguese | |
|---|---|
| Ela **completou** o trabalho. | She **completed** the work (preterite). |
| Ela tem **completado** o trabalho. | She has **completed** the work (past participle). |
| O trabalho **completado**. | The **completed** work (past participle used as an adjective, although you can also use 'completo'). |
| Eu tenho **feito** tudo o que ele me pediu | I have **done** all that he asked of me (past participle – irregular). |
| Eu **fiz** tudo o que ele me pediu. | I **did** all that he asked of me (preterite – irregular). |

## Regular and Irregular Past Participles

I am sure you will be delighted to know, that some Portuguese verbs have more than one past participle (one regular, and one irregular). In fact, some verbs have only regular past participles, some have only irregular ones, and others have both regular and irregular! Where there are 2 past participle forms to choose from, the irregular one is used only when combined with one of the auxiliary verbs: ser, estar, or ficar.

So, 'foi aceite' means 'it was accepted' ('aceite' is the irregular past participle[*], and is used here because the preceding verb is 'foi', which comes from 'ser'), but 'tenho aceitado' means 'I have accepted' ('aceitado' is the regular past participle, and is used here because the auxiliary verb is 'tenho' from 'ter').

For a better understanding of the use of Portuguese past participles, we present here a couple of tables:

| *Table 27.3: A list of verbs with irregular Past Participles only* | | |
|---|---|---|
| *Verb* | *Past Participle* | *Meaning in English* |
| abrir | aberto | opened |
| cobrir | coberto | covered |
| dizer | dito | said / told |
| descobrir | descoberto | discovered |
| descrever | descrito | described |
| escrever | escrito | written |
| fazer | feito | done / made |
| ganhar | ganho | won |
| gastar | gasto | spent |
| impor | imposto | imposed |
| inscrever | inscrito | enrolled |
| pagar | pago | paid |
| pôr | posto | put |

---

[*] In Brazil, the irregular past participle of 'aceitar' is 'aceito'.

| Verb | Past Participle | Meaning in English |
|---|---|---|
| satisfazer | satisfeito | satisfied |
| ver | visto | seen |
| vir | vindo | come |

**Table 27.3: A list of verbs with both regular and irregular Past Participles**

| Verb | Regular Past Participle with 'ter' as auxiliary verb | Irregular Past Participle with 'ser', 'estar' or 'ficar' as auxiliary verb | Meaning in English |
|---|---|---|---|
| aceitar | aceitado | aceite (aceito [BR]) | accepted |
| acender | acendido | aceso | switched on |
| eleger | elegido | eleito | elected |
| emergir | emergido | emerso | immersed |
| entregar | entregado | entregue | delivered |
| envolver | envolvido | envolto | involved / wrapped |
| expulsar | expulsado | expulso | expelled |
| exprimir | exprimido | expresso | expressed |
| extinguir | extinguido | extinto | extinguished |
| imprimir | imprimido | impresso | printed |
| matar | matado | morto | killed |
| morrer | morrido | morto | died |
| prender | prendido | preso | arrested |
| romper | rompido | roto | torn |
| salvar | salvado | salvo | saved |
| secar | secado | seco | dried |
| soltar | soltado | solto | released |
| suspender | suspendido | suspenso | suspended |

## Exercise 18: Past Participle

## Exercício 18: Particípio Passado

*Answers on page 300.*

As we have seen, in Portuguese, verbs with regular past participles end with '...ado' (for first conjugation verbs) and '...ido'(for both second and third conjugation verbs). There are other verbs with both a regular and an irregular past participle.

**18.1.** Let's check out how good you are at using the past participles in Portuguese, by filling in the gaps with the correct one for the verb given.

18.1.1. O filme foi _____ (ver) por milhares de pessoas.
*(The film was **seen** by thousands of people.)*

18.1.2. As flores que ela me deu estão _____ (estragar).
*(The flowers she gave me are **damaged**.)*

18.1.3. A carta já foi _____ (enviar).
*(The letter has been **sent**.)*

18.1.4. Quando eu cheguei à oficina, o meu carro já tinha sido

_____ (arranjar).
*(When I arrived at the garage, my car had already been **fixed**.)*

18.1.5.  As teorias científicas serão _____ (apresentar) na reunião.
*(The scientific theories will be **presented** at the meeting.)*

18.1.6. Em tribunal provou-se que ele tinha _____ (dizer) a verdade.
*(In court it was proved that he had **told** the truth.)*

18.1.7. Ele e eu temos _____ (trabalhar) muito esta semana.
*(He and I have **worked** hard this week.)*

18.1.8. Quando ele chegou ao aeroporto, o avião já tinha _____ (partir).
*(When he arrived at the airport, the plane had already **left**.)*

18.1.9. Uma nova música foi _____ (cantar) pelos artistas no concerto.

*(A new song was **sung** by the artists at the concert.)*

18.1.10. Ele não se interessa pelos prémios que tem _____ (ganhar).

*(He doesn't care about the prizes he has **won**.)*

# 28. Subjects and Objects

Differentiation between subjects and objects has a significant impact on the way we speak, so it is important to understand what they are.

The subject of a sentence is the person or thing referred to as carrying out or performing the action described by the verb. For example, in the sentence 'The cat scratched the curtains' ('O gato arranhou as cortinas') – the subject of the sentence is the cat – 'o gato' – because he was the one who did the scratching. The first thing to do then, is to identify the verb. Then ask yourself 'who or what is performing the activity represented by this verb?' The answer is the subject of the sentence, and this can be any type of noun (proper noun [i.e. a name], noun, noun phrase, or pronoun).

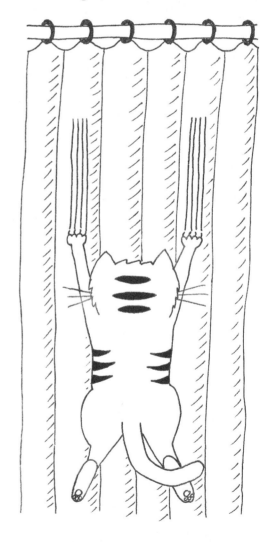

Often, but not always, an action as described by a verb, is performed on, to, or for someone or something: the object. In the above example, it was the curtains that were scratched by the cat, so the curtains are the object of the sentence. To identify the object then, ask yourself who or what was affected by the verb's action – again, the object is always a type of noun.

By the way, if a verb *requires* an object before it will make sense (e.g. the verb 'to sell' – something that is sold has to be sold *to* somebody), it is known as 'transitive'. If it is not really possible to use an object noun with a particular verb (e.g. 'to arrive'), the verb is said to be 'intransitive'.

*"O gato arranhou as cortinas."*

One example of how subjects and objects affect word choice in English, is seen in the difference between the words 'who' and 'whom'. The word 'who' should only ever be used when referencing the subject, and 'whom' when referencing the object ('who does what to whom') – although this rule is gradually being eroded from the English language, so that the word 'who' is beginning to be accepted as a correct way of referring to an object (the technically incorrect use of 'who' as an object often sounds more natural, and conversational).

Likewise in Portuguese, subjects and objects have a bearing on the choice of pronoun, but knowing what they are is also helpful when it comes to understanding reflexive verbs (coming up next).

# 29. Reflexive Verbs

When the object of a verb refers to the same individual as the subject, the verb is said to be reflexive. In English, this means using a pronoun that ends with 'self' or 'selves' (for example, 'she cut herself'; 'they behaved themselves'). Portuguese also has a set of pronouns that are used to make verbs reflexive, and we will look at those in more detail further down.

There are a lot more reflexive verbs in Portuguese than there are in English, and they often seem a little odd to us at first. It is a common habit for us learners to forget to use the pronoun of a reflexive verb (and therefore not use it reflexively), but this can be dangerous because it can cause the verb to take on a different meaning.

A good example of what reflexive verbs are all about is the Portuguese verb 'lembrar-se'. The '-se' on the end of the infinitive is a reflexive pronoun, and it is this pronoun which makes the verb reflexive. The English translation of 'lembrar-se' is 'to remember'. However, if you use the verb non-reflexively – i.e. 'lembrar' (rather than 'lembar-se'), it means 'to remind'. So whereas in English, we use two completely separate verbs ('to remember', and 'to remind'), the Portuguese just use one ('lembrar') with the option of making it reflexive ('lembrar-se'). Although 'lembrar-se' means 'to remember', it might be more helpful to think of a literal translation: 'to remind oneself'.

When conjugating a reflexive verb, you use the same rules as for other verbs – 'lembrar-se' is still a first conjugation verb (only the 1st person plural conjugation changes slightly), but you have to amend the pronoun on the end to reflect the correct 'person'. Here is the full conjugation of a reflexive verb:

***Present Indicative tense of the irregular first conjugation verb: lembrar-se (to remember)***

| | |
|---|---|
| lembro-me | lembramo-nos |
| lembras-te | lembrais-vos |
| lembra-se | lembram-se |

Here are some common reflexive verbs...

**Table 29.1: Some Common Portuguese Reflexive Verbs**

| Portuguese | English | Literal Translation |
|---|---|---|
| lembrar-se | to remember | to remind oneself |
| levantar-se | to get up | to get oneself up |
| sentar-se | to sit down | to sit oneself down |
| sentir-se | to feel | to feel inside oneself (e.g. 'sinto-me bem' = 'I feel well') |
| servir-se | to help oneself | to help oneself |
| vestir-se | to dress | to dress oneself |

The pronoun can be attached to the start of the verb instead of the end (e.g. 'não me lembro' = 'I don't remember' – the hyphen is not used when prefixing), and sometimes this is a requirement of the grammar. Brazilians usually prefix in this way anyway, so if you want to prefix it all the time I won't complain. The Portuguese however, usually suffix the verb with the pronoun except:

1. When speaking negatively, e.g. 'Eu **não me lembro**.' – 'I don't remember.'
2. When you ask a question with an interrogative pronoun (more on those later), e.g. '**Quem se lembra** do Tony?' – 'Who remembers Tony?'
3. When you use a relative pronoun, e.g. 'Eu sei **quem se lembra** do Tony.' – 'I know who remembers Tony.'
4. When you use adverbs before the verb, e.g. 'Eu **nunca me lembro** de ligar ao Tony.' – 'I never remember to call Tony.'
5. When using an indefinite pronoun (a pronoun that does not relate to a specific person, but is used in a general sense, such as 'nobody', 'someone', 'anyone', etc.), e.g. '**Nenhuma** casa **se constroi** de cima para baixo' – 'No house is built from the top down'.

# 30. The Subjunctive Mood

We've dealt with several tenses in the indicative mood, and had a look at the conditional, so let's take a closer look at the subjunctive (also sometimes referred to as 'conjunctive'). As noted in the section on moods, the subjunctive differs from the indicative in that it implies a measure of uncertainty in the action of the verb. This occurs when the action of the verb is dependent on something else or denotes a desire, hope, thought, doubt, fear, request, or demand (in other words something that is not necessarily real, at least, not yet).

English speakers have particular difficulty with the subjunctive because although we do use it in English (and Americans use it more than the British), it is not very common, and we often revert to the indicative or conditional instead, especially in speech (the subjunctive can sound rather formal). Also, we don't have a separate set of verb endings for the subjunctive, so it is not always naturally obvious to us even when we are using it (we like to borrow from the infinitive).

In Portuguese though, the subjunctive is used a lot, and they do have separate verb endings for it. So there's a whole load more stuff to learn and memorise, sorry! Still, you can make yourself understood perfectly well without using the subjunctive (you will sound 'foreign', but your meaning will still be clear), so if you can't be bothered with it, feel free to skip this section.

# Present Subjunctive

Before delving into Portuguese subjunctives, I think it is worth taking a look at some examples of the present subjunctive in English just to help clarify what the subjunctive is. Let's start with conjugating a regular verb in the present subjunctive:

### *Present Subjunctive of the English regular verb 'to work'.*

| | |
|---|---|
| I work | we work |
| you work | you work |
| he/she/it work | they work |

Note that this conjugation only differs from the present indicative in that the he/she/it verb form is missing the final 's' (but it might be more helpful to think of it as using the infinitive form for all conjugations). To put that in context, you could use the subjunctive in a sentence like 'I suggest that he work harder'.

For irregular verbs, in English we also use the infinitive form (without the 'to') for all conjugations:

### *Present Subjunctive of the English irregular verb 'to be'*

| | |
|---|---|
| I be | we be |
| you be | you be |
| he/she/it be | they be |

You can often identify the present subjunctive by the use of the word 'that' (or 'que' in Portuguese) followed by a noun or pronoun, followed by what looks like an infinitive in English (but is actually subjunctive). For example, 'Can I ask that I **be** excused?' – in this case the verb 'to be' is subjunctive ('that', followed by a pronoun ['I'], followed by subjunctive verb ['be']).

As Portuguese subjunctives have their own verb forms, it is much easier to identify a subjunctive verb when you come across one – what is not so easy for the English speaker is to decide when it is appropriate to use them, but as you get used to hearing them, it will become more obvious to you. The main thing to ask yourself is whether the action of the verb is definitely carried out or not. If the verb relates to something which might or might not actually happen, you need to use the subjunctive.

Before I give you some examples, here are the conjugations of the present subjunctive for regular verbs in Portuguese:

### Present Subjunctive of the first conjugation regular verb: trabalhar (to work)

| | |
|---|---|
| trabalhe | trabalhemos |
| trabalhes | trabalheis |
| trabalhe | trabalhem |

### Present Subjunctive of the first conjugation regular verb: pensar (to think)

| | |
|---|---|
| pense | pensemos |
| penses | penseis |
| pense | pensem |

### Present Subjunctive of the second conjugation regular verb: comer (to eat)

| | |
|---|---|
| coma | comamos |
| comas | comais |
| coma | comam |

### Present Subjunctive of the second conjugation regular verb: escrever (to write)

| | |
|---|---|
| escreva | escrevamos |
| escrevas | escrevais |
| escreva | escrevam |

### Present Subjunctive of the third conjugation regular verb: garantir (to guarantee)

| | |
|---|---|
| garanta | garantamos |
| garantas | garantais |
| garanta | garantam |

### Present Subjunctive of the third conjugation regular verb: assistir (to attend; to watch [BR])

| | |
|---|---|
| assista | assistamos |
| assistas | assistais |
| assista | assistam |

Irregular present subjunctives…

***Present Subjunctive of the irregular first conjugation verb: estar (to be)***

| | |
|---|---|
| esteja | estejamos |
| estejas | estais |
| esteja | estejam |

***Present Subjunctive of the irregular second conjugation verb: ser (to be)***

| | |
|---|---|
| seja | sejamos |
| sejas | sejais |
| seja | sejam |

***Present Subjunctive of the irregular third conjugation verb: ir (to go)***

| | |
|---|---|
| vá | vamos |
| vás | vades |
| vá | vão |

Here are some examples of sentences in Portuguese that use the present subjunctive (the subjunctive verb is shown in italics). Note that in each case the action of the verb is not certain to occur – even if a demand is made, it is not a foregone conclusion that the demand will be met, so it is still uncertain and therefore expressed in the subjunctive.

***Table 30.1: Examples of the Present Subjunctive in Portuguese***

| Portuguese | English | Notes |
|---|---|---|
| Espero que o senhor *esteja* bem. | I hope you are well. | Literally: I hope that the gentleman *be* well. |
| Eu insisto que *fiques* aqui. | I insist that you *stay* here. | Informal, e.g. to a child. |
| Quero que ela *diga* isso novamente. | I want her to say it again. | Literally: I want that she *say* it again. |
| Sugiro que *tentemos* outra coisa. | I suggest we *try* something else. | |
| É importante que eles *assistam*. | It is important that they *attend*. | |

Other common expressions that require the use of the present subjunctive are:

| | |
|---|---|
| a menos que … | unless … |
| antes (de) que … | before … |
| assim que … | as soon as … |
| até que … | until … (in the future) |
| con tal (de) que … | provided that … |
| depois (de) que … | after … (in the future) |
| duvidar que … | to doubt that … |
| é bom que … | it's good that … |
| é importante que … | it's important that … |
| é improvável que … | it's unlikely that … |
| é necessário que … | it's necessary that … |
| é possível que … | it's possible that … |
| embora … | although |
| enquanto … | as long as … (in the future) |
| esperar que … | to hope / expect / wish that … |
| ficar contente que … | to be happy that … |
| insistir em que … | to insist that … |
| lamentar que … | to regret that … |
| mais vale que … | it's better that … |
| não acreditar que … | not to believe that … |
| negar que … | to deny that … |
| ojalá / oxalá … | hopefully … |
| para que … | in order that … |
| pedir que … | to ask that … |
| preferir que … | to prefer that … |
| quando … | when … (in the future) |
| recomendar que … | to recommend that … |
| sugerir que … | to suggest that … |
| talvez … | maybe … |

# Future Subjunctive

To talk about things that might or might not occur in the future, we have a whole new set of conjugations (this is made a little easier due to all the regular forms starting with the full infinitive, the same as with the future indicative). In English, we don't use the future subjunctive at all, and it has fallen out of favour in Spanish too – but Portuguese still uses it consistently. Still, just ask yourself whether the action of the verb is certain to occur or not. If it is, use the indicative, if it isn't, use the subjunctive.

### *Future Subjunctive of the first conjugation regular verb: trabalhar (to work)*

| | |
|---|---|
| trabalhar | trabalharmos |
| trabalhares | trabalhardes |
| trabalhar | trabalharem |

### *Future Subjunctive of the first conjugation regular verb: pensar (to think)*

| | |
|---|---|
| pensar | pensarmos |
| pensares | pensardes |
| pensar | pensarem |

### *Future Subjunctive of the second conjugation regular verb: comer (to eat)*

| | |
|---|---|
| comer | comermos |
| comeres | comerdes |
| comer | comerem |

### *Future Subjunctive of the second conjugation regular verb: escrever (to write)*

| | |
|---|---|
| escrever | escrevermos |
| escreveres | escreverdes |
| escrever | escreverem |

### *Future Subjunctive of the third conjugation regular verb: garantir (to guarantee)*

| | |
|---|---|
| garantir | garantirmos |
| garantires | garantirdes |
| garantir | garantirem |

*Future Subjunctive of the third conjugation regular verb: assistir (to attend; to watch [BR])*

| | |
|---|---|
| assistir | assistirmos |
| assistires | assistirdes |
| assistir | assistirem |

Irregular future subjunctives…

*Future Subjunctive of the irregular first conjugation verb: estar (to be)*

| | |
|---|---|
| estiver | estivermos |
| estiveres | estiverdes |
| estiver | estiverem |

*Future Subjunctive of the irregular second conjugation verb: ser (to be)*

| | |
|---|---|
| for | formos |
| fores | fordes |
| for | forem |

*Future Subjunctive of the irregular third conjugation verb: ir (to go)*

| | |
|---|---|
| for | formos |
| fores | fordes |
| for | forem |

As with the preterite indicative, ser and ir share the same forms for the future subjunctive.

Time for some examples of the future subjunctive – again, to make it clearer, the future subjunctive verbs are shown in italics:

**Table 30.2: Examples of the Future Subjunctive in Portuguese**

| Portuguese | English | Notes |
|---|---|---|
| Se *chover*, vamos ficar em casa. | If it rains, let's stay at home. | |
| Diga-me quando ele *chegar*. | Tell me when he arrives. | Diga is the present subjunctive, but is being used here imperatively (as a command), chegar is future subjunctive as we cannot be certain he will arrive. |
| Pode colocá-lo aonde *quiser*. | You can put it wherever you like. | You can think of 'quiser' as meaning 'you may desire' (it comes from the verb 'querer', meaning 'to want'). |
| Enquanto eles não *pararem*, não podemos comer. | Until they stop, we cannot eat. | Lit. 'while they don't stop' |
| Se *fizer* bom tempo amanhã, sairei. | If the weather is nice tomorrow, I will go out. | |

## Imperfect Subjunctive

There is no direct equivalent of the preterite indicative in the subjunctive mood in Portuguese – instead, we have to use either the imperfect, or a compound form such as the present perfect or past perfect (more on these forms later). The imperfect subjunctive is just like the imperfect indicative, but as with all subjunctives, the verb carries uncertainty.

So if you are referring to something that might have happened but wasn't certain to have happened, and it relates to an unspecified time in the past, you use the imperfect subjunctive.

In practice, this usually takes the form of 'se' (if), followed by the imperfect subjunctive, followed by a conditional verb. For example, 'Se eu ganhasse na loteria, teria comprado uma moto' ('If I had won the lottery, I would have bought a motorbike'). Here we have 'se', followed by 'ganhasse' (the imperfect subjunctive of 'ganhar' ['to win']), followed by 'teria' ('would have'), which is conditional.

Less often, it can take the form of a preterite or imperfect indicative verb followed by 'que' (that), followed by the imperfect subjunctive. For example, 'Ela pediu que eu ficasse' ('She asked that I stay') – 'pediu' being the preterite from 'pedir' (to ask), followed by 'que' followed by 'ficasse' (1st person singular imperfect subjunctive of the verb 'ficar', ['to stay']).

Note that in English, it is not obvious from the verb (stay) whether the request to stay is still in force or not – that would have to be inferred from the context. In Portuguese though, the imperfect subjunctive form (ficasse) tells us that the request to stay is now over. So although these extra verb forms are a pain in the neck to learn, they do lead to less ambiguity in the language.

If all that makes your head spin, don't worry, you're not alone! You should only worry about subjunctives if you are already comfortable with indicatives and have some experience at listening to Portuguese. If it won't 'click' for you just yet, try coming back to it in a few weeks' or months' time.

Time for the conjugations:

*Imperfect Subjunctive of the first conjugation regular verb: trabalhar (to work)*

| | |
|---|---|
| trabalhasse | trabalhássemos |
| trabalhasses | trabalhásseis |
| trabalhasse | trabalhassem |

*Imperfect Subjunctive of the first conjugation regular verb: pensar (to think)*

| | |
|---|---|
| pensasse | pensássemos |
| pensasses | pensásseis |
| pensasse | pensassem |

*Imperfect Subjunctive of the second conjugation regular verb: comer (to eat)*

| | |
|---|---|
| comesse | comêssemos |
| comesses | comêsseis |
| comesse | comessem |

*Imperfect Subjunctive of the second conjugation regular verb: escrever (to write)*

| | |
|---|---|
| escrevesse | escrevêssemos |
| escrevesses | escrevêsseis |
| escrevesse | escrevessem |

*Imperfect Subjunctive of the third conjugation regular verb: garantir (to guarantee)*

| | |
|---|---|
| garantisse | garantíssemos |
| garantisses | garantísseis |
| garantisse | garantissem |

*Imperfect Subjunctive of the third conjugation regular verb: assistir (to attend; to watch [BR])*

| | |
|---|---|
| assistisse | assistíssemos |
| assistisses | assistísseis |
| assistisse | assistissem |

Irregular imperfect subjunctives…

### *Imperfect Subjunctive of the irregular first conjugation verb: estar (to be)*

| | |
|---|---|
| estivesse | estivéssemos |
| estivesses | estivésseis |
| estivesse | estivessem |

### *Imperfect Subjunctive of the irregular second conjugation verb: ser (to be)*

| | |
|---|---|
| fosse | fôssemos |
| fosses | fôsseis |
| fosse | fossem |

### *Imperfect Subjunctive of the irregular third conjugation verb: ir (to go)*

| | |
|---|---|
| fosse | fôssemos |
| fosses | fôsseis |
| fosse | fossem |

Some examples, with the imperfect subjunctive shown in italics:

### Table 30.3: Examples of the Imperfect Subjunctive in Portuguese

| Portuguese | English | Notes |
|---|---|---|
| O que faria se eles *ficassem*? | What would you do if they [had] stayed? | 'ficassem' is the imperfect subjunctive of 'ficar' (to stay). |
| Se ela *quisesse* falar, falaria. | If she wanted to speak, she would speak. | 'quisesse' is from the verb 'querer' (to want). |
| Eles insistiram que eu *trabalhasse*. | They insisted that I work. | |
| Ele quis que *comêssemos*. | He wanted us to eat. | 'quis' is the preterite of 'querer' (to want). |
| Eu teria ido se *fosse* possível. | I would have gone if it were possible. | |

# Exercise 19: Subjunctive

# Exercício 19: Conjuntivo (Subjuntivo)

*Answers on page 301.*

The indicative (as the word says) indicates a fact, and the subjunctive in turn is used to express non-factual situations. These situations may be in the present, in the past or in the future, but are always non-factual.

In order for you to use the subjunctive, you need to look out for a specific word or expression that requires its use.

### *O Presente do Conjuntivo / The Present Subjunctive*

**19.1.** From the expressions shown in Table 30.4, please find the one that best suits each sentence as in the example given.

| Table 30.4: Phrases that can be paired with the present subjunctive | |
|---|---|
| *Portuguese* | *English* |
| caso | in case |
| mal | as soon as |
| para que | in order that |
| a não ser que | unless |
| embora | although |
| mesmo que | even if |
| talvez | maybe |
| oxalá | let's hope |
| espero que | I hope that |
| não acho que | I don't think that |
| é possível que | it's possible that |

*Example:* __É possível que__ o António abra a carta.
***(It's possible that** Antonio is opening the letter.)*

19.1.1. _____ tu não gostes, não mostres má cara.
*(**Even if** you don't like it, don't pull a face.)*

19.1.2. Eu não posso ir ao concerto _____ goste da banda.
*(I can't go to the concert **although** I like the band.)*

19.1.3. Ele vai falar com ele _____ acabe de comer.
*(He will speak with him **as soon as** he finishes eating.)*

19.1.4. _____ você tenha tempo, podemos tomar um café juntos.
*(If [or '**in case**'] you have time, we can go and have a coffee together.)*

19.1.5. Vou mandar um e-mail à Dina _____ ela tenha toda a informação necessária.
*(I'm going to send an e-mail to Dina, **in order for** her to have all the necessary information.)*

19.1.6. Nós amanhã vamos à praia, _____ chova!
*(We'll go to the beach tomorrow, **unless** it rains!)*

19.1.7. _____ ele venha à festa hoje. Ele está doente.
*(**I don't think** he's coming to the party today. He's ill.)*

19.1.8. _____ ele ganhe um prémio pelo seu trabalho notável.
*(**Maybe** he wins a prize for his remarkable work.)*

19.1.9. _____ tudo corra bem na consulta com o médico.
*(**Let's hope** everything will be fine in the appointment with the doctor.)*

19.1.10. _____ que o sol brilhe amanhã.
*(**I hope** the sun will shine tomorrow.)*

**19.2.** Please fill in the gaps with the verbs given in the present tense of the subjunctive mood. The words and expressions that require the subjunctive mood are underlined. Watch out! Some of the verbs are irregular.

19.2.1. <u>Embora</u> ela _____ (ser) pobre, conseguiu comprar uma casa.
*(Although she **is** poor, she managed to buy a house.)*

19.2.2. <u>Caso</u> vocês o _____ (ver), digam-lhe que eu preciso de falar com ele.
*(In case you **see** him, tell him I need to talk to him.)*

19.2.3. Eu preciso de um advogado <u>que</u> me _____ (ajudar).
*(I need a lawyer who **can help** me.)*

19.2.4. <u>É preciso que</u> nós _____ (organizar) tudo antes de ela chegar.
*(We must **organise** everything before she arrives.)*

19.2.5. Porquê é que <u>ele quer que eu</u> lhe _____ (entregar) o relatório hoje?
*(Why does he want me to **hand in** the report today?)*

19.2.6. <u>Quer</u> _____ (fazer) bom ou mau tempo, eu hoje vou correr 5 quilómetros.
*(Whether **it's** good or bad weather, I'm going to run 5 kilometres today.)*

19.2.7. <u>Espero</u> que eles _____ (estar) em casa hoje.
*(I hope they **are** at home today.)*

19.2.8. Compre os bilhetes para o concerto <u>antes que</u> _____ (esgotar).
*(Please buy the tickets for the concert before they **run out**.)*

19.2.9. Ela fala com toda a gente, <u>embora</u> não _____ (conhecer) ninguém.
*(She talks with everyone, even though she doesn't **know** anyone.)*

19.2.10. <u>É necessário que</u> eu _____ (saber) a verdade agora.
*(It's necessary that I **know** the truth now.)*

### O Futuro do Conjuntivo / The Future Subjunctive

The future subjunctive reflects a possible action in the future. As before, this subjunctive tense requires certain expressions.

**19.3.** Please choose from Table 30.5, the one that best suits each sentence.

| Table 30.5: Phrases that can be paired with the future subjunctive | |
|---|---|
| *Portuguese* | *English* |
| se | if |
| quando | whenever |
| logo que | as soon as |
| enquanto | as long as |
| conforme | in accordance with |
| como | as |
| onde | wherever |
| quem | whoever |

19.3.1. Para _____ ela for, ela avisa sempre os pais.
*(**Wherever** she goes, she always tells her parents.)*

19.3.2. Vocês podem escrever o relatório _____ vocês quiserem.
*(You can write the report **as** you wish.)*

19.3.3. Eu vou fazer o trabalho _____ as ordens que eu receber.
*(I'm going to do the job **in accordance with** the orders I receive.)*

19.3.4. _____ chegares ao escritório, liga para o teu irmão.
*(**Whenever** you arrive at the office, call your brother.)*

19.3.5. _____ a lei proteger a corrupção, a situação do país nunca vai melhorar.
*(**As long as** the law protects corruption, the situation of the country will never improve.)*

19.3.6. Eu posso preparar um café agora _____ o senhor quiser.
*(Sir, I can prepare a coffee now, **if** you wish.)*

19.3.7. Sr. Ministro, _____ o senhor jogar o nosso jogo, nunca terá problemas de dinheiro.
*(Mr Minister, **as long as** you play our game, you'll never have money problems.)*

19.3.8. Nós vos avisaremos _____ chegarmos ao nosso destino.
*(We will let you (guys) know, **as soon as** we arrive at our destination.)*

19.3.9. _____ chover nós ficamos em casa.
*(**If** it rains, we will stay at home.)*

19.3.10. Vocês nunca devem fazer o vosso trabalho _____ ele vos disser. Vocês devem ser originais.
*(You should never do your job **the way** he tells you. You must be original.)*

**19.4.** Now, check the verbs in the Future tense of the Subjunctive mood and when you are done, fill in the gaps below.

19.4.1. Quando eles _____ (chegar), vai estar tudo pronto.
*(When they **arrive**, everything will be ready.)*

19.4.2. Onde quer que elas _____ (ir) de férias, elas vão mandar um postal.
*(Wherever they **go** on holiday, they will send a postcard.)*

19.4.3. Quanto mais tu _____ (trabalhar), menos tempo tens para saber o que se passa no mundo.
*(The more you **work**, the less time you have to know what is going on in the world.)*

19.4.4. Quanto menos bagagem nós _____ (levar), mais fácil será a viagem.
*(The less luggage we **take**, the easier the trip will be.)*

19.4.5. Se nós _____ (correr) muito, podemos ganhar a corrida.
*(If we **run** a lot, we can win the race.)*

19.4.6. Se eles _____ (abrir) a janela, o ar fresco vai poder entrar.
*(If they **open** the window, the fresh air can come in.)*

19.4.7. Eles poderão organizar melhor a vida se _____ (controlar) o consumismo.
*(They can organise their life better if they **control** their consumerism.)*

19.4.8. Quando você _____ (terminar) o seu curso, poderá ajudar muita gente.
*(When you **finish** your course, you will be able to help many people.)*

19.4.9. Ninguém vai perceber nada, se (vocês) não _____ (prestar) atenção.
*(Nobody will understand anything, unless you **pay** attention.)*

19.4.10. É necessário nós estarmos atentos quando a verdadeira notícia

_____ (chegar).
*(It's necessary for us to be alert when the real news **arrives**.)*

### *O Imperfeito do Conjuntivo / The Imperfect Subjunctive*

Normally, the imperfect subjunctive is used in two situations: Either as part of a condition, or as part of reported speech.

**a)** When part of the condition the formula is:
**Se + Imperfect Subjunctive + Conditional** *or*
**Se + Imperfect Subjunctive + Imperfect Indicative**

For example:

1. **Se** eu **quisesse** eu **organizaria** uma festa hoje. (With the conditional)
*(If I wanted I would organize a party today.)*
2. **Se** eu **quisesse** eu **organizava** uma festa hoje. (With the imperfect indicative)
*(If I wanted I would organize a party today.)*

**b)** When it's part of reported speech it works like this:

Ela pediu-me que eu **fosse** ao cinema com ela.
*(She asked me to go to the cinema with her.)*

**19.5.** Taking this into account, please fill in the gaps with the imperfect subjunctive of the given verbs.

19.5.1. Se eles _____ (deixar) avançar mais a tecnologia, teríamos uma vida melhor.
*(If they were to **let** the technology improve more, we would have a better life.)*

19.5.2. Se tu _____ (comparar) os jornais com a internet, terias outra visão do mundo.
*(If you **compared** the newspapers with the Internet, you would have another perspective of the world.)*

19.5.3. Agradecia que o senhor me _____ (dar) o seu nome e o seu número de contacto.
*(I would be grateful if you **could** please **let me have** your name and your contact number.)*

19.5.4. O patrão pediu-nos que _____ (trazer) o carro hoje.
*(The boss asked us **to bring** the car today.)*

19.5.5. Gostava de comprar um carro que _____ (ser) completamente elétrico.
*(I would have liked to buy a car that **was** totally electric.)*

19.5.6. Estou a morrer de fome! E se _____ (ir) almoçar?
*(I'm starving! What about if we **went** for lunch?)*

19.5.7. Se eu _____ (ter) tempo, faria uma viagem ao mundo por um ano.
*(If I **had** the time, I would do a round-the-world trip for a year.)*

19.5.8. Se eu _____ (poder) escolher viver noutro país, escolheria o Uruguai.
*(If I **could** choose to live in another country, I would choose Uruguay.)*

19.5.9. Se eu não _____ (ter) possibilidade de ter uma casa, vivia numa caravana.

*(If I **didn't have** the chance to have a house, I would live in a camper-van.)*

19.5.10. Eu praticava surf se _____ (viver) perto do mar.
*(I would do surfing if I **lived** close to the sea.)*

# 31. Imperative

As already mentioned in the section on 'moods', the imperative mood and its tense refer to commands, instructions, or requests for action (there is only one tense in the imperative mood, so the term 'imperative tense' is rarely used – it is usually just referred to as the 'imperative mood').

The imperative forms of verbs cannot be conjugated in the first person singular, because you can't really request or command yourself to do something (but if you did want to do so rhetorically, or you just like talking to yourself, you can use the present subjunctive instead). It is also quite rare for the imperative to be used in the first person plural, but it does happen with a limited number of verbs (e.g. 'vamos' = 'let's go'; 'vejamos' = 'let's see') – technically, this is really the present subjunctive form, but it is used imperatively. Usually, to say 'let's do something or other', you use 'vamos' + the infinitive of the required verb. So 'let's eat' would be 'vamos comer'.

There is no real need for a true imperative form with the third person, since you can't really command someone who is not party to the conversation, but due to Portuguese using the third person as a polite way of addressing someone, the need for a third person conjugation is introduced. As with the second person plural, Portuguese borrows from the present subjunctive for this.

Technically then, the imperative only relates to the second person singular and plural, and even then, only for affirmative actions, so some reference works will only give you 2 words for the imperative. We will look at the full conjugations though (borrowing from the present subjunctive for the other forms), as it is helpful to think of these additional forms as being imperative.

The rules for creating imperative forms are a bit topsy-turvy. It's probably 50/50 whether it takes more time to learn the rules or just to memorise the endings as with any other conjugation. It certainly won't do any harm to try studying the rules though, and it might help you to remember the endings, so here goes…

For first conjugation verbs, use the present indicative tense, but swap the 'a' for an 'e' in the ending. For second and third conjugation verbs, you also use the present indicative, but swap the 'e' or 'i' for an 'a' in the ending. The exception to this is the second person – where you don't exchange the vowels, but you do knock of the last 's'.

So…

trabalhar = infinitive (to work)
trabalh = stem (work)
trabalhas = second person singular present indicative (you work)
**trabalha** = second person singular **imperative** (work!)
trabalham = third person plural present indicative (they work)
**trabalhem** = third person plural **imperative** ([all of you] work!)

escrever = infinitive (to write)
escrev = stem (write)
escrevemos = first person plural present indicative (we write)
**escrevamos** = first person plural **imperative** (let's write!) – note this would be a very
formal way of saying this. More common would be 'vamos escrever'.
escreve = third person singular present indicative (he writes)
**escreva** = third person singular **imperative** (write!)

assistir = infinitive (to attend)
assist = stem (attend)
assiste = third person singular (she attends)
**assista** = third person singular **imperative** (attend!)

For most irregular verbs, the imperative is constructed by taking **the first person
singular** from the present indicative (which ends with the letter 'o'), dropping the 'o',
and appending 'e/emos/em' or 'a/amos/am' depending on which conjugation is being
dealt with (although not all irregulars follow this pattern, the majority do).

So, in keeping with the tables supplied for the other tenses, here are the full
conjugations for the imperative:

***Imperative of the first conjugation regular verb: trabalhar (to work)***

|            | trabalhemos |
|------------|-------------|
| trabalha   | trabalhai   |
| trabalhe   | trabalhem   |

***Imperative of the first conjugation regular verb: pensar (to think)***

|         | pensemos |
|---------|----------|
| pensa   | pensai   |
| pense   | pensem   |

*Imperative of the second conjugation regular verb: comer (to eat)*

|        | comamos |
|--------|---------|
| come   | comei   |
| coma   | comam   |

*Imperative of the second conjugation regular verb: escrever (to write)*

|          | escrevamos |
|----------|------------|
| escreve  | escrevei   |
| escreva  | escrevam   |

*Imperative of the third conjugation regular verb: garantir (to guarantee)*

|          | garantamos |
|----------|------------|
| garante  | garanti    |
| garanta  | garantam   |

*Imperative of the third conjugation regular verb: assistir (to attend; to watch [BR])*

|         | assistamos |
|---------|------------|
| assiste | assisti    |
| assista | assistam   |

Irregular imperatives…

*Imperative of the irregular first conjugation verb: estar (to be)*

|        | estejamos |
|--------|-----------|
| está   | estai     |
| esteja | estejam   |

*Imperative of the irregular second conjugation verb: ser (to be)*

|       | sejamos |
|-------|---------|
| sê    | sede    |
| seja  | sejam   |

### *Imperative of the irregular third conjugation verb: ir (to go)*

|      | vamos |
|------|-------|
| vá   | ide   |
| vai  | vão   |

As noted above, the imperative is only used for affirmative actions – e.g. 'fica aqui' (stay here [informal]). For negative commands, you have to use the present subjunctive – e.g. 'nao fiques aqui' (don't stay here [informal]). However, even some native speakers (especially in Brazil) are unaware of this rule, and fail to differentiate between negative and positive commands.

# Exercise 20: Imperative

# Exercício 20: Imperativo

*Answers on page 303.*

As we have seen, the imperative is the mood that allows you to give commands to other people. Although the use of 'por favor' or 'se faz favor' is polite, in Portuguese you don't necessarily need to say it all the time.

**20.1.** Let's pretend that you are the boss now. Please instruct your employees about the work that has to be done today.

    20.1.1. Carlos e Pedro _____ (trabalhar) mais!
        *(Carlos and Pedro, please **work** harder!)*

    20.1.2. Américo, _____-me (mostrar) o que já fez.
        *(Americo, **show** me what you've done so far.)*

    20.1.3. Maria, não _____ (beber) enquanto trabalha!
        *(Maria, please **don't drink** while you work!)*

    20.1.4. António, por favor _____ (fazer) uma lista do material necessário.
        *(Antonio, please **make** a list of the needed material.)*

    20.1.5. Cristina, _____-me (mandar) a informação por e-mail.
        *(Christina, **send** me the information by email.)*

    20.1.6. Não _____ (falar) comigo agora! Estou muito nervoso!
        *(**Don't talk** to me now! I'm very upset!)*

    20.1.7. João, _____ (organizar) os documentos para a reunião.
        *(John, please **organize** the documents for the meeting.)*

    20.1.8. Ó Pedro, _____ ([informal 'tu'] dar) uma vista de olhos nisto.
        *(Hey Pedro, **take a look** at this.)*

20.1.9. Amigos _____ (vir) comigo!
*(Guys, **come** with me!)*

20.1.10. Pedro, não _____ (comprar) o carro mais caro.
*(Pedro, **don't buy** the more expensive car.)*

# 32. Personal Infinitive

The infinitive tense we have already discussed is the 'impersonal infinitive', and it is called that because it has no reference to any particular grammatical 'person' (see 'grammatical persons' on page 86). The personal infinitive is similar but *does* relate to a grammatical person. We don't have a direct equivalent in English, so it can be a bit difficult to get your head around it!

Although we don't have a personal infinitive form in English, we do still need to construct sentences involving a grammatical person and the infinitive – in which case we either use the impersonal infinitive, or the gerund (the present participle, or 'ing' form). Typically this would take the form: preposition + pronoun + infinitive or gerund.

For example, 'It was difficult for me to understand'. In this case we have 'for' (a preposition), 'me' (a pronoun), and 'to understand' (the impersonal infinitive). Another example would be 'Without them knowing'. 'Without' (preposition) + 'them' (pronoun) + 'knowing' (gerund). Whenever you see this pattern (preposition, pronoun, infinitive/gerund) in English, you know that you have a good candidate for using the personal infinitive in Portuguese.

In Portuguese, the above examples would be:

- 'Foi difícil para mim entender' – 'para' is a preposition, 'mim' is a pronoun, and 'entender' is the personal infinitive.
- 'Sem eles saberem': 'Sem' (preposition) + 'eles' (pronoun) + 'saberem' (personal infinitive).

These phrases are often preceded by 'it is' or 'it was' (e.g., 'it is important for me to know' – 'é importante eu saber', 'it was good for them to see' – 'foi bom eles verem', etc.), so there's another clue.

The personal infinitive is often used as an alternative to the present subjunctive in Portuguese, although you never use the word 'que' ('that') with the personal infinitive like you would with the present subjunctive. For example, instead of saying 'it is important that I know' – 'é importante que eu saiba' (for which you would use the present subjunctive), you can say 'it is important for me to know' 'é importante eu saber' (for which you use the personal infinitive). It can even be used sometimes as an alternative to the imperative – it sounds a little 'softer', less direct, and a little more polite.

We are not going to go through all the conjugations here (there are full conjugations in the reference section at the end of the book), because the impersonal infinitive is conjugated in exactly the same way as regular verbs in the future subjunctive (see page 149).

It is important to note though, that even irregular verbs follow the same pattern as regular verbs when it comes to the personal infinitive (even though they have irregular forms in the future subjunctive). So you can think of *all* verbs as being regular in the personal infinitive, which is great!

Having said all that, often, Portuguese speakers will replace the personal infinitive with the impersonal infinitive. For example, instead of saying 'quanto a nós, é melhor **vivermos** aqui' ('as for us, it is better for us to live here'), they might instead say 'quanto a nós, é melhor **viver** aqui'. Whilst technically it would be more accurate to use the personal infinitive, use of the impersonal is quite a common practice, so don't be alarmed if the personal becomes impersonal from time to time!

## Exercise 21: Personal Infinitive
## Exercício 21: Infinitivo Pessoal

*Answers on page 303.*

The Portuguese personal infinitive has its own set of conjugations, however, as a shortcut, it is often replaced with the infinitive itself (the actual verb like falar, comer, ser, abrir, etc).

**21.1.** Please fill in the gaps with the personal infinitive of the given verbs.

21.1.1. A Sofia ficou muito feliz ao _____ (saber) que foi promovida.
    *(Sofia was very happy **knowing** she was promoted.)*

21.1.2. Não preparem o jantar até eu _____ (voltar).
    *(Please, don't prepare the dinner until I **come back**.)*

21.1.3. Sem nós _____ (saber) falar português é difícil viver em Angola.
    *(Without us **knowing** how to speak Portuguese it's difficult to live in Angola.)*

21.1.4. Apesar de eles _____ (fazer) barulho, os vizinhos não reclamam.
    *(Despite them **making** noise, their neighbours don't complain.)*

21.1.5. Não é muito provável amanhã _____ (estar) bom tempo.
    *(It's not very likely that the weather **will be** good tomorrow [or more literally, '**for it to be** good weather'].)*

21.1.6. Temos que arrumar a casa depois da festa _____ (terminar).
    *(We must tidy up the house after the party **is finished**.)*

21.1.7. Depois das pessoas _____ (ir embora) podemos conversar.
    *(After everybody **has gone** we can talk.)*

21.1.8. Antes dos convidados _____ (chegar) temos de ter tudo pronto.

*(Before the guests **arrive** we must have everything ready.)*

21.1.9. O José não vem trabalhar hoje por _____ (estar) doente.

*(José is not coming to work today due to **being** ill.)*

21.1.10. O Francisco e a Cláudia estão a estudar português para

_____ (viver) no Brasil.

*(Francisco and Claudia are studying Portuguese **to live** in Brazil.)*

# 33. Other Tenses

There are a few other tenses that you don't really need to learn, either because you will likely never use them, or because you already know enough to use them without thinking about it. This is because they are compound forms (forms with two or more words) which follow the same pattern as their equivalents in English, using combinations of forms that we have already covered. Still, for the sake of completeness, let's run through them now.

## Simple Pluperfect Indicative

This is one you are never likely to need to use yourself, but if you want to read some old Portuguese literature, you might come across it (legend has it some isolated regions of Portugal still use it, but it is certainly not encountered very often). It is a way of speaking about things that happened and were completed in the past. These days, we use the past perfect tense for that (in both English and Portuguese). It is also known as the preterite pluperfect indicative.

The past perfect is a compound tense (i.e. it requires an auxiliary verb), whereas the simple pluperfect is a separate verb form with its own conjugations and doesn't require an auxiliary. The meaning of the 2 forms is identical though. See the verb tables at the end of the book for the conjugations.

## Present Perfect (Indicative/Subjunctive)

The present perfect tense is a kind of mixture between the preterite and the imperfect – it describes past events that have been completed but without a definite time period specified. It might seem odd that a tense that deals with the past should include the word 'present'! The reason for that will become clearer in a moment. The Portuguese tend not to use the present perfect much – they prefer to use either the preterite or the imperfect instead. We use it quite a lot in English though.

In the indicative mood, the present perfect tense takes the appropriate form of the verb 'to have' in the present indicative (hence the use of the word 'present' in the name of the tense), followed by the past participle of the verb you want to express in the present perfect. This is true in both English and Portuguese, so it is natural to translate directly without needing to learn more conjugations.

The present perfect also appears in the subjunctive mood, so sometimes you need to use the subjunctive form of 'to have' followed by the past participle. As with other subjunctives, this only happens if the action is not definitely real.

In Portuguese, the present perfect construction can also be used where we would use the present perfect continuous in English. So 'Eles têm trabalhado' can be translated as both 'They have worked' and 'They have been working'.

### Table 33.1: Examples of the Present Perfect Indicative in Portuguese

| Portuguese | English |
|---|---|
| tenho estado | I have been |
| têm trabalhado | they have worked / they have been working |
| ela tem comido | she has eaten / she has been eating |

### Table 33.2: Examples of the Present Perfect Subjunctive in Portuguese

| Portuguese | English |
|---|---|
| que eu tenha comido | that I have eaten |
| espero que ele tenha trabalhado | I hope he has worked |
| é importante que eles tenham sido | it is important that they have been |

## Past Perfect (or Pluperfect) (Indicative/Subjunctive)

'Pluperfect' is a nice posh word. It means 'more than perfect'. As you may have noticed by now, 'perfect' refers to something that is completed. Pluperfect is not just completed, but was already completed in the past. So if you are already talking in the past tense (using the imperfect and/or preterite), and want to refer to something that had already happened before then, you use the pluperfect.

In both English and Portuguese, the pluperfect again uses the auxiliary verb 'to have', but in the past tense, followed by the past participle of the verb whose action is being portrayed in the past perfect. The slight deviation between English and Portuguese comes from the fact that we use the preterite form of 'to have' in English ('had'), but Portuguese uses the imperfect ('tinha', 'tinhas', 'tinha', 'tínhamos', 'tinham'). As you may remember, we don't have a separate imperfect form in English.

Again, it appears in both the indicative and the subjunctive mood in Portuguese. In the subjunctive, the imperfect subjunctive form of 'ter' ('tenha', 'tenhas', 'tenha', 'tenhamos', 'tenham') is followed by the past participle.

**Table 33.3: Examples of the Pluperfect Indicative in Portuguese**

| Portuguese | English |
|---|---|
| eu tinha estado | I had been |
| tinham trabalhado | they had worked |
| tínhamos comido | we had eaten |

**Table 33.4: Examples of the Pluperfect Subjunctive in Portuguese**

| Portuguese | English |
|---|---|
| se eu tivesse estado | if I had been |
| se eles tivessem trabalhado | if they had worked |
| era importante que tivéssemos comido | it was important that we had eaten |

## Future Perfect (Indicative/Subjunctive)

To express that something will be completed in the future, we use the future perfect. In both English and Portuguese, the auxiliary verb 'to have' is used in the future tense (this can be indicative or subjunctive in Portuguese, although use of the future perfect subjunctive is not common), followed again by the past participle.

**Table 33.5: Examples of the Future Perfect Indicative in Portuguese**

| Portuguese | English |
|---|---|
| teremos estado | we will have been |
| terão comido | they will have eaten |
| terei trabalhado | I will have worked |

| Table 33.6: Examples of the Future Perfect Subjunctive in Portuguese | |
|---|---|
| *Portuguese* | *English* |
| se tu tiveres trabalhado | if you will have worked [informal] |
| se eles tiverem comido | if they will have eaten |
| se eu tiver estado | if I will have been |

## Conditional Perfect

The conditional perfect combines the conditional form of 'to have' with the past participle of the verb in question, and again follows the same pattern in both English and Portuguese. As with the conditional tense, there is no subjunctive form (because any uncertainty is directly quantified by the condition).

| Table 33.7: Examples of the Conditional Perfect in Portuguese | |
|---|---|
| *Portuguese* | *English* |
| teriam trabalhado | they would have worked |
| eu teria comido | I would have eaten |
| ela teria estado | she would have been |

## Present Perfect Continuous

This is a combination of the present perfect (mentioned above) and the present participle (the gerund, or '…ing' form). It indicates an action that started in the past but which may or may not still be going on. For example 'He has been working.' In Portuguese, this could be translated literally as 'Ele tem estado a trabalhar', but as noted above, it is possible to substitute the present perfect here ('Ele tem trabalhado'). This tense is also known as the present perfect progressive.

## Past Perfect Continuous

This is almost the same as the present perfect continuous, but the auxiliary verb ('to have') is placed in the past tense, meaning that the action was ongoing in the past but is now finished. For example, 'He had been working'. In Portuguese, the imperfect form of 'ter' is used: 'Ele tinha estado a trabalhar'. This tense is also known as the past perfect progressive.

## Exercise 22: Pluperfect Indicative

## Exercício 22: Pretérito Mais-Que-Perfeito do Indicativo

*Answers on page 303.*

The pluperfect reflects an action in the past that occurred before another past action. It is formed with the Imperfect indicative of 'ter' + past participle of the main verb.

**22.1.** Please fill in the gaps with the pluperfect like in the given example.

Example:     Antes da reunião começar eu já **tinha preparado** o relatório.
*(Before the meeting started, I **had** already **prepared** the report).*

22.1.1. Quando nós chegámos à sala a reunião já _____ (começar).
*(When we arrived at the room the meeting **had** already **started**.)*

22.1.2. Ontem preparei um filme bom para vermos mas a Maria já o

_____ (ver).
*(Yesterday I prepared a good movie for us to watch but Maria **had** already **seen** it.)*

22.1.3. O comboio já _____ (partir) quando eles chegaram à estação.
*(The train **had** already **left** when they got to the station.)*

22.1.4. Elas _____ (acabar) de sair com o Pedro quando o táxi chegou.
*(They **had just** left with Pedro when the taxi arrived.)*

22.1.5. Quando ele chegou ao escritório, a secretária já _____ (enviar) o e-mail.
*(When he arrived at the office, his secretary **had** already **sent** the e-mail.)*

22.1.6. Quando precisei de pagar o meu café, vi que me _____ (esquecer) do dinheiro.
*(When I needed to pay for my coffee, I realised that I **had forgotten** the money.)*

22.1.7. O teste foi fácil porque eu _____ (estudar) bem a matéria.
*(The test was easy because I **had studied** the subject well.)*

22.1.8. Eu queria telefonar ao Zé, mas não sabia onde _____ (pôr) o número dele.
*(I wanted to call Zé, but I didn't know where I **had put** his number.)*

22.1.9. Eu não comprei os bilhetes hoje porque eu já os _____ (comprar) antes.
*(I didn't buy the tickets today because I **had** already **bought** them before.)*

22.1.10. A Maria já _____ (fazer) o chá quando eles chegaram.
*(Maria **had** already **made** the tea when they arrived.)*

# 34. Portuguese Pronouns

Portuguese has approximately one squillion and three different pronouns. In English, we tend to use the same few words for all the different types of pronoun, so we often don't even realise that there are so many different types.

We don't have that luxury in Portuguese though, so we have to delve a bit deeper into these interesting little words. Using pronouns correctly is quite difficult – even the Portuguese themselves use them incorrectly sometimes, so try not to punish yourself too hard if you occasionally get your indirect objects mixed up with your prepositionals.

## Subject Pronouns

Pronouns are usually specific to subjects or objects. For example, the pronoun 'I' is only used for a subject, whereas 'me' is only used for an object. Likewise, the word 'he' only relates to subjects, and 'him' only relates to objects. Certain pronouns can therefore be spoken of as 'subject pronouns', or 'object pronouns'. The pronoun 'you', in modern English, can be used for both subjects and objects. In Shakespeare's time though, the words 'thou' and 'thee' were used – 'thou' only ever referring to a subject, and 'thee' to an object. The following table lists all of the subject pronouns in both English and Portuguese.

| *Table 34.1: Subject Pronouns* | | |
|---|---|---|
| *English* | *Portuguese* | *Notes* |
| I | eu | |
| we | nós<br>a gente<br>uma pessoa<br>um gajo<br>um indivíduo | 'A gente', 'uma pessoa', 'um gajo', and 'um indivíduo' are colloquial expressions that can mean 'we', but any verbs following them use the third person singular form (e.g. 'a gente trabalha' = 'we work', or more literally 'people [in general] work'). |
| you (singular) | tu<br>você<br>o senhor<br>a senhora | |
| you (plural) | vocês<br>vós<br>os senhores<br>as senhoras | 'Vós' is now obsolete, but can still be found in some older literature. 'Vocês' is the most commonly used form and nowadays it practically replaces 'vós'. |
| he/it (masculine) | ele | |
| she/it (feminine) | ela | |
| they | eles<br>elas | |

## Object Pronouns

A pronoun referring to the object on which a verb is performed is, logically enough, an object pronoun. However, a further distinction needs to be made between types of object pronoun. Object pronouns can be direct or indirect, and this has an appreciable effect on the Portuguese language. It can be quite difficult to discern whether a pronoun is direct or indirect, as it depends not only on the verb, but also on how it is being used.

The basic rule is: an indirect object pronoun has something done to or for it. A direct object pronoun has something performed on it. With indirect object pronouns, we often use the word 'to' or 'for' in English between the verb and the object whereas direct object pronouns usually appear immediately after the verb.

For example: 'He wrote to **me** every day' – 'Ele escreveu-**me** todos os dias' – the writing was done to or for 'me', so 'me' is an indirect object pronoun. On the other hand, to say 'He kicked **it**' – 'Ele chutou-**o**' – involves an action being directly performed on 'it', so 'it' is a direct object pronoun.

The confusion arises when the word 'to' or 'for' is omitted even though the object pronoun is indirect. This is done quite often in English. For example, in the sentence 'He wrote **me** a letter every day.' – 'Ele escreveu-**me** uma carta todos os dias' (PT) / 'Ele **me** escreveu uma carta todos os dias' (BR) – the writing is still being done to or for 'me', so 'me' is still an indirect object pronoun. However, there is no word 'to' in the sentence like there was in the previous example, so it could be difficult to spot that the object pronoun is indirect. The thing to remember, is that for indirect object pronouns, the word 'to' or 'for', even if it is omitted, is still implied.

Unfortunately, with some verbs the object pronoun is direct in English, but indirect in Portuguese, and vice-versa (for example, in Portuguese, you 'ask to' someone, which is indirect, whereas in English we use a direct object). I'm afraid there's no easy way to learn which ones are which – you just have to be patient, and hopefully with the passage of time, you will learn them.

For some further explanation on these object pronouns, please visit:

- www.learn-portuguese-with-rafa.com/european-portuguese-pronouns.html – for European Portuguese Object Pronouns
- www.learn-portuguese-with-rafa.com/brazilian-portuguese-pronouns.html – for Brazilian Portuguese Object Pronouns.

## Table 34.2: Direct Object Pronouns

| English | Portuguese | Notes |
|---|---|---|
| me | me | Remember to pronounce the Portuguese version differently to the English! (Sort of a weak 'muh', rather than a 'mee'). |
| us | nos | Note that the subject pronoun (we) has an acute accent ('nós') whereas the direct object pronoun (us) does not ('nos'). It's pronounced 'noosh'. |
| you (singular) | te<br>o<br>a<br>lo<br>la | 'te' is used informally. 'o' and 'a' are used formally, for male and female objects respectively. 'lo' and 'la' are also used formally, but only if the object is placed immediately after the infinitive form of a verb (in which case, the spelling of the verb is altered – see below). |
| you (plural) | os<br>los / nos<br>as<br>las / nas | More information on 'nos' and 'nas' from page 193 onwards. |
| him/it (masculine) | o<br>lo / no | More information on 'no' from page 193 onwards. |
| her/it (feminine) | a<br>la / na | More information on 'na' from page 193 onwards. |
| them | os<br>los / nos<br>as<br>las / nas | More information on 'nos' and 'nas' from page 193 onwards. |

The direct object pronouns 'lo', 'la', 'los', and 'las' are used after an infinitive verb form. The addition of the 'l' serves to make the articulation easier. When this happens though, the spelling of the verb is affected as shown below:

First conjugation verbs: drop the final 'r', and put an acute accent on the 'a'.
Second conjugation verbs: drop the final 'r', and put a circumflex on the 'e'.
Third conjugation verbs: just drop the final 'r'.
Having changed the infinitive, the pronoun is attached to it with a hyphen.

For example:

| | |
|---|---|
| levar + os = levá-los | to take them |
| fazer + a = fazê-la | to make her |
| destruir + o = destrui-lo | to destroy it |

If the pronoun comes before the verb, this restructuring is not necessary, and the plain old pronouns are used:

| | |
|---|---|
| os levar | to take them |
| a fazer | to make her |
| o destruir | to destroy it |

### Table 34.3: Indirect Object Pronouns

| English | Portuguese | Notes |
|---|---|---|
| [to/for] me | me<br>para mim | All of these indirect pronouns have an alternative using the word 'para' ('to'). In speech, Brazilians often shorten the word 'para' to just 'pra'. Particularly when writing, the 'para' can be replaced with the word 'a', which means the same thing. |
| [to/for] us | nos<br>para nós | Note the acute accent on 'nós' (indicating an open 'nosh' sound) when using the 'para nós' variation. |
| [to/for] you (singular) | te<br>para ti<br>lhe<br>para você | 'te' and 'para ti' are informal. 'lhe' and 'para você' are formal. |
| [to/for] you (plural) | lhes<br>para vocês | |
| [to/for] him/it (masculine) | lhe<br>para ele<br>para o senhor | |

| English | Portuguese | Notes |
|---|---|---|
| [to/for] her/it (feminine) | lhe<br>para ela<br>para a senhora | |
| [to/for] them | lhes<br>para eles<br>para elas | |

## Prepositional Pronouns

Where a preposition is followed immediately by a pronoun, the pronoun follows a similar pattern to the indirect object pronouns listed previously. At times though, the preposition and the pronoun are contracted into a single word.

For example, 'with us' would be translated literally as 'com nós', but it is often contracted into a single word: 'connosco' (which is spelt with a single 'n' by Brazilians). Similarly, 'from him', which would be 'de ele' can be contracted to 'dele'. These contractions are optional, and some are used more commonly than others.

So, first of all, I'll give you another table with the regular prepositional pronouns, following which we will take a look at the most common contractions.

| Table 34.4: Prepositional Pronouns | |
|---|---|
| *English* | *Portuguese* |
| me | mim |
| us | nós<br>a gente |
| you (singular) | ti<br>si<br>você<br>o senhor<br>a senhora |
| you (plural) | vocês |
| him | ele |
| her | ela |
| them | eles<br>elas |

**Table 34.5: Contraction of Preposition 'with' and Prepositional Pronouns**

| English | Portuguese | Notes |
|---|---|---|
| with me | comigo | |
| with us | connosco | Spelt 'conosco' in Brazil. |
| with you (singular) | contigo consigo | 'contigo' is informal, 'consigo' is formal; 'com o senhor' / 'com a senhora' / 'com você' are more common in Brazil than 'consigo', which is commonly used in Portugal. |
| with you (plural) | convosco | |

**Table 34.6: Contraction of Preposition 'of/from' and Prepositional Pronouns**

| English | Portuguese | Notes |
|---|---|---|
| of/from us | da gente | More often, 'de nós'. |
| of/from you (singular) | do senhor da senhora | Alternatively 'de você'. |
| of/from him | dele | |
| of/from her | dela | |
| of/from them | deles delas | |

**Table 34.7: Contraction of Preposition 'by/for' and Prepositional Pronouns**

| English | Portuguese | Notes |
|---|---|---|
| by/for us | pela gente | 'por nós' is more common. |
| by/for you (singular) | pelo senhor pela senhora | Or 'por você'. |

| English | Portuguese | Notes |
|---------|-----------|-------|
| *Table 34.8: Contraction of Preposition 'in/on' and Prepositional Pronouns* | | |
| in/on us | na gente | Or 'em nós'. |
| in/on you (singular) | no senhor<br>na senhora | Or 'em você'. |
| in/on him | nele | |
| in/on her | nela | |
| in/on them | neles<br>nelas | |

## Possessive Pronouns

We use possessive pronouns when identifying a person or thing as being the owner of a noun. For example, my; his; your; its; their. In Portuguese, things are complicated a bit by the fact that both the possessor and the thing possessed have a gender. Some possessive pronouns reflect the gender and quantity of the possessor, and others relate to the thing possessed.

**Table 34.9: Possessive Pronouns which reflect the gender and quantity of the thing possessed**

| English | Portuguese | Notes |
|---|---|---|
| my/mine (singular possession) | o meu<br>a minha | The definite article ('o'; 'a'; 'os'; 'as') is not required for 'mine' and is not always required for 'my' (especially in Brazil) – the same principle applies to all of these possessive pronouns. |
| my/mine (plural possession) | os meus<br>as minhas | |
| our/ours (singular possession) | o nosso<br>a nossa | |
| our/ours (plural possession) | os nossos<br>as nossas | |
| your/yours (singular possession) | o teu<br>a tua<br>o vosso<br>a vossa<br>o seu<br>a sua | 'seu' and 'sua' are sometimes avoided in speech because they can easily be confused between the second and third person (the same form is used for both) – 'dele' and 'dela' are not so ambiguous (see below). This is less of a problem when writing. 'Vosso' and 'vossa' refer to multiple possessors of a single possession. |
| your/yours (plural possession) | os teus<br>as tuas<br>os vossos<br>as vossas<br>os seus<br>as suas | |

| English | Portuguese | Notes |
|---|---|---|
| their/theirs (singular possession) | o seu<br>a sua | |
| their/theirs (plural possession) | os seus<br>as suas | |

**Table 34.10: Possessive Pronouns which reflect the gender of the possessor**

| English | Portuguese | Notes |
|---|---|---|
| our (of us/ours) | da gente | 'nosso' is more common. |
| your (of you/yours) | do senhor<br>da senhora | literally 'of the gentleman' or 'of the lady'. |
| his (of him) | dele | literally 'of him', but equivalent of the English word 'his'. |
| her/hers (of her) | dela | |
| their (of them) | deles<br>delas | |

There are many occasions where we use possessive pronouns in English but the Portuguese don't. For example, when referring to parts of the body: Whereas we would say 'my arm', 'my head', or 'its wheel' the Portuguese would say 'the arm' ('o braço') 'the head' ('a cabeça'), or 'the wheel' ('a roda'). The same is true of items of clothing ('my coat' becomes 'the coat'). The possessive pronoun could still be used if you wanted to emphasize whose item you were referring to (e.g. '*my* arm, not yours').

For example, 'Vou buscar o casaco' = 'I'll get my coat'.

The possessive pronouns that reflect the gender of the possessor ('dele', 'dela', 'deles', 'delas') are often used to avoid confusion over who is being referred to because using the words 'seu', 'sua', 'seus', or 'suas' ('your', 'his', 'her', or 'their') can be ambiguous if the identity of the possessor is not obvious from the context.

# Reflexive pronouns

Reflexive pronouns are the ones that are used with reflexive verbs (see reflexive verbs section on page 142). They are used when the subject and object both refer to the same individual, and in English are usually words that end in 'self' or 'selves' (e.g., 'he behaves **himself**' – 'ele comporta-se' [PT] / 'ele se comporta' [BR], 'they amuse **themselves**' – 'Eles divertem-se' [PT] / 'Eles se divertem' [BR]). The same pronouns are used for reciprocal actions – that is, where subject and object act on each other (e.g., '**they** hate **each other**' – 'eles odeiam-se' [PT] / 'eles se odeiam' [BR], '**we** respect **each other**' – 'nós respeitamo-nos' [PT] / 'nós nos respeitamos' [BR]).

The same group of pronouns are also known as 'pronominal' – which basically means that they are there for no particular reason! Some verbs take pronominal pronouns in the same way as reflexive verbs take reflexive pronouns – it's just that the pronouns do not actually serve any particular purpose. Since the pronouns for all 3 groups (reflexive, reciprocal, and pronominal) are identical, it is easier just to think of pronominal and reciprocal pronouns as being reflexive. The distinction is only made for the purposes of keeping pedantic grammarians happy.

OK, here they are:

| Table 34.11: Reflexive, Reciprocal, and Pronominal Pronouns | | |
|---|---|---|
| *English* | *Portuguese* | *Notes* |
| myself | me | |
| ourselves | nos | |
| yourself | te<br>se | As you can probably guess by now, 'te' is informal, and 'se' is formal. |
| yourselves | se<br>vos | 'vos' is pretty much obsolete nowadays. |
| himself | se | |
| herself | se | |
| themselves | se | |

## Exercise 23: Pronouns

## Exercício 23:  Pronomes

*Answers on page 304.*

The role of a pronoun is to replace a noun. There are a lot of different types of pronoun to learn about: personal pronouns, reflexive pronouns, direct object pronouns, indirect object pronouns, indefinite pronouns.

Here we are going to exercise each one of these categories separately.

### *Pronomes Pessoais – Personal Pronouns*

Personal pronouns are pronouns that represent people or objects, such as eu *(I)*, você *(you)*, nós *(we)*, eles *(they)*, etc.

**23.1.** Translate the following pronouns from English to Portuguese:

1. we  _____

2. me  _____

3. she  _____

4. they (group of females) _____

5. I  _____

6. you (informal)  _____

7. you sir  _____

8. they (group of males)  _____

9. he  _____

10. you madam  _____

11. one  _____

12. you ladies  _____

13. you gentlemen  _____

***Pronomes Reflexos – Reflexive Pronouns.***

Reflexive pronouns are associated with reflexive verbs (see page 142).

**23.2.** Fill in the gaps below by using the correct reflexive pronouns either before of after the verb. The verb is given in brackets after each sentence.

23.2.1. Eu _____ chamo _____ António. *(chamar-se = to be called)*
*(My name is Antonio.)*

23.2.2. Nós _____ reunimo(s) _____ depois do almoço. *(reunir-se = to meet up)*
*(We meet up after lunch.)*

23.2.3. Ele _____ lembra _____ do seu tempo de escola. *(lembrar-se = to remember)*
*(He remembers his school time.)*

23.2.4. A senhora _____ chama _____ Maria Castro? *(chamar-se = to be called)*
*(Madam, is your name Maria Castro?)*

23.2.5. Elas _____ encontram _____ sempre no restaurante. *(encontrar-se = to meet up)*
*(They always meet at the restaurant.)*

23.2.6. No cinema, gosto de _____ sentar _____ perto dos meus amigos. *(sentar-se = to sit down)*
*(At the cinema, I like to sit next to my friends.)*

23.2.7. Tu nunca _____ lembras _____ do Rafael. *(lembrar-se = to remember)*
*(You never remember Rafael.)*

23.2.8. Eles _____ atrasaram _____ e perderam o princípio do filme. *(atrasar-se = to fall behind or become late)*
*(They were late and they missed the beginning of the film.)*

23.2.9. Nós _____ sentimo(s) _____ bem. (sentir-se)
*(We feel well.)*

23.2.10. Porquê o senhor _____ preocupa _____ tanto? *(preocupar-se = to worry)*
*(Why do you worry so much, sir?)*

### *Pronomes de Complemento Direto / Direct Object Pronouns.*

There are only 8 pronouns under this category in European Portuguese. These pronouns are words that allow you to ask a certain verb a couple of questions:

**O que?** (What?)
**Quem?** (Who? / Whom?)

Direct object pronouns are used all the time in conversations and they are:

'**me**', which corresponds to '**me**' in english;
'**te**', which corresponds to an informal '**you**' in english;
'**o**', which corresponds to '**him**' or '**it**' when an object is masculine;
'**a**' which corresponds to '**her**' or '**it**' when an object is feminine;
'**nos**', which corresponds to '**us**';
'**vos**' / '**vocês**', which corresponds to plural '**you**' (as 'you guys');
'**os**', which corresponds to a masculine '**them**', be they people or objects;
'**as**', which also corresponds to a feminine '**them**', be they people or objects.

Along with knowing the pronouns themselves, we also need to get familiar with the rules that guide their usage, and they are:

1.  Mainly in European Portuguese, the pronoun comes after the verb separated by a hyphen (Brazilians use it mostly in front of the verb).

    e.g. 'Eu como **o bolo** todo.' → 'Eu como-**o** todo.'
    *(I eat all **the cake**. → I eat **it** all.)*

2.  In European Portuguese, the pronoun needs to be placed before the verb when the verb comes after:

    **a)** Adverbs like 'também', 'sempre', 'já', 'ainda', etc.

    e.g. 'Eu também comi **o bolo**.' → 'Eu também **o** comi.'
    *(I also ate **the cake**. → I also ate **it**.).*
    (Here the word 'o' means 'it' [o bolo] as a masculine object.)

**b)** A negative statement.

> e.g. 'Ele não come **o bolo**.' → 'Ele não **o** come.'
> *(He doesn't eat **the cake**. → He doesn't eat **it**.)*

**c)** Interrogative (with a question word like 'quando', 'quem', 'onde', etc.).

> e.g. 'Quem come **o bolo** hoje?' → 'Quem **o** come hoje?'
> *(Who eats **the cake** today? → Who eats **it** today?)*

**d)** Relative pronouns – remember them as words you would normally use to ask questions, but which you can use in statements as well. e.g., 'que' (who, that, which, whom), 'quando' (when), 'onde' (where), etc.

> e.g. 'Ele disse que comeu **o bolo** todo.' → 'Ele disse que **o** comeu todo.'
> *(He said he ate all **the cake**. → He said he ate **it** all.)*

**e)** Prepositions (like 'de', 'para', 'por', 'em', 'até', etc.).

> e.g. 'Ela gosta de beber **o café** com leite.' → 'Ela gosta de **o** beber com leite.'
> *(She likes drinking **the coffee** with milk. → She likes drinking **it** with milk.)*

But, there are other important rules we must consider:

3.  If the verb you are using ends with the letters **s**, **z**, or **r**, the last letters of the verb – s, z or r – fall off and you **add an l** to the pronouns 'o' 'a', 'os' 'as'.

> e.g. Tu come**s** **o bolo** todo. → Tu **come-lo** todo.
> *(You eat all **the cake**. → You **eat it** all.)*

And in this case, we need to figure out 4 things:

i.   When does a verb end with '**s**'?

      When you use the persons 'Tu' and 'Nós' in the present tense, for instance.
            e.g. Nós chamamos **o Manuel**. → Nós chamamo-**lo**.
            *(We call Manuel. → We call **him**.)*

ii.  When does a verb end with '**z**'?

      Only irregular verbs like Trazer, Fazer, Dizer, end with 'z' in the 3rd person.

            e.g. Ele traz **o carro** agora. → Ele trá-**lo** agora.
            *(He brings **the car** now. → He brings **it** now.)*

      In this case, we need to place an accent on the 'á' because the original word has its phonetic stress on the last syllable (words ending with a 'z'), so we need to keep the word stress where it was originally.

iii. When does a verb end with '**r**'?

      Always when it's in its infinitive form e.g., comer, falar, beber, fazer, etc. A verb will likely be in its infinitive form if it uses another verb as an auxiliary.

            e.g. Eu vou **comer** um bolo hoje.  → Eu vou **comê-lo** hoje.
            *(I'm going **to eat** a cake today. → I'm going to eat **it** today.)*

      Verbs ending in 'er' normally get a circumflex accent (^) on the last syllable, instead of an acute accent (´) because, any verb in its original infinitive form must be stressed in the last syllable (and obviously, it ends with an 'r').

iv.  Finally, when the verb of your sentence **ends with a nasal sound** (which happens with the persons 'eles', 'elas', 'vocês', 'os senhores' and 'as senhoras'), we need to keep the verb as it is and add an '**n**' to the pronoun.

            e.g. 'Eles bebem **o vinho** todo.' → 'Eles bebem-**no** todo.'
            *(They drink all **the wine**. →They drink **it** all.)*

**23.3.** Now that you've read all that, please fill in the gaps of the sentences below with the correct pronoun as in the example. Be careful about whether you place the pronoun before or after the verb.

> *Example:* A Sonia viu o Pedro, mas o Pedro não ___a viu___ (ver).
> *(Sonia saw Pedro, but Pedro didn't **see her**.)*

23.3.1. Eu quero comprar este livro. Eu quero _____ (comprar) barato.
> *(I want to buy this book. I want to **buy it** cheap.)*

23.3.2. Ela leva o Manuel ao cinema. Ela _____ (levar) de carro.
> *(She takes Manuel to the cinema. She **takes him** by car.)*

23.3.3. Eles trazem os livros no saco. Eles _____ (trazer) todos.
> *(They bring the books in the bag. They **bring them** all.)*

23.3.4. Tu tens que avisar o Paulo. Tens que _____ (avisar) hoje!
> *(You have to warn Paulo. You have to **warn him** today!)*

23.3.5. O senhor levou o carro para o escritório. O senhor

_____ (levar) cedo.
> *(Sir, you took the car to the office. You **took it** early.)*

23.3.6. As senhoras querem água fresca, ou _____ (querer) natural?
> *(Ladies, would you like cold water, or would you **like it** at room temperature?)*

23.3.7. Eu não quero a salada simples. Eu _____ (querer) com tomate e cebola.
> *(I don't want a plain salad. I **want it** with tomatoes and onions.)*

23.3.8. Eu entendo o Pedro, mas quando ele fala rápido eu não

_____ (entender).
> *(I understand Pedro, but when he speaks quickly I don't **understand him**.)*

23.3.9. Na festa, nós bebemos vinho, mas nós não _____ (beber) todo.

> *(At the party we drank wine, but we didn't **drink it** all.)*

23.3.10. Afinal comprei o carro. _____ (comprar) ontem.

> *(In the end I bought the car. I **bought it** yesterday.)*

23.3.11. Eu vou trazer o livro em breve. Eu vou _____ (trazer) até ao fim da semana.

> *(I'll bring back the book soon. I'll **bring it** by the end of the week.)*

23.3.12. Hoje as empresas comandam os governos. Elas _____ (comandar) todos.

> *(Nowadays the corporations run the governments. They **run them** all.)*

23.3.13. Os programas de TV controlam a mente. Eles _____ (controlar) a todos.

> *(The TV programs control the mind. They **control us** all.)*

23.3.14. O Manuel quer comprar um barco. Ele quer _____ (comprar) novo.

> *(Manuel wants to buy a boat. He wants to **buy it** brand new.)*

### *Pronomes de Complemento Indireto / Indirect Object Pronouns*

Indirect object pronouns follow the same rules as direct object pronouns but only as far as their position is concerned (they can be positioned either before or after the verb). The advantage of these pronouns is that no letters are added to or taken away from the verb. These pronouns reply to the questions: 'a quem?', 'para quem?' (to whom?).

If, when you ask about the verb, it is not possible to ask the full question 'to whom', but only 'whom', the following pronouns **do not apply** (the ones that apply in that case are the ones above – direct object pronouns).
There are 6 indirect object pronouns, and they are:

1.  'me', which corresponds to 'to me' in english;
2.  'te', which corresponds to an informal 'to you';
3.  'lhe', which corresponds to 'to him', 'to her', or 'to it' (one of the rare occasions where English makes a gender distinction but Portuguese doesn't!);

4. '**nos**', which corresponds to '**to us**';
5. '**vos**' / '**para vocês**', which corresponds to the plural '**to you**' (to you guys);
6. '**lhes**', which corresponds to '**to them**', be they people or objects (male or female).

OK, let's do some exercises.

**23.4.** Please fill in the gaps of the sentences below with the correct pronoun as in the example. You'll find two spaces, one before and another after the verb, in order for you to decide where to place the pronoun.

*Example:* A Sonia enviou um e-mail ao Pedro, mas o Pedro não ___lhe___

respondeu _____.
      *(Sonia sent an e-mail to Pedro, but Pedro didn't reply **to her**.)*

23.4.1. A Paula e o Ivo gostam do vinho. Eu vou _____ dar _____ mais vinho.
      *(Paula and Ivo like the wine. I'm going to **give them** more wine.)*

23.4.2. Ele quis a informação hoje. Eu _____ enviei _____ as informações imediatamente.
      *(He wanted the information today. I sent **him** the information straight away. [Note: unlike English, in Portuguese, the word 'information' has a separate plural form.])*

23.4.3. Eles querem conhecer a Joana. Vou _____ apresentar _____ a Joana na festa.
      *(They want to meet Joana. I'm going to introduce Joana **to them** at the party.)*

23.4.4. Eu tenho o meu carro avariado. Ele _____ empresta _____ o carro dele hoje.
      *(My car has broken down. He is lending **me** his car today.)*

23.4.5. Porque nós gostamos de livros, ele _____ dar _____ um livro no nosso aniversário.
      *(Because we like books, he offers **us** a book for our anniversary.)*

23.4.6. Quando tu precisas de dinheiro, eu _____ dou _____ algum dinheiro.
*(When you need money, I give **you** some money.)*

23.4.7. Dr. fonseca, o seu quarto é lá em cima. Eu _____ mostro _____ o quarto.
*(Dr. Fonseca, **your** room is upstairs. I'll show **you** the room.)*

23.4.8. A Tânia precisa de comer fruta. Maçãs _____ fazem _____ bem.
*(Tania needs to eat fruits. Apples do **her** good.)*

23.4.9. Sei que ela _____ escreveu _____ uma carta porque eu vi ele ler a carta.
*(I know she wrote **him** a letter because I saw him reading the letter.)*

23.4.10. Eu preciso de uma caneta. Podes _____ emprestar _____ a tua?
*(I need a pen. Can you lend **me** yours, please?)*

### *Pronomes Indefinidos / Indefinite Pronouns*

In Portuguese, there are two kinds of indefinite pronouns (an indefinite pronoun is one that represents an unspecified person, thing, or group – for example in the phrase 'nobody likes me', the word 'nobody' is an indefinite pronoun, since we are not being specific about the identity of the noun): the variable ones (which agree in gender and number with the unspecified person, place, or thing) and the invariable ones (that never change, regardless).

Interestingly, these invariable pronouns force other pronouns to be placed before the verb. For example, in the sentence 'Nesta turma **ninguém** se chama Pedro' ('In this class, **nobody** is called Pedro.'), the reflexive pronoun ('se') must come before the verb ('chama'). The same would be true of a direct or indirect object pronoun – normally they can be placed after the verb, but when used with an invariable indefinite pronoun, they must come before it.

**Table 34.12: Variable Indefinite Pronouns**

| Portuguese | | | | English |
|---|---|---|---|---|
| Singular | | Plural | | |
| Masculine | Feminine | Masculine | Feminine | |
| algum | alguma | alguns | algumas | some / any |
| nenhum | nenhuma | nenhuns | nenhumas | none / not any / no [+ noun] |
| muito | muita | muitos | muitas | Many / a lot / much / several |
| pouco | pouca | poucos | poucas | little / few |
| todo o | toda a | todos os | todas as | all the / the whole / every |
| tanto | tanta | tantos | tantas | so many / so much |
| outro | outra | outros | outras | other / another (one) |

**Table 34.13: Invariable Indefinite Pronouns**

| Portuguese | English |
|---|---|
| tudo | everything |
| nada | nothing / not anything |
| alguma coisa | something / anything |
| alguém | someone / somebody / anyone |
| ninguém | no one  / nobody |

The following exercises will allow you to focus on one set of the indefinite pronouns at a time.

**23.5.** Fill in the gaps with **algum / alguma / alguns / algumas / alguma coisa / alguém**.

23.5.1. David, você viu _____ estranha no escritório hoje?
(*David, did you see **anything** weird in the office today?*)

23.5.2. Eu vi _____ copos usados na mesa e

_____ secretárias fora do lugar.
*(I saw **some** used glasses on the table and **some** desks out of place.)*

23.5.3. A Maria também viu _____ que não conhecia.
*(Maria also saw **someone** she didn't know.)*

23.5.4. Claro! Quando eu entro no escritório, vejo _____ pão,
e doce por todo o lado!
*(Of course! When I come in to the office, I see **some** bread, and jam everywhere!)*

23.5.5. O José também viu _____ água no chão.
*(José also saw **some** water on the floor.)*

23.5.6. Vamos ter _____ problemas para limpar tudo.
*(We are going to have **some** problems cleaning everything up.)*

23.5.7. _____ tem que nos ajudar.
*(**Someone** has to help us out.)*

**23.6.** Fill in the gaps with **nenhum / nenhuma / nenhuns / nenhumas / nada /
ninguém**.

23.6.1. _____ sabe o que aconteceu ontem à noite.
*(**Nobody** knows what happened last night.)*

23.6.2. Não há evidência de _____ assalto.
*(There is no evidence of **any** robbery.)*

23.6.3. As pessoas dos escritórios vizinhos não viram _____
também.
*(The people from the neighbouring offices did not see **anything** either.)*

23.6.4. Estranho! _____ documento desapareceu.
*(Weird! **No** document disappeared.)*

23.6.5. Bem, pelo menos não temos _____ consequências.
*(Well, at least, we do not have **any** consequences.)*

23.6.6. _____ das instalações foi danificada.
*(**None** of the premises were damaged.)*

23.6.7. No fundo, _____ aconteceu.
*(In the end, **nothing** happened.)*

**23.7.** Now use **muito / muita / muitos / muitas / pouco / pouca / poucos / poucas**.

23.7.1. _____ gente fala Português.
*(**Many** people speak Portuguese.)*

23.7.2. _____ alunos que estudam e praticam frequentemente alcançam bons resultados.
*(**Many** students that study and practice often achieve good results.)*

23.7.3. O Jamie tem _____ amigas bonitas?
*(Does Jamie have **many** beautiful female friends?)*

23.7.4. Não. Ele tem _____ amigas bonitas, mas elas são simpáticas.
*(No. He has **few** beautiful female friends, but they are pleasant.)*

23.7.5. Eu tenho _____ dinheiro para comprar um carro novo.
*(I have **little** money to buy a brand new car.)*

23.7.6. Ela quer fazer um bolo, mas tem _____ ingredientes.
*(She wants to make a cake, but she has **few** ingredients.)*

23.7.7. Eles têm _____ tempo para terminar o trabalho.
*(They have **little** time to finish the job.)*

23.7.8. _____ gente sabe que a cultura só serve os interesses de certas entidades.
*(**Few** people know that culture only serves certain entities' interests.)*

**23.8.** Now use **todo (o) / toda (a) / todos (os) / todas (as) / tudo**.

23.8.1. Eu conheço _____ países da América Latina.
*(I've been to **all the** Latin-American countries.)*

23.8.2. Ela arrumou a casa _____ para a festa.
*(She tided up the **whole** house for the party.)*

23.8.3. Ela organizou _____.
*(She organized **everything**.)*

23.8.4. Quando eles lêem, eles reconhecem _____ palavras em português.
*(When they read, they recognise **all the** words in Portuguese.)*

23.8.5. Nós gostamos de puzzles. É divertido juntar _____ peças.
*(We like puzzles. It's fun to assemble **all the** pieces.)*

23.8.6. _____ línguas estão sujeitas a interpretação subjetiva.
*(**All** languages are open to subjective interpretation.)*

23.8.7. Quando eu visitar o México, eu quero fotografar _____.
*(When I visit Mexico, I want to photograph **everything**.)*

**23.9.** Fill in the gaps by using **tanto / tanta / tantos / tantas**.

23.9.1. Há _____ pessoas na miséria, enquanto que outras desperdiçam recursos.
*(There are **so many** people living in misery, while others waste resources.)*

23.9.2. Ela tem _____ amigos que às vezes se esquece do nome deles.
*(She has **so many** friends that sometimes she forgets their names.)*

23.9.3. No Algarve há _____ turistas no verão!
*(In the Algarve there are **so many** tourists in the summer!)*

23.9.4. Ele tem _____ trabalho que não pode falar com ninguém agora.

*(He has **so much** work that he cannot talk to anyone right now.)*

23.9.5. Nas ruas de Lisboa há _____ carros que quase não há espaço para as pessoas.

*(On the streets of Lisbon there are **so many** cars that there is almost no room for the people.)*

23.9.6. Esta semana temos demasiado trabalho. Temos _____ reuniões!

*(This week we have too much work. We have **so many** meetings!)*

23.9.7. Um tornado causa _____ destruição que às vezes é impossível calcular os danos.

*(A tornado causes **so much** destruction that sometimes it's impossible to evaluate the damage.)*

**23.10.** Fill in the gaps by using **outro / outra / outros / outras**.

23.10.1. Este carro já está velho. Eu preciso de comprar _____.
*(This car is too old. I need to buy **another one**.)*

23.10.2. Umas vezes ela vai ao cinema, _____ vezes ela vai ao teatro.
*(Sometimes she goes to the cinema, **other** times she goes to the theatre.)*

23.10.3. Nós não gostamos desta casa. Preferimos a _____.
*(We don't like this house. We prefer **the other** one.)*

23.10.4. Este dicionário é bom, mas o _____ é muito melhor.
*(This dictionary is good, but the **other one** is much better.)*

23.10.5. O senhor tem de apresentar este impresso, não o _____.
*(Sir, you have to present this form, not the **other one**.)*

23.10.6. Eu queria _____ cerveja, por favor.
*(I'd like **another** beer, please.)*

23.10.7. Este sistema está corrupto. Precisamos de _____ totalmente novo.

> *(This system is corrupt. We need **another** completely new one.)*

**23.11.** Now that you've mastered them all, rewrite the following sentences with the opposites like in the example given.

Question:  Está **alguém** em casa? *(Is  anybody home?)*
Answer:    **Ninguém** está em casa. *(**Nobody** is home.)*

23.11.1. Temos **alguma** sala vaga? *(Do we have **a [any]** vacant room?)*

_____.

*(We do **not** have **a [any]** vacant room.)*

23.11.2. Ele bebe **muita** cerveja? *(Does he drink **much** beer?)*

_____.

*(He drinks **little** beer.)*

23.11.3. Hoje nós tivemos **muito** trabalho. *(Today we had **much** work to do.)*

_____.

*(Today we had **little** work to do.)*

23.11.4 **Alguém** telefonou? *(Did **anybody** call?)*

_____.

*(**Nobody** called.)*

23.11.5. **Muita** gente admira Jacque Fresco. *(**Many** people admire Jacque Fresco.)*

_____.

*(**Few** people admire Jacque Fresco.)*

23.11.6. **Alguém** fez o exercício? *(Did **anybody** do the exercise?)*

_____.

*(**Nobody** did the exercise.)*

## Exercise 24: Possessives

## Exercício 24: Possessivos

*Answers on page 307.*

Possessives can be used under two categories: pronouns and adjectives. Normally you can distinguish the possessive pronoun from the possessive adjective by adding a determinant to it. So, to say 'my car' you simply say 'o meu carro', whereas 'the car is mine' is 'o carro é meu'.

**24.1.** Please fill in the gaps with either the right possessive pronoun or the right possessive adjective.

24.1.1. Sr António, onde está _____ telefone?
*(Mr Antonio, where is **your** telephone?)*

24.1.2. _____ telefone está no meu bolso.
*(**My** telephone is in my pocket.)*

24.1.3. Eu vi o Sr António com o telefone _____.
*(I saw Mr Antonio with **his** phone.)*

24.1.4. Dona Maria, onde estão _____ filhas?
*(Ms Maria, where are **your** daughters?)*

24.1.5. _____ filhas estão na piscina.
*(**My** daughters are at the swimming pool.)*

24.1.6. Dona Ana, como estão _____ sogros?
*(Ms Ana, how are **your** in-laws?)*

24.1.7. _____ sogros estão bem, obrigada.
*(**My** in-laws are fine, thanks.)*

24.1.8. A Maria já arranjou o carro _____?
*(Has Maria fixed **her** car yet?)*

24.1.9. O pai _____ tem que pagar primeiro.
*(**Her** father must pay first.)*

24.1.10. João e Pedro, como estão _____ pais?
*(John and Peter, how are **your** parents?)*

24.1.11. _____ pais estão bem, obrigado.
*(**Our** parents are well, thank you.)*

24.1.12. Esta bola é _____?
*(Is this ball **yours**, guys?)*

24.1.13. Sim, essa bola é _____ obrigado.
*(Yes, that ball is **ours**, thanks.)*

24.1.14. Este carro é _____ Sr Ivo?
*(Is this car **yours**, Mr Ivo?)*

24.1.15. Não. O carro é de um amigo _____.
*(No, The car belongs to a friend of **mine**.)*

## Exercise 25: Demonstratives

## Exercício 25: Demonstrativos

*Answers on page 308.*

The demonstrative pronouns in Portuguese present 3 different categories:

a) the ones you use when **the object is next to the speaker:**

| Table 34.14: Demonstrative Pronouns for objects next to the speaker | | |
|---|---|---|
| *Gender/Plurality* | *Portuguese* | *English* |
| Singular masculine | este | this (one) |
| Singular feminine | esta | |
| Plural masculine | estes | these (ones) |
| Plural feminine | estas | |
| Neutral (indefinite) | isto | this thing |

b) the ones you use when **the object is next to the listener:**

**Table 34.15: Demonstrative Pronouns for objects next to the listener**

| Gender/Plurality | Portuguese | English |
|---|---|---|
| Singular masculine | esse | that (one) |
| Singular feminine | essa | |
| Plural masculine | esses | those (ones) |
| Plural feminine | essas | |
| Neutral (indefinite) | isso | that thing |

c) the ones you use when **the object is far from both, the speaker and the listener**:

**Table 34.15: Demonstrative Pronouns for objects far from both speaker and listener**

| Gender/Plurality | Portuguese | English |
|---|---|---|
| Singular masculine | aquele | that (one) over there |
| Singular feminine | aquela | |
| Plural masculine | aqueles | those (ones) over there |
| Plural feminine | aquelas | |
| Neutral (indefinite) | aquilo | that thing over there |

**25.1.** Please fill in the gaps with **este, esta, estes, estas**.

1. _____ livro
*(this book)*

2. _____ casa
*(this house)*

3. _____ guitarras
*(these [electric] guitars)*

4. _____ mesas
*(these tables)*

5. _____ óculos
*(these eye-glasses)*

6. _____ cadeiras
*(these chairs)*

7. _____ flores
*(these flowers)*

8. _____ bolos
*(these cakes)*

9. _____ quadro
*(this board)*

10. _____ mulheres
*(these women)*

11. _____ cidade
*(this city)*

12. _____ estradas
*(these roads)*

13. _____ homens
*(these men)*

14. _____ filme
*(this film)*

15. _____ moto
*(this motorcycle)*

16. _____ dicionário
*(this dictionary)*

**25.2.** Please fill in the gaps with **esse, essa, esses, essas**.

1. _____ livro
*(that book)*

2. _____ casa
*(that house)*

3. _____ guitarras
*(those [electric] guitars)*

4. _____ mesas
*(those tables)*

5. _____ óculos
*(those eye-glasses)*

6. _____ cadeiras
*(those chairs)*

7. _____ flores
*(those flowers)*

8. _____ bolos
*(those cakes)*

9. _____ quadro
*(that board)*

10. _____ mulheres
*(those women)*

11. _____ cidade
*(that city)*

12. _____ estradas
*(those roads)*

13. _____ homens
*(those men)*

14. _____ filme
*(that film)*

15. _____ moto
*(that motorcycle)*

16. _____ dicionário
*(that dictionary)*

**25.3.** Please fill in the gaps with **aquele, aquela, aqueles, aquelas**.

1. _____ livro
*(that book over there)*

2. _____ casa
*(that house over there)*

3. _____ guitarras
*(those guitars over there)*

4. _____ mesas
*(those tables over there)*

5. _____ óculos
*(those eye-glasses over there)*

6. _____ cadeiras
*(those chairs over there)*

7. _____ flores
*(those flowers over there)*

8. _____ bolos
*(those cakes over there)*

9. _____ quadro
*(that board over there)*

10. _____ mulheres
*(those women over there)*

11. _____ cidade
*(**that** city over there)*

12. _____ estradas
*(**those** roads over there)*

13. _____ homens
*(**those** men over there)*

14. _____ filme
*(**that** film over there)*

15. _____ moto
*(**that** motorcycle over there)*

16. _____ dicionário
*(**that** dictionary over there)*

# 35. Negatives

Making negative statements is fairly easy in Portuguese (at last, something easy!). To make a sentence negative, you can just prefix the verb with the word 'não'. That's it. There are of course, other ways of making things negative, but using 'não' is by far the most common, and easiest.

Here are some examples of making negative statements using 'não':

| | |
|---|---|
| Eu não como … | I do not eat … |
| Eles não me escrevem | They do not write to me |
| Não trabalhamos aqui | We do not work here |

There are a few more things you should know about negatives. One thing you may come across is the negative usage of a strange little word: 'algum'. This word literally means 'some' (as in 'some day') or 'one' ('one day'). The feminine form of the word is 'alguma', and the plurals are 'alguns' and 'algumas' respectively. The equivalent of the English word 'something' is 'alguma coisa'.

Why does this matter? Well, 'algum' can sometimes be used to form a negative, which may seem a little odd. For example:

| | |
|---|---|
| de modo algum | by no means (lit. 'of means some [none]') |
| de forma alguma | in no way (lit. 'of way some [none]') |
| coisa alguma | nothing (lit. 'thing some [none]') |

Strange eh? Especially how swapping the words 'alguma' and 'coisa' yields completely the opposite result.

*Alguma Coisa*

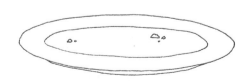

*Coisa Alguma*

Here are a few more negative words that you should be aware of:

| Table 35.1: Negative words | |
|---|---|
| *Portuguese* | *English* |
| nada | nothing; anything (Another weird one – to be explained in a minute!) |
| nenhum/nenhuma | no; not one; not any (always followed by a noun – e.g. 'nenhum lugar' means 'nowhere' – lit. 'not any place') |
| nem | neither; nor |
| ninguém | nobody; no one |
| nunca | never; ever |
| jamais | never; ever |
| proibido | forbidden; prohibited |
| proibido fumar | no smoking (lit. 'prohibited to smoke') |
| sem | without |
| sem dúvida | no doubt |
| indubitável | undoubted (formal – only used when writing) |
| contra | against |
| incapaz | unable |
| de modo algum | by no means |

Some explanation is in order! Let's take the word 'nada'. A literal translation of this would be 'nothing'. As a one-word answer to a question, this would be acceptable (e.g. – 'O que comes?' – 'Nada.' = 'What are you eating?' – 'Nothing.'). However, 'nada' is often used in conjunction with 'não' – which might seem to us like a double negative, but is normal practice in Portuguese.

For example: '**Não** comemos **nada**' (We are **not** eating **anything**).

In fact, in this type of sentence, the word 'não' is essential to make sense in Portuguese. Effectively then, the word 'nada' is being used in a way that we might use the word 'anything' – 'we are not eating anything' makes a little more sense (grammatically) than 'we are not eating nothing'.

Note though, that 'nada' is only used to mean 'anything' when the sentence is negative. If a positive statement is being made (e.g. 'I eat anything'), the words 'qualquer coisa' are used rather than 'nada' ('Eu como qualquer coisa'), although often, the Portuguese will use 'something' (alguma coisa) in places where the English would use 'anything' (qualquer coisa). 'Alguma coisa' is also normally used when asking questions. Perhaps a few more examples will help…

| | |
|---|---|
| Ele não bebe **nada** | He does not drink **anything** |
| Não escrevo **nada** | I do not write **anything** |
| Ele bebe **qualquer coisa** | He drinks **anything** |
| Está a ver **alguma coisa**? (PT) Você está assistindo **alguma coisa**? (BR) | Are you watching **anything**? (more on questions in a minute…) |

Similarly, the words 'nunca' and 'jamais' can mean 'never' or 'ever':

| | |
|---|---|
| **Nunca** mais | **Never** again |
| Mais que **nunca** | More than **ever** |
| Ninguém **jamais** pensa | Nobody **ever** thinks |

By the way, 'nunca 'is used more often than 'jamais' – 'jamais' being rather more emphatic than 'nunca'.

Note that the word 'nem' can be used in place of both 'neither' and 'nor' – so when we say 'neither x nor y' in English, the Portuguese translation could be 'nem x nem y' (an alternative translation would be 'não x [where x involves a verb] nem y', for example: 'Ele não come peixe nem carne.' – 'He eats neither fish nor meat'.).

While we are on the subject of negatives, remember that as noted in the section on imperatives (page 163), when giving negative commands, instead of using the true imperative form for the 2nd person, you switch to the present subjunctive (the same as for other 'persons').

## Exercise 26: Negatives

## Exercício 26: Negativas

*Answers on page 309.*

**26.1.** Fill in the gaps below with the missing word(s) from Table 35.1. Some of them can appear more then once.

26.1.1. Eu não consegui comer _____.
*(I was not able to eat **anything**.)*

26.1.2. Eu nunca vi _____ série de TV em espanhol.
*(I've never seen **any** TV series in Spanish.)*

26.1.3. Nem eu _____ ele gostámos do filme.
*(Neither I **nor** he liked the film.)*

26.1.4. Nós não fomos a lado _____.
*(We did not go **anywhere**.)*

26.1.5. Na polícia ele _____ disse nada!
*(At the Police (station) he **never** said anything!)*

26.1.6. Eu _____ comeria carne nem peixe. Gosto demais dos animais.
*(I would **not** eat meet or fish **ever**. I love animals too much.)*

26.1.7. _____ jamais se lembra das mentiras que ele nos disse.
*(**Nobody** ever remembers the lies he told us.)*

26.1.8. Eu não me importo _____ de levar o Tiago ao hospital.
*(**By no means** would I mind taking Tiago to hospital.)*

26.1.9. Nós _____ trabalhámos com energias alternativas, mas gostávamos muito!
*(We **never** worked with alternative energies, but we would very much like to!)*

26.1.10. Eu não posso fechar a casa _____ ele sair de casa.
*(I cannot lock the house **without** him leaving the house.)*

# 36. Questions

Forming basic questions is easy enough. Just phrase what you want to say in the same way as you would a statement, but make it obvious that it is a question by the inflection in your voice (or by a question mark if writing). For example…

| | |
|---|---|
| Você trabalha aqui? | Do you work here? |
| Não comemos agora? | Don't we eat now? |

Easy eh? You also need to be aware of other ways of asking questions in Portuguese. Merely turning a statement into a question, whilst useful, does not provide a mechanism for every type of question that you might want to ask. For example 'why do you walk home?'; 'what are you eating?' – these types of question make use of interrogative pronouns and adverbs: why; what; where; when; which; who; how. Here are their equivalents in Portuguese:

| *Table 36.1: Interrogative Pronouns and Adverbs* | |
|---|---|
| *Portuguese* | *English* |
| porquê? | why? – lit. 'for what?' If used as part of a longer question (e.g. 'por que estamos à espera?'), it is 2 separate words with no circumflex on the 'e' |
| que…? | what…? (if used on its own, a circumflex is added to the 'e') |
| o que (é)? | what (is it)? |
| para quê? | for what / what for? |
| a que horas? | what time? |
| há quanto tempo? | how long for? |
| onde? | where? |
| de onde / donde? | from where? |
| quando? | when? |
| quanto / quanta? | how much? |
| quantos / quantas? | how many? |
| de que cor? | what colour? |

| Portuguese | English |
|---|---|
| qual? | which / what? (singular) |
| quais? | which / what? (plural) |
| quem? | who? |
| como? | how? |
| quão…? | how…? (only used as an adverb – e.g., 'how tall are you?', 'how tall you are!') |

We may find it useful to explain here the difference between 'que', 'o que', 'qual', and 'quais', as they all commonly translate as 'what' in English. So here are the rules:

- **'que'** is followed by a noun or proper noun, e.g. 'Que carro tem?' ('What car do you have?')
- **'qual'** / **'quais'** are followed by a noun as well, but the aim of using these words is to find out 'what' or 'which one(s)' among a list of possibilities, e.g. 'Qual é o seu nome?' ('What's your name?' [among a long list of names]) or 'Quais são os seus sapatos?' ('Which are your shoes?' [among many]).
- **'o que'** is followed by a verb, e.g. 'O que (vocês) fazem hoje à noite?' ('What are you (guys) doing tonight?')

One more that you need to know is 'será que…', which can be used to start a question requiring a yes or no answer. Literally, this means 'it will be that…', but a better translation might be 'is it true that…?'. It can also be translated as 'I wonder if…?'. We don't really have a direct equivalent in English, but virtually any question that has a yes or no answer could probably be phrased using 'será que…'. For example:

Será que eles vão a pé para casa? – Do they walk home? (is it so that they walk home?)
Será que comemos agora? – I wonder if we eat now?

## Exercise 27: Question words
## Exercício 27: Interrogativos

*Answers on page 309.*

If you know how to ask questions, you can sustain a conversation for a long time.

**27.1.** Please fill in the gaps below with the correct question word from Table 36.1.

27.1.1. _____ é o concerto?
*(When is the concert?)*

27.1.2. _____ é o seu carro?
*(What colour is your car?)*

27.1.3. _____ é o diretor do jornal?
*(Who is the Director of the newspaper?)*

27.1.4. _____ é que não pode vir à festa?
*(Why is it that you can't come to the party?)*

27.1.5. _____ é a Maria originalmente?
*(Originally, where is Maria from?)*

27.1.6. _____ pessoas vão ao jantar?
*(How many people are going to the dinner?)*

27.1.7. _____ é o meu copo? Estão aqui tantos!
*(Which one is my glass? There are so many here!)*

27.1.8. _____ vocês vivem em Lisboa?
*(How long have you guys lived in Lisbon?)*

27.1.9. _____ é a reunião?
*(What time is the meeting?)*

27.1.10. _____ é que ele precisa disso?
*(What does he need that for?)*

# Part 4 – Vocabulary and Reference

*"You do not really understand something unless you can explain it to your grandmother." – Albert Einstein*

This section includes some words and phrases organised by theme to help increase your vocabulary, and other useful odds and ends like dates, times, and dealing with numbers. There are also some fully conjugated verb tables representing all of the tenses we have discussed, with a selection of regular and the most common irregular verbs – handy to dip into.

# 37. Colours

| | |
|---|---|
| red | vermelho (masculine) / vermelha (feminine) |
| blue | azul (singular) / azuis (plural) |
| yellow | amarelo/a |
| green | verde |
| orange | cor-de-laranja; laranja (lit. colour of orange [that is, the fruit]) |
| purple | roxo/a; púrpura; violeta |
| pink | cor-de-rosa; rosa (lit. colour of rose) |
| brown | castanho/a ('marrom' in Brazil) |
| black | preto/a |
| white | branco/a |
| grey | cinzento/a (lit. ashen – 'cinza' (ash) in Brazil) |
| beige | bege |
| crimson | carmesim; purpúreo/a |
| | |
| light | claro/a |
| dark | escuro/a |
| | |
| light blue | azul-claro/a |
| dark green | verde-escuro/a |

# 38. Numbers

There is some variation in the spelling of numbers between European and Brazilian Portuguese. The numbers given below should be sufficient to enable you to work out all of the numbers in-between. Numbers that are not in bold-type are given as examples of how you would combine the bold-type components.

Instead of using a full stop to indicate a decimal point, the Portuguese language requires a comma (or 'vírgula' in Portuguese). So a number containing a decimal fraction (take for example, '2.34'), is written and spoken with a comma like this: 2,34 = dois vírgula três quatro.

In a similar vein, whereas in English we use a comma to separate our thousands from our millions, etc., the Portuguese use a full stop (or 'ponto'). So one million and three is written like this: '1.000.003'. In order to help you get used to this, the numerals below are written using the Portuguese style.

## *Cardinal Numbers (Números Cardinais)*

| | |
|---|---|
| **0** | **zero** |
| **1** | **um/uma** |
| **2** | **dois/duas** |
| **3** | **três** |
| **4** | **quatro** |
| **5** | **cinco** |
| **6** | **seis** |
| **7** | **sete** |
| **8** | **oito** |
| **9** | **nove** |
| **10** | **dez** |
| **11** | **onze** |
| **12** | **doze** |
| **13** | **treze** |
| **14** | **catorze (Brazilians sometimes use quatorze)** |
| **15** | **quinze** |

| 16 | **dezasseis (Brazilian: dezesseis)** |
| 17 | **dezassete (Brazilian: dezessete)** |
| 18 | **dezoito** |
| 19 | **dezanove (Brazilian: dezenove)** |
| 20 | **vinte** |
| 21 | vinte e um/uma |
| 22 | vinte e dois/duas |
| 23 | vinte e três |
| 30 | **trinta** |
| 31 | trinta e um/uma |
| 40 | **quarenta** |
| 50 | **cinquenta (Brazilians might still use a diaeresis: cinqüenta)** |
| 60 | **sessenta** |
| 70 | **setenta** |
| 80 | **oitenta** |
| 90 | noventa |
| 100 | **cem (note: 'cem' is only used if the next 2 digits are zeros – otherwise, use 'cento')** |
| 101 | cento e um/uma |
| 102 | cento e dois/duas |
| 120 | cento e vinte |
| 121 | cento e vinte e um/uma |
| 122 | cento e vinte e dois/duas |
| 200 | **duzentos/duzentas** |
| 201 | duzentos/duzentas e um/uma |
| 300 | **trezentos/trezentas** |
| 400 | **quatrocentos/quatrocentas** |
| 500 | **quinhentos/quinhentas** |
| 600 | **seiscentos/seiscentas** |
| 700 | **setecentos/setecentas** |
| 800 | **oitocentos/oitocentas** |
| 900 | **novecentos/novecentas** |

| | |
|---|---|
| **1.000** | **mil** |
| 1.001 | mil e um/uma |
| 1.985 | mil novecentos e oitenta e cinco (the first 'e' is dropped) |
| 2.000 | dois mil/duas mil |
| 3.000 | três mil |
| 10.000 | dez mil |
| 100.000 | cem mil |
| 100.001 | cem mil e um/uma |
| 101.000 | cento e um/uma mil |
| 125.000 | cento e vinte e cinco mil |
| 500.000 | quinhentos mil |
| 735.346 | setecentos e trinta e cinco mil trezentos e quarenta e seis |
| **1.000.000** | **um milhão (unlike 'mil', the preceeding number [in this case, um] is required with milhão and bilião)** |
| 1.537.469 | um milhão quinhentos e trinta e sete mil quatrocentos e sessenta e nove |
| 1.000.000.000 | mil milhão **(um bilhão in Brazil)** |
| **1.000.000.000.000** | **um bilião (um trilhão in Brazil)** |

The word 'e' (meaning 'and'), as used when speaking or writing numbers in full, appears more frequently in Portuguese than in English. It is generally used between all major components (the bold-type numbers), but for every group of 3 numbers (thousand, million, billion, etc.), the 'e' is dropped unless the last 2 digits of the group are both zero. Hence…

| | |
|---|---|
| 1.200.300 | um milhão **e** duzentos mil **e** trezentos |
| 1.214.379 | um milhão, duzentos **e** catorze mil, trezentos **e** setenta **e** nove |
| 1.200.379 | um milhão **e** duzentos mil, trezentos **e** setenta **e** nove |
| 1.214.300 | um milhão, duzentos **e** catorze mil **e** trezentos |

Note: If you want to state a million / billion people, you need to add 'de' – ('of') after the number, e.g. 'Um milhão **de** pessoas'. The same would apply to other units: 'A billion dollars' – 'Um bilião **de** dólares' (PT) / 'Um bilhão **de** dólares' (BR).

## *Ordinal Numbers (Números Ordinais)*

| English Notation | Portuguese Notation | Portuguese Words |
|---|---|---|
| 1st | 1º/1ª | primeiro/primeira |
| 2nd | 2º/2ª | segundo/segunda |
| 3rd | 3º/3ª | terceiro/terceira ('terça' is sometimes used as a short-cut, particularly in compound words – e.g. 'terça-feira') |
| 4th | 4º/4ª | quarto/quarta |
| 5th | 5º/5ª | quinto/quinta |
| 6th | 6º/6ª | sexto/sexta |
| 7th | 7º/7ª | sétimo/sétima |
| 8th | 8º/8ª | oitavo/oitava |
| 9th | 9º/9ª | nono/nona |
| 10th | 10º/10ª | décimo/décima |
| 11th | 11º/11ª | décimo primeiro/décima primeira |
| 12th | 12º/12ª | décimo segundo/décima segunda |
| 20th | 20º/20ª | vigésimo/vigésima |
| 21st | 21º/21ª | vigésimo primeiro/vigésima primeira |
| 30th | 30º/30ª | trigésimo/trigésima |
| 40th | 40º/40ª | quadragésimo/quadragésima |
| 50th | 50º/50ª | quinquagésimo/quinquagésima (Brazilians might still use the diaeresis: qüinquagésimo/a) |
| 60th | 60º/60ª | sexagésimo/sexagésima |
| 70th | 70º/70ª | septuagésimo/septuagésima (the 'p' is virtually silent – Brazilian spelling: setuagésimo/a) |
| 80th | 80º/80ª | octagésimo/octagésima |
| 90th | 90º/90ª | nonagésimo/nonagésima |
| 100th | 100º/100ª | centésimo/centésima |

So, 'one fifth' is 'um quinto', 'one eighth' is 'um oitavo', etc. ('one third' uses the shortened form 'um terço'). Note though, that the Portuguese use cardinal numbers for dates, not ordinal like we do in English (see section on days, dates and times, below).

# Exercise 28: Cardinal Numbers
# Exercício 28: Números Cardinais

*Answers on page 309.*

**28.1.** Knowing the numbers is essential to speak portuguese. Please write the following numbers in full, as per the example.

Example: **12.345,67**

Doze mil, trezentos e quarenta e cinco, vírgula sessenta e sete.

28.1.1. **40.444,44**

_____

28.1.2. **20.222,22**

_____

28.1.3. **60.666,66**

_____

28.1.4. **50.555,55**

_____

28.1.5. **70.777,77**

_____

28.1.6. **30.333,33**

_____

28.1.7. **90.999,99**

_____

28.1.8. **80.888,88**

28.1.9. **100.001,10**

28.1.10. **4.370.444,44**

# 39. Letters of the Alphabet

Up until recently, there were only 23 letters in the Portuguese alphabet (not including diacritics). The other 3 letters of the English alphabet were viewed as 'foreign' in Portuguese, but they were still used for certain 'imported' words such as 'whiskey' (they sometimes spell this more phonetically using their own alphabet: 'uísque'). Since the 1990 orthographic agreement went into effect though (which was in January 2009), the 'w', 'k', and 'y' are now officially included.

***The Portuguese Alphabet (O Alfabeto Português)***

| | |
|---|---|
| A | (ah) |
| B | (beh) |
| C | (seh) |
| D | (deh) |
| E | (eh) |
| F | (eff) |
| G | (ge[ay] – hard g as in 'gold'; sometimes zhe[ay]) |
| H | (agah) – hard g as in 'gold'; |
| I | (ee) |
| J | (zhota) |
| L | (el) |
| M | (em) |
| N | (en) |
| O | (oh) – as in 'soft' |
| P | (peh) |
| Q | (keh) |
| R | (err) |
| S | (ess) |
| T | (teh) |
| U | (oo) |
| V | (veh) |
| X | (sheesh) – 'shees' in Brazil (hence some fast-food places refer to a 'x-burger'!) |
| Z | (zeh) |

***Foreign Letters (Letras Estrangeiras) – now part of the portuguese alphabet after the Portuguese Spelling Agreement.***

K          (kappa) – sometimes just 'ka' (esp. in Brazil)

W          (doopluveh or dablyu)

Y          (ípsilon) – also known as 'i grego' (Greek 'i')

# 40. Days, Dates, and Times

## The Days of the Week (Os Dias da Semana)

| Portuguese | English |
|---|---|
| segunda-feira | Monday (lit. 'second market day') |
| terça-feira | Tuesday ('third market day' etc.) |
| quarta-feira | Wednesday |
| quinta-feira | Thursday |
| sexta-feira | Friday |
| sábado | Saturday (lit. 'sabbath') |
| domingo | Sunday |

## The Months of the Year (Os Meses do Ano)

| Portuguese | English |
|---|---|
| janeiro | January |
| fevereiro | February |
| março | March |
| abril | April |
| maio | May |
| junho | June |
| julho | July |
| agosto | August |
| setembro | September |
| outubro | October |
| novembro | November |
| dezembro | December |

Neither days of the week, nor months of the year start with a capital letter in Portuguese. Please also note that the months in Portuguese do not have a gender, so you mustn't use 'o' or 'a' in front of them.

The year is given as a complete number in Portuguese. So for example, 1999 is given as 'one thousand nine hundred and ninety nine' rather than 'nineteen ninety nine'. The day of the year is given as the cardinal number rather than ordinal, (for example, they say the equivalent of 'day 4' rather than 'the fourth') – although Brazilians make an exception for the first, which is ordinal ('primeiro').

| English | Portuguese |
|---|---|
| 21st February 1763 | 21 de fevereiro de 1763 (Dia vinte e um de fevereiro, de mil setecentos e sessenta e três) |
| 19th July 1974 | 19 de julho de 1974 (Dia dezanove de julho, de mil novecentos e setenta e quatro) |
| 1st May 2002 | 1 de maio de 2002 (Dia um de maio, de dois mil e dois (PT); Primeiro de maio, de dois mil e dois (BR)) |

Going back further into history, you may need to refer to dates as 'AC' (Antes [de] Cristo) which means 'BC' or 'Before Christ', and 'DC' (Depois [de] Cristo) – which means 'AD' (Anno Domini – 'the year of our lord').

| English | Portuguese |
|---|---|
| 1336 BC | 1336 AC (Mil trezentos e trinta e seis antes [de] Cristo) |
| 305 AD | 305 DC (Trezentos e cinco depois [de] Cristo) |

### The Seasons (As Estações)

| English | Portuguese |
|---|---|
| spring | a primavera |
| summer | o verão |
| autumn | o outono |
| winter | o inverno |

### The Time (A Hora)

| English | Portuguese |
|---|---|
| one o'clock | uma hora |
| two o'clock | duas horas |
| three o'clock | três horas |
| midday | meio-dia |

| | |
|---|---|
| midnight | meia-noite |
| half past one | uma e meia |
| half past two | duas e meia |
| quarter past one | uma e um quarto (quarters are not used in Brazil) |
| quarter past two | duas e um quarto |
| quarter to one | uma menos um quarto |
| quarter to two | duas menos um quarto |
| five past one | uma e cinco |
| five past two | duas e cinco |
| ten to one | dez para uma |
| ...or... | uma menos dez (not used in Brazil) |
| ten to two | dez para duas |
| ...or... | duas menos dez (not used in Brazil) |

# 41. Medical Terms

When using medical or scientific terms, if you are not sure of a word, try using both body language and the Latin-based English word, as this is more likely to be understood by a Portuguese speaker. For example, instead of saying 'breathing', say 'respiration' (which is closer to the Portuguese word 'respiração'), or instead of 'womb', say 'uterus' (which is closer to the Portuguese word 'útero').

### Parts of the Body

| English | Portuguese |
|---|---|
| head | a cabeça |
| brain | o cérebro |
| eyes | os olhos |
| ears | os ouvidos (inner) / as orelhas (outer) |
| nose | o nariz |
| mouth | a boca |
| tongue | a língua |
| teeth | os dentes |
| throat | a garganta |
| neck | o pescoço |
| shoulder | o ombro |
| arm | o braço |
| elbow | o cotovelo |
| hand | a mão |
| finger | o dedo |
| thumb | o polegar |
| chest | o peito |
| heart | o coração |
| lungs | os pulmões |
| breast | o seio |
| back | as costas (in Portuguese, 'back' is plural – referring to the vertebrae) |
| side | o lado |
| ribs | as costelas |

| | |
|---|---|
| stomach | o estômago |
| belly | a barriga |
| abdomen | o abdómen |
| liver | o fígado |
| kidneys | os rins |
| bowels | os intestinos |
| womb | o útero |
| bottom | o traseiro |
| legs | as pernas |
| knee | o joelho |
| feet | os pés |
| toes | os dedos do pé |

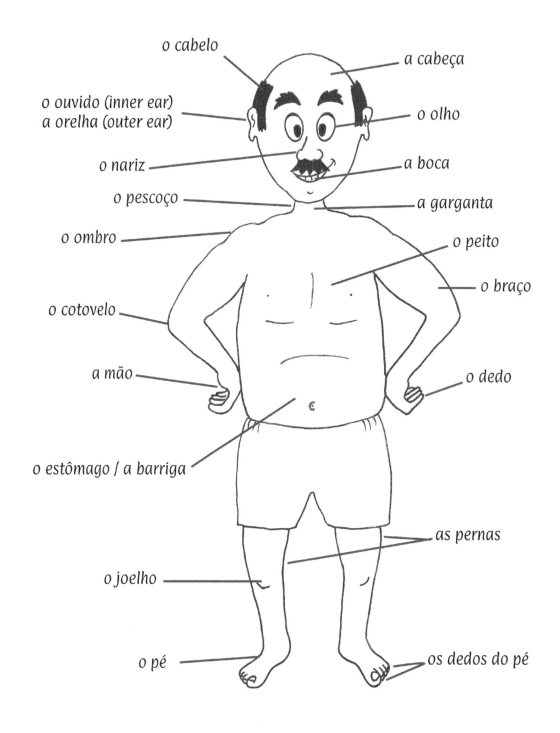

o cabelo

a cabeça

o ouvido (inner ear)
a orelha (outer ear)

o olho

o nariz

a boca

o pescoço

a garganta

o ombro

o peito

o braço

o cotovelo

a mão

o dedo

o estômago / a barriga

as pernas

o joelho

o pé

os dedos do pé

## Illnesses/complaints

The names of illnesses are often Latin-based, so the word is usually quite similar in English/Portuguese. So if you don't know the word, just use English and you will probably be understood.

| English | Portuguese |
| --- | --- |
| acne | o acne |
| allergy | a alergia |
| arthritis | a artrite |
| asthma | a asma |
| bronchitis | a bronquite |
| cold | a constipação (not to be confused with constipation!) |
| bad cold/flu | a gripe |
| cancer | o cancro (PT) / câncer (BR) |
| chicken pox | a varicela (PT) / catapora (BR) |
| constipation | a prisão de ventre (lit: 'prison of belly') |
| a cough | uma tosse |
| to cough | tossir |
| cyst | o cisto / o quisto / o nódulo |
| cystitis | a cistite |
| depression | a depressão |
| diabetes | a diabetes |
| diarrhoea | a diarreia |
| fever | a febre |
| gout | gota |
| hay fever | a febre do feno |
| headache | a dor de cabeça |
| heartburn | a azia |
| indigestion | a indigestão |
| infection | a infecção |
| insomnia | a insónia |
| to itch | picar / estar com comichão |
| measles | o sarampo |

| | |
|---|---|
| migraine | a enxaqueca |
| nausea | a náusea |
| sore throat | a dor de garganta |
| tired | cansado ('cansada' for a woman) |

### Related Words

| *English* | *Portuguese* |
|---|---|
| pain | a dor |
| painful | doloroso |
| illness/sickness | a doença |
| ill/sick | doente |
| medicine | a medicina |
| remedy | o remédio |
| doctor | o médico |
| doctor (as a title – e.g. Dr. Smith, or 'thank you doctor!') | doutor |
| to examine | examinar |
| a sample | uma amostra |
| blood | o sangue |
| urine | a urina |
| pregnant | grávida |
| pregnancy | a gravidez |
| prescription | a receita |
| where is the pain? | onde é a dor? |
| open your mouth | abra a boca |
| I'm going to refer you to a specialist | vou encaminhá-lo a um especialista |
| hospital | o hospital |
| you need… | você precisa de… |
| …rest | …descanso |
| …excercise | …exercício |
| …antibiotics | …antibióticos |
| …an operation | …uma operação |
| …a healthy diet | …uma dieta saudável |

# 42. Traffic and Directions

| | |
|---|---|
| north | o norte |
| south | o sul |
| east | o leste |
| west | o oeste |
| north-east | o nordeste |
| north-west | o noroeste |
| south-east | o sudeste |
| south-west | o sudoeste |
| left | a esquerda |
| right | a direita |
| straight on | sempre em frente |
| turn left | volte à esquerda |
| turn right | volte à direita |
| stop | pare (formal) / pára (informal) |
| pull over, please | encoste (formal) / encosta (informal), por favor |
| go | vá (formal) / vai (informal) |
| follow | siga (formal) / segue (informal) |
| traffic light | o sinal luminoso / o semáforo |
| roundabout (traffic circle) | o rotunda (PT) / a rotatória (BR) |
| traffic jam | o engarrafamento |
| directions | as instruções |
| near [to] | perto [de] |
| far [from] | longe [de] |
| where is ...? | onde fica ...? |
| is there ... near here? | há ... aqui perto? |
| a bank | um banco |
| a supermarket | um supermercado |
| a chemist (pharmacy) | uma farmácia |
| a sign | um sinal |
| road | a estrada |
| street | a rua |

# 43. Animals, Birds, Insects

### Animals and Birds

| English | Portuguese |
|---|---|
| dog | o cão (cachorro in Brazil) |
| cat | o gato |
| mouse | o ratinho (the same word is used for other small rodents) |
| sheep | a ovelha |
| pig | o porco |
| cow | a vaca |
| horse | o cavalo |
| snake | a cobra |
| fish | o peixe |
| frog | o sapo (or a rã) |
| lion | o leão |
| tiger | o tigre |
| bear | o urso |
| elephant | o elefante |
| bird | o pássaro |
| chicken | o frango; a galinha (hen) |
| blackbird | o melro |
| sparrow | o pardal |
| starling | o estorninho |
| parrot | o papagaio |
| penguin | o pinguim |

### Insects and Arachnids

| English | Portuguese |
|---|---|
| bee | a abelha |
| spider | a aranha |
| ant | a formiga |
| wasp | a vespa |
| fly | a mosca |

# 44. Summary of Tenses

Here is a quick reference guide to the tenses covered in this book, with a single example of each tense (using only the third person singular for the personal tenses) in both English and Portuguese.

| *Table 44.1: Summary of Tenses* | | |
|---|---|---|
| *Tense* | *English Example* | *Portuguese Example* |
| Impersonal Infinitive | to work | trabalhar |
| Personal Infinitive | [for] him to work | [para] ele trabalhar |
| Present Indicative | he works | ele trabalha |
| Present Subjunctive | he work | ele trabalhe |
| Present Continuous Indicative | he is working | ele está a trabalhar (PT) ele está trabalhando (BR) |
| Present Continuous Subjunctive | he be working | ele esteja a trabalhar (PT) ele esteja trabalhando (BR) |
| Conditional | he would work | ele trabalharia |
| Conditional Perfect | he would have worked | ele teria trabalhado |
| Preterite Indicative | he worked | ele trabalhou |
| Imperfect Indicative | he worked/used to work | ele trabalhava |
| Imperfect Subjunctive | he may have worked | ele trabalhasse |
| Past Continuous Indicative | he was working | ele estava a trabalhar (PT) ele estava trabalhando (BR) |
| Past Continuous Subjunctive | he may have been working | ele estivesse a trabalhar (PT) ele estivesse trabalhando (BR) |
| Present Perfect Indicative | he has worked | ele tem trabalhado |
| Present Perfect Subjunctive | he may have worked | ele tenha trabalhado |
| Present Perfect Continuous | he has been working | ele tem estado a trabalhar (PT) ele tem estado trabalhando (BR) |

| Tense | English Example | Portuguese Example |
|---|---|---|
| Past Perfect Continuous | he had been working | ele tinha estado a trabalhar (PT) ele tinha estado trabalhando (BR) |
| Simple Pluperfect Indicative | he had worked | trabalhara |
| Past Perfect Indicative | he had worked | ele tinha trabalhado |
| Past Perfect Subjunctive | he had [possibly] worked | ele tivesse trabalhado |
| Future Indicative | he will work | ele trabalhará |
| Future Subjunctive | he may work [in future] | ele trabalhar |
| Future Perfect Indicative | he will have worked | ele terá trabalhado |
| Future Perfect Subjunctive | he [possibly] will have worked | ele tiver trabalhado |
| Imperative | work | trabalhe |

**Notes:**

- Past Perfect is also known as Pluperfect.
- Continuous is also known as Progressive (some languages distinguish between continuous and progressive aspects, but neither English nor Portuguese do so).
- Preterite is sometimes referred to as Simple Past.
- When forming perfect tenses in Portuguese, sometimes the verb 'haver' is used instead of 'ter' ('haver' is much more formal and is only used when writing, mainly in Brazil).

# 45. Verb Conjugation Reference

For easy reference, all conjugations of the tenses are listed here for a sample of regular verbs (in conjugation order, i.e. …ar, …er, …ir), followed by the most common irregulars (in alphabetical order).

Each conjugation is spread over 2 pages – indicative and subjunctive forms are shown side by side first, followed by tenses in other moods. Each tense shows a page number which you can refer back to for an explanation of how the tense is used.

### First Conjugation Regular Verb: trabalhar (to work) – Part 1

Stem: *trabalh*;  Present participle: *trabalhando*;  Past participle: *trabalhado*

| Indicative Mood | | Subjunctive Mood | |
|---|---|---|---|
| **Present Indicative** *(p. 108)* | | **Present Subjunctive** *(p. 145)* | |
| trabalho | trabalhamos | trabalhe | trabalhemos |
| trabalhas | trabalhais | trabalhes | trabalheis |
| trabalha | trabalham | trabalhe | trabalhem |
| **Imperfect Indicative** *(p. 116)* | | **Imperfect Subjunctive** *(p. 152)* | |
| trabalhava | trabalhávamos | trabalhasse | trabalhássemos |
| trabalhavas | trabalháveis | trabalhasses | trabalhásseis |
| trabalhava | trabalhavam | trabalhasse | trabalhassem |
| **Future Indicative** *(p. 125)* | | **Future Subjunctive** *(p. 149)* | |
| trabalharei | trabalharemos | trabalhar | trabalharmos |
| trabalharás | trabalhareis | trabalhares | trabalhardes |
| trabalhará | trabalharão | trabalhar | trabalharem |
| **Present Perfect Indicative** *(p. 173)* | | **Present Perfect Subjunctive** *(p. 173)* | |
| tenho trabalhado | temos trabalhado | tenha trabalhado | tenhamos trabalhado |
| tens trabalhado | tendes trabalhado | tenhas trabalhado | tenhais trabalhado |
| tem trabalhado | têm trabalhado | tenha trabalhado | tenham trabalhado |
| **Past Perfect (Pluperfect) Indicative** *(p. 174)* | | **Past Perfect (Pluperfect) Subjunctive** *(p. 174)* | |
| tinha trabalhado | tínhamos trabalhado | tivesse trabalhado | tivéssemos trabalhado |
| tinhas trabalhado | tínheis trabalhado | tivesses trabalhado | tivésseis trabalhado |
| tinha trabalhado | tinham trabalhado | tivesse trabalhado | tivessem trabalhado |
| **Future Perfect Indicative** *(p. 175)* | | **Future Perfect Subjunctive** *(p. 175)* | |
| terei trabalhado | teremos trabalhado | tiver trabalhado | tivermos trabalhado |
| terás trabalhado | tereis trabalhado | tiveres trabalhado | tiverdes trabalhado |
| terá trabalhado | terão trabalhado | tiver trabalhado | tiverem trabalhado |

### First Conjugation Regular Verb: trabalhar (to work) – Part 2

| Indicative Mood | | Subjunctive Mood | |
|---|---|---|---|
| **Present Continuous Indicative** (p. 108) | | **Present Continuous Subjunctive** (p. 108) | |
| estou a trabalhar | estamos a trabalhar | esteja a trabalhar | estejamos a trabalhar |
| estás a trabalhar | estais a trabalhar | estejas a trabalhar | estejais a trabalhar |
| está a trabalhar | estão a trabalhar | esteja a trabalhar | estejam a trabalhar |
| **Past Continuous Indicative** (p. 119) | | **Past Continuous Subjunctive** (p. 119) | |
| estava a trabalhar | estávamos a trabalhar | estivesse a trabalhar | estivéssemos a trabalhar |
| estavas a trabalhar | estáveis a trabalhar | estivesses a trabalhar | estivésseis a trabalhar |
| estava a trabalhar | estavam a trabalhar | estivesse a trabalhar | estivessem a trabalhar |

| Indicative Mood | | Infinitive Mood | |
|---|---|---|---|
| **Preterite Indicative** (p. 111) | | **Impersonal Infinitive** (p. 77) | |
| trabalhei | trabalhámos | trabalhar | |
| trabalhaste | trabalhastes | | |
| trabalhou | trabalharam | | |
| **Simple Pluperfect Indicative** (p. 173) | | **Personal Infinitive** (p. 169) | |
| trabalhara | trabalháramos | trabalhar | trabalharmos |
| trabalharas | trabalháreis | trabalhares | trabalhardes |
| trabalhara | trabalharam | trabalhar | trabalharem |

| Conditional Mood | | | |
|---|---|---|---|
| **Conditional** (p. 129) | | **Conditional Perfect** (p. 176) | |
| trabalharia | trabalharíamos | teria trabalhado | teríamos trabalhado |
| trabalharias | trabalharíeis | terias trabalhado | teríeis trabalhado |
| trabalharia | trabalhariam | teria trabalhado | teriam trabalhado |

| Imperative Mood | | | |
|---|---|---|---|
| **Imperative** (p. 163) | | | |
| | trabalhemos | | |
| trabalha | trabalhai | | |
| trabalhe | trabalhem | | |

## Second Conjugation Regular Verb: comer (to eat) – Part 1

Stem: *com*;  Present participle: *comendo*;  Past participle: *comido*

| Indicative Mood | | Subjunctive Mood | |
|---|---|---|---|
| **Present Indicative** *(p. 108)* | | **Present Subjunctive** *(p. 145)* | |
| como | comemos | coma | comamos |
| comes | comeis | comas | comais |
| come | comem | coma | comam |
| **Imperfect Indicative** *(p. 116)* | | **Imperfect Subjunctive** *(p. 152)* | |
| comia | comíamos | comesse | comêssemos |
| comias | comíeis | comesses | comêsseis |
| comia | comiam | comesse | comessem |
| **Future Indicative** *(p. 125)* | | **Future Subjunctive** *(p. 149)* | |
| comerei | comeremos | comer | comermos |
| comerás | comereis | comeres | comerdes |
| comerá | comerão | comer | comerem |
| **Present Perfect Indicative** *(p. 173)* | | **Present Perfect Subjunctive** *(p. 173)* | |
| tenho comido | temos comido | tenha comido | tenhamos comido |
| tens comido | tendes comido | tenhas comido | tenhais comido |
| tem comido | têm comido | tenha comido | tenham comido |
| **Past Perfect (Pluperfect) Indicative** *(p. 174)* | | **Past Perfect (Pluperfect) Subjunctive** *(p. 174)* | |
| tinha comido | tínhamos comido | tivesse comido | tivéssemos comido |
| tinhas comido | tínheis comido | tivesses comido | tivésseis comido |
| tinha comido | tinham comido | tivesse comido | tivessem comido |
| **Future Perfect Indicative** *(p. 175)* | | **Future Perfect Subjunctive** *(p. 175)* | |
| terei comido | teremos comido | tiver comido | tivermos comido |
| terás comido | tereis comido | tiveres comido | tiverdes comido |
| terá comido | terão comido | tiver comido | tiverem comido |

## Second Conjugation Regular Verb: comer (to eat) – Part 2

| Indicative Mood | | Subjunctive Mood | |
|---|---|---|---|
| **Present Continuous Indicative** (p. 108) | | **Present Continuous Subjunctive** (p. 108) | |
| estou a comer | estamos a comer | esteja a comer | estejamos a comer |
| estás a comer | estais a comer | estejas a comer | estejais a comer |
| está a comer | estão a comer | esteja a comer | estejam a comer |
| **Past Continuous Indicative** (p. 119) | | **Past Continuous Subjunctive** (p. 119) | |
| estava a comer | estávamos a comer | estivesse a comer | estivéssemos a comer |
| estavas a comer | estáveis a comer | estivesses a comer | estivésseis a comer |
| estava a comer | estavam a comer | estivesse a comer | estivessem a comer |

| Indicative Mood | | Infinitive Mood | |
|---|---|---|---|
| **Preterite Indicative** (p. 111) | | **Impersonal Infinitive** (p. 77) | |
| comi | comemos | | |
| comeste | comestes | comer | |
| comeu | comeram | | |
| **Simple Pluperfect Indicative** (p. 173) | | **Personal Infinitive** (p. 169) | |
| comera | comêramos | comer | comermos |
| comeras | comêreis | comeres | comerdes |
| comera | comeram | comer | comerem |

| Conditional Mood | | | |
|---|---|---|---|
| **Conditional** (p. 129) | | **Conditional Perfect** (p. 176) | |
| comeria | comeríamos | teria comido | teríamos comido |
| comerias | comeríeis | terias comido | teríeis comido |
| comeria | comeriam | teria comido | teriam comido |

| Imperative Mood | | | |
|---|---|---|---|
| **Imperative** (p. 163) | | | |
| | comamos | | |
| come | comei | | |
| coma | comam | | |

### Third Conjugation Regular Verb: garantir (to guarantee) – Part 1

Stem: *garant*; Present participle: *garantindo*; Past participle: *garantido*

| Indicative Mood | | Subjunctive Mood | |
|---|---|---|---|
| **Present Indicative** (p. 108) | | **Present Subjunctive** (p. 145) | |
| garanto | garantimos | garanta | garantamos |
| garantes | garantis | garantas | garantais |
| garante | garantem | garanta | garantam |
| **Imperfect Indicative** (p. 116) | | **Imperfect Subjunctive** (p. 152) | |
| garantia | garantíamos | garantisse | garantíssemos |
| garantias | garantíeis | garantisses | garantísseis |
| garantia | garantiam | garantisse | garantissem |
| **Future Indicative** (p. 125) | | **Future Subjunctive** (p. 149) | |
| garantirei | garantiremos | garantir | garantirmos |
| garantirás | garantireis | garantires | garantirdes |
| garantirá | garantirão | garantir | garantirem |
| **Present Perfect Indicative** (p. 173) | | **Present Perfect Subjunctive** (p. 173) | |
| tenho garantido | temos garantido | tenha garantido | tenhamos garantido |
| tens garantido | tendes garantido | tenhas garantido | tenhais garantido |
| tem garantido | têm garantido | tenha garantido | tenham garantido |
| **Past Perfect (Pluperfect) Indicative** (p. 174) | | **Past Perfect (Pluperfect) Subjunctive** (p. 174) | |
| tinha garantido | tínhamos garantido | tivesse garantido | tivéssemos garantido |
| tinhas garantido | tínheis garantido | tivesses garantido | tivésseis garantido |
| tinha garantido | tinham garantido | tivesse garantido | tivessem garantido |
| **Future Perfect Indicative** (p. 175) | | **Future Perfect Subjunctive** (p. 175) | |
| terei garantido | teremos garantido | tiver garantido | tivermos garantido |
| terás garantido | tereis garantido | tiveres garantido | tiverdes garantido |
| terá garantido | terão garantido | tiver garantido | tiverem garantido |

## Third Conjugation Regular Verb: garantir (to guarantee) – Part 2

| Indicative Mood | | Subjunctive Mood | |
|---|---|---|---|
| **Present Continuous Indicative** *(p. 108)* | | **Present Continuous Subjunctive** *(p. 108)* | |
| estou a garantir | estamos a garantir | esteja a garantir | estejamos a garantir |
| estás a garantir | estais a garantir | estejas a garantir | estejais a garantir |
| está a garantir | estão a garantir | esteja a garantir | estejam a garantir |
| **Past Continuous Indicative** *(p. 119)* | | **Past Continuous Subjunctive** *(p. 119)* | |
| estava a garantir | estávamos a garantir | estivesse a garantir | estivéssemos a garantir |
| estavas a garantir | estáveis a garantir | estivesses a garantir | estivésseis a garantir |
| estava a garantir | estavam a garantir | estivesse a garantir | estivessem a garantir |

| Indicative Mood | | Infinitive Mood | |
|---|---|---|---|
| **Preterite Indicative** *(p. 111)* | | **Impersonal Infinitive** *(p. 77)* | |
| garanti | garantimos | garantir | |
| garantiste | garantistes | | |
| garantiu | garantiram | | |
| **Simple Pluperfect Indicative** *(p. 173)* | | **Personal Infinitive** *(p. 169)* | |
| garantira | garantíramos | garantir | garantirmos |
| garantiras | garantíreis | garantires | garantirdes |
| garantira | garantiram | garantir | garantirem |

| Conditional Mood | | | |
|---|---|---|---|
| **Conditional** *(p. 129)* | | **Conditional Perfect** *(p. 176)* | |
| garantiria | garantiríamos | teria garantido | teríamos garantido |
| garantirias | garantiríeis | terias garantido | teríeis garantido |
| garantiria | garantiriam | teria garantido | teriam garantido |

| Imperative Mood | | | |
|---|---|---|---|
| **Imperative** *(p. 163)* | | | |
| | garantamos | | |
| garante | garanti | | |
| garanta | garantam | | |

**First Conjugation Irregular Verb: dar (to give) – Part 1**

Stem: *d*;  Present participle: *dando*;  Past participle: *dado*

| Indicative Mood | | Subjunctive Mood | |
|---|---|---|---|
| **Present Indicative** *(p. 108)* | | **Present Subjunctive** *(p. 145)* | |
| dou | damos | dê | dêmos |
| dás | dais | dês | deis |
| dá | dão | dê | dêem |
| **Imperfect Indicative** *(p. 116)* | | **Imperfect Subjunctive** *(p. 152)* | |
| dava | dávamos | desse | déssemos |
| davas | dáveis | desses | désseis |
| dava | davam | desse | dessem |
| **Future Indicative** *(p. 125)* | | **Future Subjunctive** *(p. 149)* | |
| darei | daremos | der | dermos |
| darás | dareis | deres | derdes |
| dará | darão | der | derem |
| **Present Perfect Indicative** *(p. 173)* | | **Present Perfect Subjunctive** *(p. 173)* | |
| tenho dado | temos dado | tenha dado | tenhamos dado |
| tens dado | tendes dado | tenhas dado | tenhais dado |
| tem dado | têm dado | tenha dado | tenham dado |
| **Past Perfect (Pluperfect) Indicative** *(p. 174)* | | **Past Perfect (Pluperfect) Subjunctive** *(p. 174)* | |
| tinha dado | tínhamos dado | tivesse dado | tivéssemos dado |
| tinhas dado | tínheis dado | tivesses dado | tivésseis dado |
| tinha dado | tinham dado | tivesse dado | tivessem dado |
| **Future Perfect Indicative** *(p. 175)* | | **Future Perfect Subjunctive** *(p. 175)* | |
| terei dado | teremos dado | tiver dado | tivermos dado |
| terás dado | tereis dado | tiveres dado | tiverdes dado |
| terá dado | terão dado | tiver dado | tiverem dado |

## First Conjugation Irregular Verb: dar (to give) – Part 2

| Indicative Mood | | Subjunctive Mood | |
|---|---|---|---|
| **Present Continuous Indicative** (p. 108) | | **Present Continuous Subjunctive** (p. 108) | |
| estou a dar | estamos a dar | esteja a dar | estejamos a dar |
| estás a dar | estais a dar | estejas a dar | estejais a dar |
| está a dar | estão a dar | esteja a dar | estejam a dar |
| **Past Continuous Indicative** (p. 119) | | **Past Continuous Subjunctive** (p. 119) | |
| estava a dar | estávamos a dar | estivesse a dar | estivéssemos a dar |
| estavas a dar | estáveis a dar | estivesses a dar | estivésseis a dar |
| estava a dar | estavam a dar | estivesse a dar | estivessem a dar |

| Indicative Mood | | Infinitive Mood | |
|---|---|---|---|
| **Preterite Indicative** (p. 111) | | **Impersonal Infinitive** (p. 77) | |
| dei | demos | | |
| deste | destes | dar | |
| deu | deram | | |
| **Simple Pluperfect Indicative** (p. 173) | | **Personal Infinitive** (p. 169) | |
| dera | déramos | dar | darmos |
| deras | déreis | dares | dardes |
| dera | deram | dar | darem |

| Conditional Mood | | | |
|---|---|---|---|
| **Conditional** (p. 129) | | **Conditional Perfect** (p. 176) | |
| daria | daríamos | teria dado | teríamos dado |
| darias | daríeis | terias dado | teríeis dado |
| daria | dariam | teria dado | teriam dado |

| Imperative Mood | | | |
|---|---|---|---|
| **Imperative** (p. 163) | | | |
| | dêmos | | |
| dá | dai | | |
| dê | dêem | | |

## Second Conjugation Irregular Verb: dizer (to say) – Part 1

Stem: *diz*;  Present participle: *dizendo*;  Past participle: *dito*

| Indicative Mood | | Subjunctive Mood | |
|---|---|---|---|
| **Present Indicative** *(p. 108)* | | **Present Subjunctive** *(p. 145)* | |
| digo | dizemos | diga | digamos |
| dizes | dizeis | digas | digais |
| diz | dizem | diga | digam |
| **Imperfect Indicative** *(p. 116)* | | **Imperfect Subjunctive** *(p. 152)* | |
| dizia | dizíamos | dissesse | disséssemos |
| dizias | dizíeis | dissesses | dissésseis |
| dizia | diziam | dissesse | dissessem |
| **Future Indicative** *(p. 125)* | | **Future Subjunctive** *(p. 149)* | |
| direi | diremos | disser | dissermos |
| dirás | direis | disseres | disserdes |
| dirá | dirão | disser | disserem |
| **Present Perfect Indicative** *(p. 173)* | | **Present Perfect Subjunctive** *(p. 173)* | |
| tenho dito | temos dito | tenha dito | tenhamos dito |
| tens dito | tendes dito | tenhas dito | tenhais dito |
| tem dito | têm dito | tenha dito | tenham dito |
| **Past Perfect (Pluperfect) Indicative** *(p. 174)* | | **Past Perfect (Pluperfect) Subjunctive** *(p. 174)* | |
| tinha dito | tínhamos dito | tivesse dito | tivéssemos dito |
| tinhas dito | tínheis dito | tivesses dito | tivésseis dito |
| tinha dito | tinham dito | tivesse dito | tivessem dito |
| **Future Perfect Indicative** *(p. 175)* | | **Future Perfect Subjunctive** *(p. 175)* | |
| terei dito | teremos dito | tiver dito | tivermos dito |
| terás dito | tereis dito | tiveres dito | tiverdes dito |
| terá dito | terão dito | tiver dito | tiverem dito |

## Second Conjugation Irregular Verb: dizer (to say) – Part 2

| Indicative Mood | | Subjunctive Mood | |
|---|---|---|---|
| **Present Continuous Indicative** *(p. 108)* | | **Present Continuous Subjunctive** *(p. 108)* | |
| estou a dizer | estamos a dizer | esteja a dizer | estejamos a dizer |
| estás a dizer | estais a dizer | estejas a dizer | estejais a dizer |
| está a dizer | estão a dizer | esteja a dizer | estejam a dizer |
| **Past Continuous Indicative** *(p. 119)* | | **Past Continuous Subjunctive** *(p. 119)* | |
| estava a dizer | estávamos a dizer | estivesse a dizer | estivéssemos a dizer |
| estavas a dizer | estáveis a dizer | estivesses a dizer | estivésseis a dizer |
| estava a dizer | estavam a dizer | estivesse a dizer | estivessem a dizer |

| Indicative Mood | | Infinitive Mood | |
|---|---|---|---|
| **Preterite Indicative** *(p. 111)* | | **Impersonal Infinitive** *(p. 77)* | |
| disse | dissemos | dizer | |
| disseste | dissestes | | |
| disse | disseram | | |
| **Simple Pluperfect Indicative** *(p. 173)* | | **Personal Infinitive** *(p. 169)* | |
| dissera | disséramos | dizer | dizermos |
| disseras | disséreis | dizeres | dizerdes |
| dissera | disseram | dizer | dizerem |

| Conditional Mood | | | |
|---|---|---|---|
| **Conditional** *(p. 129)* | | **Conditional Perfect** *(p. 176)* | |
| diria | diríamos | teria dito | teríamos dito |
| dirias | diríeis | terias dito | teríeis dito |
| diria | diriam | teria dito | teriam dito |

| Imperative Mood | | | |
|---|---|---|---|
| **Imperative** *(p. 163)* | | | |
| | digamos | | |
| diz | dizei | | |
| diga | digam | | |

## First Conjugation Irregular Verb: estar (to be) – Part 1

Stem: *est*;  Present participle: *estando*;  Past participle: *estado*

| Indicative Mood | | Subjunctive Mood | |
|---|---|---|---|
| **Present Indicative** (p. 108) | | **Present Subjunctive** (p. 145) | |
| estou | estamos | esteja | estejamos |
| estas | estais | estejas | estejais |
| está | estão | esteja | estejam |
| **Imperfect Indicative** (p. 116) | | **Imperfect Subjunctive** (p. 152) | |
| estava | estávamos | estivesse | estivéssemos |
| estavas | estáveis | estivesses | estivésseis |
| estava | estavam | estivesse | estivessem |
| **Future Indicative** (p. 125) | | **Future Subjunctive** (p. 149) | |
| estarei | estaremos | estiver | estivermos |
| estarás | estareis | estiveres | estiverdes |
| estará | estarão | estiver | estiverem |
| **Present Perfect Indicative** (p. 173) | | **Present Perfect Subjunctive** (p. 173) | |
| tenho estado | temos estado | tenha estado | tenhamos estado |
| tens estado | tendes estado | tenhas estado | tenhais estado |
| tem estado | têm estado | tenha estado | tenham estado |
| **Past Perfect (Pluperfect) Indicative** (p. 174) | | **Past Perfect (Pluperfect) Subjunctive** (p. 174) | |
| tinha estado | tínhamos estado | tivesse estado | tivéssemos estado |
| tinhas estado | tínheis estado | tivesses estado | tivésseis estado |
| tinha estado | tinham estado | tivesse estado | tivessem estado |
| **Future Perfect Indicative** (p. 175) | | **Future Perfect Subjunctive** (p. 175) | |
| terei estado | teremos estado | tiver estado | tivermos estado |
| terás estado | tereis estado | tiveres estado | tiverdes estado |
| terá estado | terão estado | tiver estado | tiverem estado |

## First Conjugation Irregular Verb: estar (to be) – Part 2

| Indicative Mood | Subjunctive Mood |
|---|---|
| **Present Continuous Indicative** (p. 108) | **Present Continuous Subjunctive** (p. 108) |
| Not applicable ('am being', 'is being' and 'are being' only apply to the verb 'ser', not 'estar' – e.g. you can say 'I am being silly', but you wouldn't say 'I am being tired'). | Not applicable |
| **Past Continuous Indicative** (p. 119) | **Past Continuous Subjunctive** (p. 119) |
| Not applicable | Not applicable |

| Indicative Mood | | Infinitive Mood | |
|---|---|---|---|
| **Preterite Indicative** (p. 111) | | **Impersonal Infinitive** (p. 77) | |
| estive | estivemos | | |
| estiveste | estivestes | estar | |
| esteve | estiveram | | |
| **Simple Pluperfect Indicative** (p. 173) | | **Personal Infinitive** (p. 169) | |
| estivera | estivéramos | estar | estarmos |
| estiveras | estivéreis | estares | estardes |
| estivera | estiveram | estar | estarem |

Conditional Mood

| **Conditional** (p. 129) | | **Conditional Perfect** (p. 176) | |
|---|---|---|---|
| estaria | estaríamos | teria estado | teríamos estado |
| estarias | estaríeis | terias estado | teríeis estado |
| estaria | estariam | teria estado | teriam estado |

Imperative Mood

| **Imperative** (p. 163) | |
|---|---|
| | estejamos |
| está | estai |
| esteja | estejam |

**Second Conjugation Irregular Verb: *fazer (to make; to do)* – Part 1**

Stem: *faz*;  Present participle: *fazendo*;  Past participle: *feito*

| Indicative Mood | | Subjunctive Mood | |
|---|---|---|---|
| **Present Indicative** *(p. 108)* | | **Present Subjunctive** *(p. 145)* | |
| faço | fazemos | faça | façamos |
| fazes | fazeis | faças | façais |
| faz | fazem | faça | façam |
| **Imperfect Indicative** *(p. 116)* | | **Imperfect Subjunctive** *(p. 152)* | |
| fazia | fazíamos | fizesse | fizéssemos |
| fazias | fazíeis | fizesses | fizésseis |
| fazia | faziam | fizesse | fizessem |
| **Future Indicative** *(p. 125)* | | **Future Subjunctive** *(p. 149)* | |
| farei | faremos | fizer | fizermos |
| farás | fareis | fizeres | fizerdes |
| fará | farão | fizer | fizerem |
| **Present Perfect Indicative** *(p. 173)* | | **Present Perfect Subjunctive** *(p. 173)* | |
| tenho feito | temos feito | tenha feito | tenhamos feito |
| tens feito | tendes feito | tenhas feito | tenhais feito |
| tem feito | têm feito | tenha feito | tenham feito |
| **Past Perfect (Pluperfect) Indicative** *(p. 174)* | | **Past Perfect (Pluperfect) Subjunctive** *(p. 174)* | |
| tinha feito | tínhamos feito | tivesse feito | tivéssemos feito |
| tinhas feito | tínheis feito | tivesses feito | tivésseis feito |
| tinha feito | tinham feito | tivesse feito | tivessem feito |
| **Future Perfect Indicative** *(p. 175)* | | **Future Perfect Subjunctive** *(p. 175)* | |
| terei feito | teremos feito | tiver feito | tivermos feito |
| terás feito | tereis feito | tiveres feito | tiverdes feito |
| terá feito | terão feito | tiver feito | tiverem feito |

## Second Conjugation Irregular Verb: fazer (to make; to do) – Part 2

| Indicative Mood | | Subjunctive Mood | |
|---|---|---|---|
| **Present Continuous Indicative** (p. 108) | | **Present Continuous Subjunctive** (p. 108) | |
| estou a fazer | estamos a fazer | esteja a fazer | estejamos a fazer |
| estás a fazer | estais a fazer | estejas a fazer | estejais a fazer |
| está a fazer | estão a fazer | esteja a fazer | estejam a fazer |
| **Past Continuous Indicative** (p. 119) | | **Past Continuous Subjunctive** (p. 119) | |
| estava a fazer | estávamos a fazer | estivesse a fazer | estivéssemos a fazer |
| estavas a fazer | estáveis a fazer | estivesses a fazer | estivésseis a fazer |
| estava a fazer | estavam a fazer | estivesse a fazer | estivessem a fazer |

| Indicative Mood | | Infinitive Mood | |
|---|---|---|---|
| **Preterite Indicative** (p. 111) | | **Impersonal Infinitive** (p. 77) | |
| fiz | fizemos | fazer | |
| fizeste | fizestes | | |
| fez | fizeram | | |
| **Simple Pluperfect Indicative** (p. 173) | | **Personal Infinitive** (p. 169) | |
| fizera | fizéramos | fazer | fazermos |
| fizeras | fizéreis | fazeres | fazerdes |
| fizera | fizeram | fazer | fazerem |

| Conditional Mood | | | |
|---|---|---|---|
| **Conditional** (p. 129) | | **Conditional Perfect** (p. 176) | |
| faria | faríamos | teria feito | teríamos feito |
| farias | faríeis | terias feito | teríeis feito |
| faria | fariam | teria feito | teriam feito |

| Imperative Mood | |
|---|---|
| **Imperative** (p. 163) | |
| | façamos |
| faz | fazei |
| faça | façam |

| **Second Conjugation Irregular Verb: haver (to be [impersonal]; to have [auxiliary]) – Part 1** | | | |
|---|---|---|---|
| Stem: *hav*;  Present participle: *havendo*;  Past participle: *havido* | | | |
| Indicative Mood | | Subjunctive Mood | |
| **Present Indicative** *(p. 108)* | | **Present Subjunctive** *(p. 145)* | |
| hei (de) | havemos (de) | | |
| hás (de) | haveis (de) | | |
| há / há (de) | hão (de) | haja | |
| **Imperfect Indicative** *(p. 116)* | | **Imperfect Subjunctive** *(p. 152)* | |
| | | | |
| | | | |
| havia | | houvesse | |
| **Future Indicative** *(p. 125)* | | **Future Subjunctive** *(p. 149)* | |
| | | | |
| | | | |
| haverá | | houver | |
| **Present Perfect Indicative** *(p. 173)* | | **Present Perfect Subjunctive** *(p. 173)* | |
| | | | |
| | | | |
| tem havido | têm havido | tenha havido | tenham havido |
| **Past Perfect (Pluperfect) Indicative** *(p. 174)* | | **Past Perfect (Pluperfect) Subjunctive** *(p. 174)* | |
| | | | |
| | | | |
| tinha havido | tinham havido | tivesse havido | tivessem havido |
| **Future Perfect Indicative** *(p. 175)* | | **Future Perfect Subjunctive** *(p. 175)* | |
| | | | |
| | | | |
| terá havido | terão havido | tiver havido | tiverem havido |

**Second Conjugation Irregular Verb: haver (to be [impersonal; to have [auxiliary]) – Part 2**

| Indicative Mood | | Subjunctive Mood | |
|---|---|---|---|
| **Present Continuous Indicative** (p. 108) | | **Present Continuous Subjunctive** (p. 108) | |
| | | | |
| | | | |
| está a haver | estão a haver | esteja a haver | estejam a haver |
| **Past Continuous Indicative** (p. 119) | | **Past Continuous Subjunctive** (p. 119) | |
| | | | |
| | | | |
| estava a haver | estavam a haver | estivesse a haver | estivessem a haver |

| Indicative Mood | | Infinitive Mood | |
|---|---|---|---|
| **Preterite Indicative** (p. 111) | | **Impersonal Infinitive** (p. 77) | |
| | | | |
| | | haver | |
| houve | | | |
| **Simple Pluperfect Indicative** (p. 173) | | **Personal Infinitive** (p. 169) | |
| | | | |
| | | | |
| houvera | | haver | |

| Conditional Mood | | | |
|---|---|---|---|
| **Conditional** (p. 129) | | **Conditional Perfect** (p. 176) | |
| | | | |
| | | | |
| haveria | | teria havido | teriam havido |

| Imperative Mood | Note: this verb is impersonal or auxiliary only, so cannot be fully conjugated, and only has its plural form when presented in a compound tense as an auxiliary verb. |
|---|---|
| **Imperative** (p. 163) | |
| Not applicable | |

**Third Conjugation Irregular Verb: ir (to go) – Part 1**

Stem: *none!*;  Present participle: *indo*;  Past participle: *ido*

| Indicative Mood | | Subjunctive Mood | |
|---|---|---|---|
| **Present Indicative** *(p. 108)* | | **Present Subjunctive** *(p. 145)* | |
| vou | vamos | vá | vamos |
| vais | ides | vás | vades |
| vai | vão | vá | vão |
| **Imperfect Indicative** *(p. 116)* | | **Imperfect Subjunctive** *(p. 152)* | |
| ia | íamos | fosse | fôssemos |
| ias | íeis | fosses | fôsseis |
| ia | iam | fosse | fossem |
| **Future Indicative** *(p. 125)* | | **Future Subjunctive** *(p. 149)* | |
| irei | iremos | for | formos |
| irás | ireis | fores | fordes |
| irá | irão | for | forem |
| **Present Perfect Indicative** *(p. 173)* | | **Present Perfect Subjunctive** *(p. 173)* | |
| tenho ido | temos ido | tenha ido | tenhamos ido |
| tens ido | tendes ido | tenhas ido | tenhais ido |
| tem ido | têm ido | tenha ido | tenham ido |
| **Past Perfect (Pluperfect) Indicative** *(p. 174)* | | **Past Perfect (Pluperfect) Subjunctive** *(p. 174)* | |
| tinha ido | tínhamos ido | tivesse ido | tivéssemos ido |
| tinhas ido | tínheis ido | tivesses ido | tivésseis ido |
| tinha ido | tinham ido | tivesse ido | tivessem ido |
| **Future Perfect Indicative** *(p. 175)* | | **Future Perfect Subjunctive** *(p. 175)* | |
| terei ido | teremos ido | tiver ido | tivermos ido |
| terás ido | tereis ido | tiveres ido | tiverdes ido |
| terá ido | terão ido | tiver ido | tiverem ido |

## Third Conjugation Irregular Verb: *ir (to go) – Part 2*

| Indicative Mood | | Subjunctive Mood | |
|---|---|---|---|
| **Present Continuous Indicative** *(p. 108)* | | **Present Continuous Subjunctive** *(p. 108)* | |
| estou a ir | estamos a ir | esteja a ir | estejamos a ir |
| estás a ir | estais a ir | estejas a ir | estejais a ir |
| está a ir | estão a ir | esteja a ir | estejam a ir |
| **Past Continuous Indicative** *(p. 119)* | | **Past Continuous Subjunctive** *(p. 119)* | |
| estava a ir | estávamos a ir | estivesse a ir | estivéssemos a ir |
| estavas a ir | estáveis a ir | estivesses a ir | estivésseis a ir |
| estava a ir | estavam a ir | estivesse a ir | estivessem a ir |

| Indicative Mood | | Infinitive Mood | |
|---|---|---|---|
| **Preterite Indicative** *(p. 111)* | | **Impersonal Infinitive** *(p. 77)* | |
| fui | fomos | | |
| foste | fostes | ir | |
| foi | foram | | |
| **Simple Pluperfect Indicative** *(p. 173)* | | **Personal Infinitive** *(p. 169)* | |
| fora | fôramos | ir | irmos |
| foras | fôreis | ires | irdes |
| fora | foram | ir | irem |

| Conditional Mood | | | |
|---|---|---|---|
| **Conditional** *(p. 129)* | | **Conditional Perfect** *(p. 176)* | |
| iria | iríamos | teria ido | teríamos ido |
| irias | iríeis | terias ido | teríeis ido |
| iria | iriam | teria ido | teriam ido |

| Imperative Mood | | | |
|---|---|---|---|
| **Imperative** *(p. 163)* | | Note: Progressive tenses are not often used for the verb 'ir'. For example, instead of 'estou a ir' (present continuous indicative), you would normally just say 'vou' (present indicative). | |
| | vamos | | |
| vai | ide | | |
| vá | vão | | |

**Second Conjugation Irregular Verb: ler (to read) – Part 1**

Stem: *l*;  Present participle: *lendo*;  Past participle: *lido*

| Indicative Mood | | Subjunctive Mood | |
|---|---|---|---|
| **Present Indicative** *(p. 108)* | | **Present Subjunctive** *(p. 145)* | |
| leio | lemos | leia | leiamos |
| lês | ledes | leias | leiais |
| lê | lêem | leia | leiam |
| **Imperfect Indicative** *(p. 116)* | | **Imperfect Subjunctive** *(p. 152)* | |
| lia | líamos | lesse | lêssemos |
| lias | líeis | lesses | lêsseis |
| lia | liam | lesse | lessem |
| **Future Indicative** *(p. 125)* | | **Future Subjunctive** *(p. 149)* | |
| lerei | leremos | ler | lermos |
| lerás | lereis | leres | lerdes |
| lerá | lerão | ler | lerem |
| **Present Perfect Indicative** *(p. 173)* | | **Present Perfect Subjunctive** *(p. 173)* | |
| tenho lido | temos lido | tenha lido | tenhamos lido |
| tens lido | tendes lido | tenhas lido | tenhais lido |
| tem lido | têm lido | tenha lido | tenham lido |
| **Past Perfect (Pluperfect) Indicative** *(p. 174)* | | **Past Perfect (Pluperfect) Subjunctive** *(p. 174)* | |
| tinha lido | tínhamos lido | tivesse lido | tivéssemos lido |
| tinhas lido | tínheis lido | tivesses lido | tivésseis lido |
| tinha lido | tinham lido | tivesse lido | tivessem lido |
| **Future Perfect Indicative** *(p. 175)* | | **Future Perfect Subjunctive** *(p. 175)* | |
| terei lido | teremos lido | tiver lido | tivermos lido |
| terás lido | tereis lido | tiveres lido | tiverdes lido |
| terá lido | terão lido | tiver lido | tiverem lido |

## Second Conjugation Irregular Verb: ler (to read) – Part 2

| Indicative Mood | | Subjunctive Mood | |
|---|---|---|---|
| **Present Continuous Indicative** (p. 108) | | **Present Continuous Subjunctive** (p. 108) | |
| estou a ler | estamos a ler | esteja a ler | estejamos a ler |
| estás a ler | estais a ler | estejas a ler | estejais a ler |
| está a ler | estão a ler | esteja a ler | estejam a ler |
| **Past Continuous Indicative** (p. 119) | | **Past Continuous Subjunctive** (p. 119) | |
| estava a ler | estávamos a ler | estivesse a ler | estivéssemos a ler |
| estavas a ler | estáveis a ler | estivesses a ler | estivésseis a ler |
| estava a ler | estavam a ler | estivesse a ler | estivessem a ler |

| Indicative Mood | | Infinitive Mood | |
|---|---|---|---|
| **Preterite Indicative** (p. 111) | | **Impersonal Infinitive** (p. 77) | |
| li | lemos | | |
| leste | lestes | ler | |
| leu | leram | | |
| **Simple Pluperfect Indicative** (p. 173) | | **Personal Infinitive** (p. 169) | |
| lera | lêramos | ler | lermos |
| leras | lêreis | leres | lerdes |
| lera | leram | ler | lerem |

| Conditional Mood | | | |
|---|---|---|---|
| **Conditional** (p. 129) | | **Conditional Perfect** (p. 176) | |
| leria | leríamos | teria lido | teríamos lido |
| lerias | leríeis | terias lido | teríeis lido |
| leria | leriam | teria lido | teriam lido |

| Imperative Mood | | | |
|---|---|---|---|
| **Imperative** (p. 163) | | | |
| | leiamos | | |
| lê | lede | | |
| leia | leiam | | |

### Third Conjugation Irregular Verb: ouvir (to hear) – Part 1

Stem: *ouv*;  Present participle: *ouvindo*;  Past participle: *ouvido*

| Indicative Mood | | Subjunctive Mood | |
|---|---|---|---|
| **Present Indicative** (p. 108) | | **Present Subjunctive** (p. 145) | |
| oiço | ouvimos | oiça | oiçamos |
| ouves | ouvis | oiças | oiçais |
| ouve | ouvem | oiça | oiçam |
| **Imperfect Indicative** (p. 116) | | **Imperfect Subjunctive** (p. 152) | |
| ouvia | ouvíamos | ouvisse | ouvíssemos |
| ouvias | ouvíeis | ouvisses | ouvísseis |
| ouvia | ouviam | ouvisse | ouvissem |
| **Future Indicative** (p. 125) | | **Future Subjunctive** (p. 149) | |
| ouvirei | ouviremos | ouvir | ouvirmos |
| ouvirás | ouvireis | ouvires | ouvirdes |
| ouvirá | ouvirão | ouvir | ouvirem |
| **Present Perfect Indicative** (p. 173) | | **Present Perfect Subjunctive** (p. 173) | |
| tenho ouvido | temos ouvido | tenha ouvido | tenhamos ouvido |
| tens ouvido | tendes ouvido | tenhas ouvido | tenhais ouvido |
| tem ouvido | têm ouvido | tenha ouvido | tenham ouvido |
| **Past Perfect (Pluperfect) Indicative** (p. 174) | | **Past Perfect (Pluperfect) Subjunctive** (p. 174) | |
| tinha ouvido | tínhamos ouvido | tivesse ouvido | tivéssemos ouvido |
| tinhas ouvido | tínheis ouvido | tivesses ouvido | tivésseis ouvido |
| tinha ouvido | tinham ouvido | tivesse ouvido | tivessem ouvido |
| **Future Perfect Indicative** (p. 175) | | **Future Perfect Subjunctive** (p. 175) | |
| terei ouvido | teremos ouvido | tiver ouvido | tivermos ouvido |
| terás ouvido | tereis ouvido | tiveres ouvido | tiverdes ouvido |
| terá ouvido | terão ouvido | tiver ouvido | tiverem ouvido |

**Third Conjugation Irregular Verb: ouvir (to hear) – Part 2**

| Indicative Mood | | Subjunctive Mood | |
|---|---|---|---|
| **Present Continuous Indicative** *(p. 108)* | | **Present Continuous Subjunctive** *(p. 108)* | |
| estou a ouvir | estamos a ouvir | esteja a ouvir | estejamos a ouvir |
| estás a ouvir | estais a ouvir | estejas a ouvir | estejais a ouvir |
| está a ouvir | estão a ouvir | esteja a ouvir | estejam a ouvir |
| **Past Continuous Indicative** *(p. 119)* | | **Past Continuous Subjunctive** *(p. 119)* | |
| estava a ouvir | estávamos a ouvir | estivesse a ouvir | estivéssemos a ouvir |
| estavas a ouvir | estáveis a ouvir | estivesses a ouvir | estivésseis a ouvir |
| estava a ouvir | estavam a ouvir | estivesse a ouvir | estivessem a ouvir |

| Indicative Mood | | Infinitive Mood | |
|---|---|---|---|
| **Preterite Indicative** *(p. 111)* | | **Impersonal Infinitive** *(p. 77)* | |
| ouvi | ouvimos | | |
| ouviste | ouvistes | ouvir | |
| ouviu | ouviram | | |
| **Simple Pluperfect Indicative** *(p. 173)* | | **Personal Infinitive** *(p. 169)* | |
| ouvira | ouvíramos | ouvir | ouvirmos |
| ouviras | ouvíreis | ouvires | ouvirdes |
| ouvira | ouviram | ouvir | ouvirem |

| Conditional Mood | | | |
|---|---|---|---|
| **Conditional** *(p. 129)* | | **Conditional Perfect** *(p. 176)* | |
| ouviria | ouviríamos | teria ouvido | teríamos ouvido |
| ouvirias | ouviríeis | terias ouvido | teríeis ouvido |
| ouviria | ouviriam | teria ouvido | teriam ouvido |

| Imperative Mood | | | |
|---|---|---|---|
| **Imperative** *(p. 163)* | | Note: in Brazil, they use 'ouç' instead of 'oiç' (e.g., ouço, ouça). | |
| | oiçamos | | |
| ouve | ouvi | | |
| oiça | oiçam | | |

**Third Conjugation Irregular Verb: pedir (to ask) – Part 1**

Stem: *ped*;  Present participle: *pedindo*;  Past participle: *pedido*

| Indicative Mood | | Subjunctive Mood | |
|---|---|---|---|
| **Present Indicative** *(p. 108)* | | **Present Subjunctive** *(p. 145)* | |
| peço | pedimos | peça | peçamos |
| pedes | pedis | peças | peçais |
| pede | pedem | peça | peçam |
| **Imperfect Indicative** *(p. 116)* | | **Imperfect Subjunctive** *(p. 152)* | |
| pedia | pedíamos | pedisse | pedíssemos |
| pedias | pedíeis | pedisses | pedísseis |
| pedia | pediam | pedisse | pedissem |
| **Future Indicative** *(p. 125)* | | **Future Subjunctive** *(p. 149)* | |
| pedirei | pediremos | pedir | pedirmos |
| pedirás | pedireis | pedires | pedirdes |
| pedirá | pedirão | pedir | pedirem |
| **Present Perfect Indicative** *(p. 173)* | | **Present Perfect Subjunctive** *(p. 173)* | |
| tenho pedido | temos pedido | tenha pedido | tenhamos pedido |
| tens pedido | tendes pedido | tenhas pedido | tenhais pedido |
| tem pedido | têm pedido | tenha pedido | tenham pedido |
| **Past Perfect (Pluperfect) Indicative** *(p. 174)* | | **Past Perfect (Pluperfect) Subjunctive** *(p. 174)* | |
| tinha pedido | tínhamos pedido | tivesse pedido | tivéssemos pedido |
| tinhas pedido | tínheis pedido | tivesses pedido | tivésseis pedido |
| tinha pedido | tinham pedido | tivesse pedido | tivessem pedido |
| **Future Perfect Indicative** *(p. 175)* | | **Future Perfect Subjunctive** *(p. 175)* | |
| terei pedido | teremos pedido | tiver pedido | tivermos pedido |
| terás pedido | tereis pedido | tiveres pedido | tiverdes pedido |
| terá pedido | terão pedido | tiver pedido | tiverem pedido |

## Third Conjugation Irregular Verb: *pedir (to ask) – Part 2*

| Indicative Mood | | Subjunctive Mood | |
|---|---|---|---|
| **Present Continuous Indicative** *(p. 108)* | | **Present Continuous Subjunctive** *(p. 108)* | |
| estou a pedir | estamos a pedir | esteja a pedir | estejamos a pedir |
| estás a pedir | estais a pedir | estejas a pedir | estejais a pedir |
| está a pedir | estão a pedir | esteja a pedir | estejam a pedir |
| **Past Continuous Indicative** *(p. 119)* | | **Past Continuous Subjunctive** *(p. 119)* | |
| estava a pedir | estávamos a pedir | estivesse a pedir | estivéssemos a pedir |
| estavas a pedir | estáveis a pedir | estivesses a pedir | estivésseis a pedir |
| estava a pedir | estavam a pedir | estivesse a pedir | estivessem a pedir |

| Indicative Mood | | Infinitive Mood | |
|---|---|---|---|
| **Preterite Indicative** *(p. 111)* | | **Impersonal Infinitive** *(p. 77)* | |
| pedi | pedimos | pedir | |
| pediste | pedistes | | |
| pediu | pediram | | |
| **Simple Pluperfect Indicative** *(p. 173)* | | **Personal Infinitive** *(p. 169)* | |
| pedira | pedíramos | pedir | pedirmos |
| pediras | pedíreis | pedires | pedirdes |
| pedira | pediram | pedir | pedirem |

| Conditional Mood | | | |
|---|---|---|---|
| **Conditional** *(p. 129)* | | **Conditional Perfect** *(p. 176)* | |
| pediria | pediríamos | teria pedido | teríamos pedido |
| pedirias | pediríeis | terias pedido | teríeis pedido |
| pediria | pediriam | teria pedido | teriam pedido |

| Imperative Mood | | | |
|---|---|---|---|
| **Imperative** *(p. 163)* | | | |
| | peçamos | | |
| pede | pedi | | |
| peça | peçam | | |

## Second Conjugation Irregular Verb: *poder (to be able to)* – Part 1

Stem: *pod*;  Present participle: *podendo*;  Past participle: *podido*

| Indicative Mood | | Subjunctive Mood | |
|---|---|---|---|
| **Present Indicative** *(p. 108)* | | **Present Subjunctive** *(p. 145)* | |
| posso | podemos | possa | possamos |
| podes | podeis | possas | possais |
| pode | podem | possa | possam |
| **Imperfect Indicative** *(p. 116)* | | **Imperfect Subjunctive** *(p. 152)* | |
| podia | podíamos | pudesse | pudéssemos |
| podias | podíeis | pudesses | pudésseis |
| podia | podiam | pudesse | pudessem |
| **Future Indicative** *(p. 125)* | | **Future Subjunctive** *(p. 149)* | |
| poderei | poderemos | puder | pudermos |
| poderás | podereis | puderes | puderdes |
| poderá | poderão | puder | puderem |
| **Present Perfect Indicative** *(p. 173)* | | **Present Perfect Subjunctive** *(p. 173)* | |
| tenho podido | temos podido | tenha podido | tenhamos podido |
| tens podido | tendes podido | tenhas podido | tenhais podido |
| tem podido | têm podido | tenha podido | tenham podido |
| **Past Perfect (Pluperfect) Indicative** *(p. 174)* | | **Past Perfect (Pluperfect) Subjunctive** *(p. 174)* | |
| tinha podido | tínhamos podido | tivesse podido | tivéssemos podido |
| tinhas podido | tínheis podido | tivesses podido | tivésseis podido |
| tinha podido | tinham podido | tivesse podido | tivessem podido |
| **Future Perfect Indicative** *(p. 175)* | | **Future Perfect Subjunctive** *(p. 175)* | |
| terei podido | teremos podido | tiver podido | tivermos podido |
| terás podido | tereis podido | tiveres podido | tiverdes podido |
| terá podido | terão podido | tiver podido | tiverem podido |

| Second Conjugation Irregular Verb: poder (to be able to) – Part 2 | |
|---|---|
| Indicative Mood | Subjunctive Mood |

| *Present Continuous Indicative (p. 108)* | *Present Continuous Subjunctive (p. 108)* |
|---|---|
| Not applicable | Not applicable |

| *Past Continuous Indicative (p. 119)* | *Past Continuous Subjunctive (p. 119)* |
|---|---|
| Not applicable | Not applicable |

| Indicative Mood | | Infinitive Mood | |
|---|---|---|---|
| *Preterite Indicative (p. 111)* | | *Impersonal Infinitive (p. 77)* | |
| pude | pudemos | poder | |
| pudeste | pudestes | | |
| pôde | puderam | | |
| *Simple Pluperfect Indicative (p. 173)* | | *Personal Infinitive (p. 169)* | |
| pudera | pudéramos | poder | podermos |
| puderas | pudéreis | poderes | poderdes |
| pudera | puderam | poder | poderem |

| Conditional Mood | | | |
|---|---|---|---|
| *Conditional (p. 129)* | | *Conditional Perfect (p. 176)* | |
| poderia | poderíamos | teria podido | teríamos podido |
| poderias | poderíeis | terias podido | teríeis podido |
| poderia | poderiam | teria podido | teriam podido |

| Imperative Mood | |
|---|---|
| *Imperative (p. 163)* | |
| | possamos |
| pode | podei |
| possa | possam |

## Second Conjugation Irregular Verb: pôr (to put) – Part 1

Stem: *p*;  Present participle: *pondo*;  Past participle: *posto*

| Indicative Mood | | Subjunctive Mood | |
|---|---|---|---|
| **Present Indicative** (p. 108) | | **Present Subjunctive** (p. 145) | |
| ponho | pomos | ponha | ponhamos |
| pões | pondes | ponhas | ponhais |
| põe | põem | ponha | ponham |
| **Imperfect Indicative** (p. 116) | | **Imperfect Subjunctive** (p. 152) | |
| punha | púnhamos | pusesse | puséssemos |
| punhas | púnheis | pusesses | pusésseis |
| punha | punham | pusesse | pusessem |
| **Future Indicative** (p. 125) | | **Future Subjunctive** (p. 149) | |
| porei | poremos | puser | pusermos |
| porás | poreis | puseres | puserdes |
| porá | porão | puser | puserem |
| **Present Perfect Indicative** (p. 173) | | **Present Perfect Subjunctive** (p. 173) | |
| tenho posto | temos posto | tenha posto | tenhamos posto |
| tens posto | tendes posto | tenhas posto | tenhais posto |
| tem posto | têm posto | tenha posto | tenham posto |
| **Past Perfect (Pluperfect) Indicative** (p. 174) | | **Past Perfect (Pluperfect) Subjunctive** (p. 174) | |
| tinha posto | tínhamos posto | tivesse posto | tivéssemos posto |
| tinhas posto | tínheis posto | tivesses posto | tivésseis posto |
| tinha posto | tinham posto | tivesse posto | tivessem posto |
| **Future Perfect Indicative** (p. 175) | | **Future Perfect Subjunctive** (p. 175) | |
| terei posto | teremos posto | tiver posto | tivermos posto |
| terás posto | tereis posto | tiveres posto | tiverdes posto |
| terá posto | terão posto | tiver posto | tiverem posto |

## Second Conjugation Irregular Verb: pôr (to put) – Part 2

| Indicative Mood | | Subjunctive Mood | |
|---|---|---|---|
| **Present Continuous Indicative** (p. 108) | | **Present Continuous Subjunctive** (p. 108) | |
| estou a pôr | estamos a pôr | esteja a pôr | estejamos a pôr |
| estás a pôr | estais a pôr | estejas a pôr | estejais a pôr |
| está a pôr | estão a pôr | esteja a pôr | estejam a pôr |
| **Past Continuous Indicative** (p. 119) | | **Past Continuous Subjunctive** (p. 119) | |
| estava a pôr | estávamos a pôr | estivesse a pôr | estivéssemos a pôr |
| estavas a pôr | estáveis a pôr | estivesses a pôr | estivésseis a pôr |
| estava a pôr | estavam a pôr | estivesse a pôr | estivessem a pôr |

| Indicative Mood | | Infinitive Mood | |
|---|---|---|---|
| **Preterite Indicative** (p. 111) | | **Impersonal Infinitive** (p. 77) | |
| pus | pusemos | | |
| puseste | pusestes | pôr | |
| pôs | puseram | | |
| **Simple Pluperfect Indicative** (p. 173) | | **Personal Infinitive** (p. 169) | |
| pusera | puséramos | pôr | pormos |
| puseras | puséreis | pores | pordes |
| pusera | puseram | pôr | porem |

| Conditional Mood | | | |
|---|---|---|---|
| **Conditional** (p. 129) | | **Conditional Perfect** (p. 176) | |
| poria | poríamos | teria posto | teríamos posto |
| porias | poríeis | terias posto | teríeis posto |
| poria | poriam | teria posto | teriam posto |

| Imperative Mood | | | |
|---|---|---|---|
| **Imperative** (p. 163) | | | |
| | ponhamos | | |
| põe | ponde | | |
| ponha | ponham | | |

## Second Conjugation Irregular Verb: querer (to want) – Part 1

Stem: *quer*;  Present participle: *querendo*;  Past participle: *querido*

| Indicative Mood | | Subjunctive Mood | |
|---|---|---|---|
| **Present Indicative** (p. 108) | | **Present Subjunctive** (p. 145) | |
| quero | queremos | queira | queiramos |
| queres | quereis | queiras | queirais |
| quer | querem | queira | queiram |
| **Imperfect Indicative** (p. 116) | | **Imperfect Subjunctive** (p. 152) | |
| queria | queríamos | quisesse | quiséssemos |
| querias | queríeis | quisesses | quisésseis |
| queria | queriam | quisesse | quisessem |
| **Future Indicative** (p. 125) | | **Future Subjunctive** (p. 149) | |
| quererei | quereremos | quiser | quisermos |
| quererás | querereis | quiseres | quiserdes |
| quererá | quererão | quiser | quiserem |
| **Present Perfect Indicative** (p. 173) | | **Present Perfect Subjunctive** (p. 173) | |
| tenho querido | temos querido | tenha querido | tenhamos querido |
| tens querido | tendes querido | tenhas querido | tenhais querido |
| tem querido | têm querido | tenha querido | tenham querido |
| **Past Perfect (Pluperfect) Indicative** (p. 174) | | **Past Perfect (Pluperfect) Subjunctive** (p. 174) | |
| tinha querido | tínhamos querido | tivesse querido | tivéssemos querido |
| tinhas querido | tínheis querido | tivesses querido | tivésseis querido |
| tinha querido | tinham querido | tivesse querido | tivessem querido |
| **Future Perfect Indicative** (p. 175) | | **Future Perfect Subjunctive** (p. 175) | |
| terei querido | teremos querido | tiver querido | tivermos querido |
| terás querido | tereis querido | tiveres querido | tiverdes querido |
| terá querido | terão querido | tiver querido | tiverem querido |

**Second Conjugation Irregular Verb: querer (to want) – Part 2**

| Indicative Mood | | Subjunctive Mood | |
|---|---|---|---|
| **Present Continuous Indicative** *(p. 108)* | | **Present Continuous Subjunctive** *(p. 108)* | |
| estou a querer | estamos a querer | esteja a querer | estejamos a querer |
| estás a querer | estais a querer | estejas a querer | estejais a querer |
| está a querer | estão a querer | esteja a querer | estejam a querer |
| **Past Continuous Indicative** *(p. 119)* | | **Past Continuous Subjunctive** *(p. 119)* | |
| estava a querer | estávamos a querer | estivesse a querer | estivéssemos a querer |
| estavas a querer | estáveis a querer | estivesses a querer | estivésseis a querer |
| estava a querer | estavam a querer | estivesse a querer | estivessem a querer |

| Indicative Mood | | Infinitive Mood | |
|---|---|---|---|
| **Preterite Indicative** *(p. 111)* | | **Impersonal Infinitive** *(p. 77)* | |
| quis | quisemos | | |
| quiseste | quisestes | querer | |
| quis | quiseram | | |
| **Simple Pluperfect Indicative** *(p. 173)* | | **Personal Infinitive** *(p. 169)* | |
| quisera | quiséramos | querer | querermos |
| quiseras | quiséreis | quereres | quererdes |
| quisera | quiseram | querer | quererem |

| Conditional Mood | | | |
|---|---|---|---|
| **Conditional** *(p. 129)* | | **Conditional Perfect** *(p. 176)* | |
| quereria | quereríamos | teria querido | teríamos querido |
| quererias | quereríeis | terias querido | teríeis querido |
| quereria | quereriam | teria querido | teriam querido |

| Imperative Mood | | | |
|---|---|---|---|
| **Imperative** *(p. 163)* | | Note: In Brazil, the 2nd person singular imperative is spelt 'quer' rather than 'quere', but that is academic really, as this verb is not normally used imperatively. | |
| | queiramos | | |
| quere | querei | | |
| queira | queiram | | |

### Second Conjugation Irregular Verb: saber (to know) – Part 1

Stem: *sab*;  Present participle: *sabendo*;  Past participle: *sabido*

| Indicative Mood | | Subjunctive Mood | |
|---|---|---|---|
| **Present Indicative** *(p. 108)* | | **Present Subjunctive** *(p. 145)* | |
| sei | sabemos | saiba | saibamos |
| sabes | sabeis | saibas | saibais |
| sabe | sabem | saiba | saibam |
| **Imperfect Indicative** *(p. 116)* | | **Imperfect Subjunctive** *(p. 152)* | |
| sabia | sabíamos | soubesse | soubéssemos |
| sabias | sabíeis | soubesses | soubésseis |
| sabia | sabiam | soubesse | soubessem |
| **Future Indicative** *(p. 125)* | | **Future Subjunctive** *(p. 149)* | |
| saberei | saberemos | souber | soubermos |
| saberás | sabereis | souberes | souberdes |
| saberá | saberão | souber | souberem |
| **Present Perfect Indicative** *(p. 173)* | | **Present Perfect Subjunctive** *(p. 173)* | |
| tenho sabido | temos sabido | tenha sabido | tenhamos sabido |
| tens sabido | tendes sabido | tenhas sabido | tenhais sabido |
| tem sabido | têm sabido | tenha sabido | tenham sabido |
| **Past Perfect (Pluperfect) Indicative** *(p. 174)* | | **Past Perfect (Pluperfect) Subjunctive** *(p. 174)* | |
| tinha sabido | tínhamos sabido | tivesse sabido | tivéssemos sabido |
| tinhas sabido | tínheis sabido | tivesses sabido | tivésseis sabido |
| tinha sabido | tinham sabido | tivesse sabido | tivessem sabido |
| **Future Perfect Indicative** *(p. 175)* | | **Future Perfect Subjunctive** *(p. 175)* | |
| terei sabido | teremos sabido | tiver sabido | tivermos sabido |
| terás sabido | tereis sabido | tiveres sabido | tiverdes sabido |
| terá sabido | terão sabido | tiver sabido | tiverem sabido |

**Second Conjugation Irregular Verb: saber (to know) – Part 2**

| Indicative Mood | | Subjunctive Mood | |
|---|---|---|---|
| **Present Continuous Indicative** (p. 108) | | **Present Continuous Subjunctive** (p. 108) | |
| estou a saber | estamos a saber | esteja a saber | estejamos a saber |
| estás a saber | estais a saber | estejas a saber | estejais a saber |
| está a saber | estão a saber | esteja a saber | estejam a saber |
| **Past Continuous Indicative** (p. 119) | | **Past Continuous Subjunctive** (p. 119) | |
| estava a saber | estávamos a saber | estivesse a saber | estivéssemos a saber |
| estavas a saber | estáveis a saber | estivesses a saber | estivésseis a saber |
| estava a saber | estavam a saber | estivesse a saber | estivessem a saber |

| Indicative Mood | | Infinitive Mood | |
|---|---|---|---|
| **Preterite Indicative** (p. 111) | | **Impersonal Infinitive** (p. 77) | |
| soube | soubemos | | |
| soubeste | soubestes | saber | |
| soube | souberam | | |
| **Simple Pluperfect Indicative** (p. 173) | | **Personal Infinitive** (p. 169) | |
| soubera | soubéramos | saber | sabermos |
| souberas | soubéreis | saberes | saberdes |
| soubera | souberam | saber | saberem |

| Conditional Mood | | | |
|---|---|---|---|
| **Conditional** (p. 129) | | **Conditional Perfect** (p. 176) | |
| saberia | saberíamos | teria sabido | teríamos sabido |
| saberias | saberíeis | terias sabido | teríeis sabido |
| saberia | saberiam | teria sabido | teriam sabido |

| Imperative Mood | | | |
|---|---|---|---|
| **Imperative** (p. 163) | | | |
| | saibamos | Some verbs, like this one, are not well suited to progressive usage ('I am knowing'), but nevertheless can be conjugated that way. | |
| sabe | sabei | | |
| saiba | saibam | | |

| Second Conjugation Irregular Verb: ser (to be) – Part 1 | | | |
|---|---|---|---|
| Stem: s;  Present participle: sendo;  Past participle: sido | | | |
| Indicative Mood | | Subjunctive Mood | |
| **Present Indicative** (p. 108) | | **Present Subjunctive** (p. 145) | |
| sou | somos | seja | sejamos |
| és | sois | sejas | sejais |
| é | são | seja | sejam |
| **Imperfect Indicative** (p. 116) | | **Imperfect Subjunctive** (p. 152) | |
| era | éramos | fosse | fôssemos |
| eras | éreis | fosses | fôsseis |
| era | eram | fosse | fossem |
| **Future Indicative** (p. 125) | | **Future Subjunctive** (p. 149) | |
| serei | seremos | for | formos |
| serás | sereis | fores | fordes |
| será | serão | for | forem |
| **Present Perfect Indicative** (p. 173) | | **Present Perfect Subjunctive** (p. 173) | |
| tenho sido | temos sido | tenha sido | tenhamos sido |
| tens sido | tendes sido | tenhas sido | tenhais sido |
| tem sido | têm sido | tenha sido | tenham sido |
| **Past Perfect (Pluperfect) Indicative** (p. 174) | | **Past Perfect (Pluperfect) Subjunctive** (p. 174) | |
| tinha sido | tínhamos sido | tivesse sido | tivéssemos sido |
| tinhas sido | tínheis sido | tivesses sido | tivésseis sido |
| tinha sido | tinham sido | tivesse sido | tivessem sido |
| **Future Perfect Indicative** (p. 175) | | **Future Perfect Subjunctive** (p. 175) | |
| terei sido | teremos sido | tiver sido | tivermos sido |
| terás sido | tereis sido | tiveres sido | tiverdes sido |
| terá sido | terão sido | tiver sido | tiverem sido |

## Second Conjugation Irregular Verb: ser (to be) – Part 2

| Indicative Mood | | Subjunctive Mood | |
|---|---|---|---|
| **Present Continuous Indicative** (p. 108) | | **Present Continuous Subjunctive** (p. 108) | |
| estou a ser | estamos a ser | esteja a ser | estejamos a ser |
| estás a ser | estais a ser | estejas a ser | estejais a ser |
| está a ser | estão a ser | esteja a ser | estejam a ser |
| **Past Continuous Indicative** (p. 119) | | **Past Continuous Subjunctive** (p. 119) | |
| estava a ser | estávamos a ser | estivesse a ser | estivéssemos a ser |
| estavas a ser | estáveis a ser | estivesses a ser | estivésseis a ser |
| estava a ser | estavam a ser | estivesse a ser | estivessem a ser |

| Indicative Mood | | Infinitive Mood | |
|---|---|---|---|
| **Preterite Indicative** (p. 111) | | **Impersonal Infinitive** (p. 77) | |
| fui | fomos | | |
| foste | fostes | ser | |
| foi | foram | | |
| **Simple Pluperfect Indicative** (p. 173) | | **Personal Infinitive** (p. 169) | |
| fora | fôramos | ser | sermos |
| foras | fôreis | seres | serdes |
| fora | foram | ser | serem |

| Conditional Mood | | | |
|---|---|---|---|
| **Conditional** (p. 129) | | **Conditional Perfect** (p. 176) | |
| seria | seríamos | teria sido | teríamos sido |
| serias | seríeis | terias sido | teríeis sido |
| seria | seriam | teria sido | teriam sido |

| Imperative Mood | | | |
|---|---|---|---|
| **Imperative** (p. 163) | | | |
| | sejamos | | |
| sê | sede | | |
| seja | sejam | | |

### Second Conjugation Irregular Verb: ter (to have) – Part 1

Stem: *t*;  Present participle: *tendo*;  Past participle: *tido*

| Indicative Mood | | Subjunctive Mood | |
|---|---|---|---|
| **Present Indicative (p. 108)** | | **Present Subjunctive (p. 145)** | |
| tenho | temos | tenha | tenhamos |
| tens | tendes | tenhas | tenhais |
| tem | têm | tenha | tenham |
| **Imperfect Indicative (p. 116)** | | **Imperfect Subjunctive (p. 152)** | |
| tinha | tínhamos | tivesse | tivéssemos |
| tinhas | tínheis | tivesses | tivésseis |
| tinha | tinham | tivesse | tivessem |
| **Future Indicative (p. 125)** | | **Future Subjunctive (p. 149)** | |
| terei | teremos | tiver | tivermos |
| terás | tereis | tiveres | tiverdes |
| terá | terão | tiver | tiverem |
| **Present Perfect Indicative (p. 173)** | | **Present Perfect Subjunctive (p. 173)** | |
| tenho tido | temos tido | tenha tido | tenhamos tido |
| tens tido | tendes tido | tenhas tido | tenhais tido |
| tem tido | têm tido | tenha tido | tenham tido |
| **Past Perfect (Pluperfect) Indicative (p. 174)** | | **Past Perfect (Pluperfect) Subjunctive (p. 174)** | |
| tinha tido | tínhamos tido | tivesse tido | tivéssemos tido |
| tinhas tido | tínheis tido | tivesses tido | tivésseis tido |
| tinha tido | tinham tido | tivesse tido | tivessem tido |
| **Future Perfect Indicative (p. 175)** | | **Future Perfect Subjunctive (p. 175)** | |
| terei tido | teremos tido | tiver tido | tivermos tido |
| terás tido | tereis tido | tiveres tido | tiverdes tido |
| terá tido | terão tido | tiver tido | tiverem tido |

**Second Conjugation Irregular Verb: ser (to be) – Part 2**

| Indicative Mood | | Subjunctive Mood | |
|---|---|---|---|
| **Present Continuous Indicative** (p. 108) | | **Present Continuous Subjunctive** (p. 108) | |
| estou a ter | estamos a ter | esteja a ter | estejamos a ter |
| estás a ter | estais a ter | estejas a ter | estejais a ter |
| está a ter | estão a ter | esteja a ter | estejam a ter |
| **Past Continuous Indicative** (p. 119) | | **Past Continuous Subjunctive** (p. 119) | |
| estava a ter | estávamos a ter | estivesse a ter | estivéssemos a ter |
| estavas a ter | estáveis a ter | estivesses a ter | estivésseis a ter |
| estava a ter | estavam a ter | estivesse a ter | estivessem a ter |

| Indicative Mood | | Infinitive Mood | |
|---|---|---|---|
| **Preterite Indicative** (p. 111) | | **Impersonal Infinitive** (p. 77) | |
| tive | tivemos | | |
| tiveste | tivestes | ter | |
| teve | tiveram | | |
| **Simple Pluperfect Indicative** (p. 173) | | **Personal Infinitive** (p. 169) | |
| tivera | tivéramos | ter | termos |
| tiveras | tivéreis | teres | terdes |
| tivera | tiveram | ter | terem |

| Conditional Mood | | | |
|---|---|---|---|
| **Conditional** (p. 129) | | **Conditional Perfect** (p. 176) | |
| teria | teríamos | teria tido | teríamos tido |
| terias | teríeis | terias tido | teríeis tido |
| teria | teriam | teria tido | teriam tido |

| Imperative Mood | | | |
|---|---|---|---|
| **Imperative** (p. 163) | | | |
| | tenhamos | | |
| tem | tende | | |
| tenha | tenham | | |

**Second Conjugation Irregular Verb: trazer (to bring) – Part 1**

Stem: *traz*;  Present participle: *trazendo*;  Past participle: *trazido*

| Indicative Mood | | Subjunctive Mood | |
|---|---|---|---|
| **Present Indicative** *(p. 108)* | | **Present Subjunctive** *(p. 145)* | |
| trago | trazemos | traga | tragamos |
| trazes | trazeis | tragas | tragais |
| traz | trazem | traga | tragam |
| **Imperfect Indicative** *(p. 116)* | | **Imperfect Subjunctive** *(p. 152)* | |
| trazia | trazíamos | trouxesse | trouxéssemos |
| trazias | trazíeis | trouxesses | trouxésseis |
| trazia | traziam | trouxesse | trouxessem |
| **Future Indicative** *(p. 125)* | | **Future Subjunctive** *(p. 149)* | |
| trarei | traremos | trouxer | trouxermos |
| trarás | trareis | trouxeres | trouxerdes |
| trará | trarão | trouxer | trouxerem |
| **Present Perfect Indicative** *(p. 173)* | | **Present Perfect Subjunctive** *(p. 173)* | |
| tenho trazido | temos trazido | tenha trazido | tenhamos trazido |
| tens trazido | tendes trazido | tenhas trazido | tenhais trazido |
| tem trazido | têm trazido | tenha trazido | tenham trazido |
| **Past Perfect (Pluperfect) Indicative** *(p. 174)* | | **Past Perfect (Pluperfect) Subjunctive** *(p. 174)* | |
| tinha trazido | tínhamos trazido | tivesse trazido | tivéssemos trazido |
| tinhas trazido | tínheis trazido | tivesses trazido | tivésseis trazido |
| tinha trazido | tinham trazido | tivesse trazido | tivessem trazido |
| **Future Perfect Indicative** *(p. 175)* | | **Future Perfect Subjunctive** *(p. 175)* | |
| terei trazido | teremos trazido | tiver trazido | tivermos trazido |
| terás trazido | tereis trazido | tiveres trazido | tiverdes trazido |
| terá trazido | terão trazido | tiver trazido | tiverem trazido |

## Second Conjugation Irregular Verb: *trazer (to bring)* – Part 2

| Indicative Mood | | Subjunctive Mood | |
|---|---|---|---|
| **Present Continuous Indicative** *(p. 108)* | | **Present Continuous Subjunctive** *(p. 108)* | |
| estou a trazer | estamos a trazer | esteja a trazer | estejamos a trazer |
| estás a trazer | estais a trazer | estejas a trazer | estejais a trazer |
| está a trazer | estão a trazer | esteja a trazer | estejam a trazer |
| **Past Continuous Indicative** *(p. 119)* | | **Past Continuous Subjunctive** *(p. 119)* | |
| estava a trazer | estávamos a trazer | estivesse a trazer | estivéssemos a trazer |
| estavas a trazer | estáveis a trazer | estivesses a trazer | estivésseis a trazer |
| estava a trazer | estavam a trazer | estivesse a trazer | estivessem a trazer |

| Indicative Mood | | Infinitive Mood | |
|---|---|---|---|
| **Preterite Indicative** *(p. 111)* | | **Impersonal Infinitive** *(p. 77)* | |
| trouxe | trouxemos | | |
| trouxeste | trouxestes | trazer | |
| trouxe | trouxeram | | |
| **Simple Pluperfect Indicative** *(p. 173)* | | **Personal Infinitive** *(p. 169)* | |
| trouxera | trouxéramos | trazer | trazermos |
| trouxeras | trouxéreis | trazeres | trazerdes |
| trouxera | trouxeram | trazer | trazerem |

| Conditional Mood | | | |
|---|---|---|---|
| **Conditional** *(p. 129)* | | **Conditional Perfect** *(p. 176)* | |
| traria | traríamos | teria trazido | teríamos trazido |
| trarias | traríeis | terias trazido | teríeis trazido |
| traria | trariam | teria trazido | teriam trazido |

| Imperative Mood | | | |
|---|---|---|---|
| **Imperative** *(p. 163)* | | | |
| | tragamos | | |
| traz | trazei | | |
| traga | tragam | | |

**Second Conjugation Irregular Verb: ver (to see) – Part 1**

Stem: *v*;  Present participle: *vendo*;  Past participle: *visto*

| Indicative Mood | | Subjunctive Mood | |
|---|---|---|---|
| **Present Indicative** (p. 108) | | **Present Subjunctive** (p. 145) | |
| vejo | vemos | veja | vejamos |
| vês | vedes | vejas | vejais |
| vê | vêem | veja | vejam |
| **Imperfect Indicative** (p. 116) | | **Imperfect Subjunctive** (p. 152) | |
| via | víamos | visse | víssemos |
| vias | víeis | visses | vísseis |
| via | viam | visse | vissem |
| **Future Indicative** (p. 125) | | **Future Subjunctive** (p. 149) | |
| verei | veremos | vir | virmos |
| verás | vereis | vires | virdes |
| verá | verão | vir | virem |
| **Present Perfect Indicative** (p. 173) | | **Present Perfect Subjunctive** (p. 173) | |
| tenho visto | temos visto | tenha visto | tenhamos visto |
| tens visto | tendes visto | tenhas visto | tenhais visto |
| tem visto | têm visto | tenha visto | tenham visto |
| **Past Perfect (Pluperfect) Indicative** (p. 174) | | **Past Perfect (Pluperfect) Subjunctive** (p. 174) | |
| tinha visto | tínhamos visto | tivesse visto | tivéssemos visto |
| tinhas visto | tínheis visto | tivesses visto | tivésseis visto |
| tinha visto | tinham visto | tivesse visto | tivessem visto |
| **Future Perfect Indicative** (p. 175) | | **Future Perfect Subjunctive** (p. 175) | |
| terei visto | teremos visto | tiver visto | tivermos visto |
| terás visto | tereis visto | tiveres visto | tiverdes visto |
| terá visto | terão visto | tiver visto | tiverem visto |

### Second Conjugation Irregular Verb: ver (to see) – Part 2

| Indicative Mood | | Subjunctive Mood | |
|---|---|---|---|
| **Present Continuous Indicative** (p. 108) | | **Present Continuous Subjunctive** (p. 108) | |
| estou a ver | estamos a ver | esteja a ver | estejamos a ver |
| estás a ver | estais a ver | estejas a ver | estejais a ver |
| está a ver | estão a ver | esteja a ver | estejam a ver |
| **Past Continuous Indicative** (p. 119) | | **Past Continuous Subjunctive** (p. 119) | |
| estava a ver | estávamos a ver | estivesse a ver | estivéssemos a ver |
| estavas a ver | estáveis a ver | estivesses a ver | estivésseis a ver |
| estava a ver | estavam a ver | estivesse a ver | estivessem a ver |

| Indicative Mood | | Infinitive Mood | |
|---|---|---|---|
| **Preterite Indicative** (p. 111) | | **Impersonal Infinitive** (p. 77) | |
| vi | vimos | | |
| viste | vistes | ver | |
| viu | viram | | |
| **Simple Pluperfect Indicative** (p. 173) | | **Personal Infinitive** (p. 169) | |
| vira | víramos | ver | vermos |
| viras | víreis | veres | verdes |
| vira | viram | ver | verem |

| Conditional Mood | | | |
|---|---|---|---|
| **Conditional** (p. 129) | | **Conditional Perfect** (p. 176) | |
| veria | veríamos | teria visto | teríamos visto |
| verias | veríeis | terias visto | teríeis visto |
| veria | veriam | teria visto | teriam visto |

| Imperative Mood | | | |
|---|---|---|---|
| **Imperative** (p. 163) | | | |
| | vejamos | | |
| vê | vede | | |
| veja | vejam | | |

### Third Conjugation Irregular Verb: vir (to come) – Part 1

Stem: *v*;  Present participle: *vindo*;  Past participle: *vindo*

| Indicative Mood | | Subjunctive Mood | |
|---|---|---|---|
| **Present Indicative** *(p. 108)* | | **Present Subjunctive** *(p. 145)* | |
| venho | vimos | venhas | venhamos |
| vens | vindes | venhas | venhais |
| vem | vêm | venha | venham |
| **Imperfect Indicative** *(p. 116)* | | **Imperfect Subjunctive** *(p. 152)* | |
| vinha | vínhamos | viesse | viéssemos |
| vinhas | vínheis | viesses | viésseis |
| vinha | vinham | viesse | viessem |
| **Future Indicative** *(p. 125)* | | **Future Subjunctive** *(p. 149)* | |
| virei | viremos | vier | viermos |
| virás | vireis | vieres | vierdes |
| virá | virão | vier | vierem |
| **Present Perfect Indicative** *(p. 173)* | | **Present Perfect Subjunctive** *(p. 173)* | |
| tenho vindo | temos vindo | tenha vindo | tenhamos vindo |
| tens vindo | tendes vindo | tenhas vindo | tenhais vindo |
| tem vindo | têm vindo | tenha vindo | tenham vindo |
| **Past Perfect (Pluperfect) Indicative** *(p. 174)* | | **Past Perfect (Pluperfect) Subjunctive** *(p. 174)* | |
| tinha vindo | tínhamos vindo | tivesse vindo | tivéssemos vindo |
| tinhas vindo | tínheis vindo | tivesses vindo | tivésseis vindo |
| tinha vindo | tinham vindo | tivesse vindo | tivessem vindo |
| **Future Perfect Indicative** *(p. 175)* | | **Future Perfect Subjunctive** *(p. 175)* | |
| terei vindo | teremos vindo | tiver vindo | tivermos vindo |
| terás vindo | tereis vindo | tiveres vindo | tiverdes vindo |
| terá vindo | terão vindo | tiver vindo | tiverem vindo |

## Third Conjugation Irregular Verb: vir (to come) – Part 2

| Indicative Mood | | Subjunctive Mood | |
|---|---|---|---|
| **Present Continuous Indicative** (p. 108) | | **Present Continuous Subjunctive** (p. 108) | |
| estou a vir | estamos a vir | esteja a vir | estejamos a vir |
| estás a vir | estais a vir | estejas a vir | estejais a vir |
| está a vir | estão a vir | esteja a vir | estejam a vir |
| **Past Continuous Indicative** (p. 119) | | **Past Continuous Subjunctive** (p. 119) | |
| estava a vir | estávamos a vir | estivesse a vir | estivéssemos a vir |
| estavas a vir | estáveis a vir | estivesses a vir | estivésseis a vir |
| estava a vir | estavam a vir | estivesse a vir | estivessem a vir |

| Indicative Mood | | Infinitive Mood | |
|---|---|---|---|
| **Preterite Indicative** (p. 111) | | **Impersonal Infinitive** (p. 77) | |
| vim | viemos | | |
| vieste | viestes | vir | |
| veio | vieram | | |
| **Simple Pluperfect Indicative** (p. 173) | | **Personal Infinitive** (p. 169) | |
| viera | viéramos | vir | virmos |
| vieras | viéreis | vires | virdes |
| viera | vieram | vir | virem |

| Conditional Mood | | | |
|---|---|---|---|
| **Conditional** (p. 129) | | **Conditional Perfect** (p. 176) | |
| viria | viríamos | teria vindo | teríamos vindo |
| virias | viríeis | terias vindo | teríeis vindo |
| viria | viriam | teria vindo | teriam vindo |

| Imperative Mood | | | |
|---|---|---|---|
| **Imperative** (p. 163) | | | |
| | venhamos | | |
| vem | vinde | | |
| venha | venham | | |

# Solutions to Exercises

## *Exercício 1: Artigos / Exercise 1: Articles*

**1.1.** Artigos definidos – Definite articles.

| | | |
|---|---|---|
| 1. **o** carro | 2. **a** casa | 3. **o** telemóvel |
| 4. **a** mulher | 5. **o** amigo | 6. **a** irmã |
| 7. **a** laranja | 8. **a** maçã | 9. **o** amendoím |
| 10. **o** garfo | 11. **o** chuveiro | 12. **o** pente |
| 13. **o** copo | 14. **o** homem | 15. **os** jogos |
| 16. **os** olhos | 17. **a** professora | 18. **os** impostos |
| 19. **os** calções | 20. **os** filhos | 21. **o** hotel |
| 22. **o** animal | 23. **a** lei | 24. **o** marido |
| 25. **a** panela | 26. **o** consultor | 27. **a** confusão |
| 28. **as** janelas | 29. **o** dinheiro | 30. **a** informação |
| 31. **os** sapatos | 32. **as** encomendas | 33. **o** campo |
| 34. **a** pasta | 35. **o** saco | 36. **os** livros |
| 37. **a** estação | 38. **as** canetas | 39. **o** bolo |

**1.2.** Artigos indefinidos (um, uma, uns, umas) – Indefinite articles (a, an, some).

| | | |
|---|---|---|
| 1. **um** senhor | 2. **uma** cultura | 3. **um** computador |
| 4. **um** relógio | 5. **uns** óculos | 6. **uns** sapatos |
| 7. **umas** saias | 8. **umas** gavetas | 9. **umas** malas |
| 10. **uma** gravata | 11. **umas** caixas | 12. **uns** copos de vinho |
| 13. **umas** famílias | 14. **um** canil | 15. **uma** marcação |
| 16. **umas** batatas fritas | 17. **um** email | 18. **um** lugar |
| 19. **umas** notas | 20. **um** troco | 21. **uns** táxis |
| 22. **uma** pastelaria | 23. **uma** cidade | 24. **umas** semanas |
| 25. **uns** negócios | 26. **umas** empresas | 27. **uma** sapataria |

| | | |
|---|---|---|
| 28. **umas** camisas | 29. **um** supermercado | 30. **uma** gorjeta |
| 31. **uns** barulhos | 32. **uma** bagagem | 33. **umas** portas |
| 34. **uma** viagem | 35. **uns** casacos | 36. **umas** saladas |
| 37. **uns** morangos | 38. **umas** bananas | 39. **uma** ligação |

**1.3.** Quando usar os artigos definidos – When to use definite articles.

1.3.1. O António é meu vizinho.     ✓ (definite article should be used)

1.3.2. Eu gosto muito de figos.     ✓ (definite article should not be used)

1.3.3. Ө Peter, venha cá por favor.     ✗ (definite article should not be used)

1.3.4. O carro dele é muito rápido.     ✓ (definite article should be used)

1.3.5. A comida está fria.     ✗ (definite article should be used)

1.3.6. O chá é bom.     ✓ (definite article should be used)

1.3.7. Ele detesta **o** café.     ✗ (definite article should be used)

1.3.8. Lisboa é uma cidade antiga.     ✓ (definite article should not be used)

1.3.9. Nө Em agosto eu vou à praia.     ✗ (definite article should not be used)

**1.4.** Nomes confusos – Confusing nouns.

| | |
|---|---|
| 1. **um** problema | 2. **uma** universidade |
| 3. **uma** consideração | 4. **uma** continuidade |
| 5. **um** poema | 6. **um** programa de televisão |
| 7. **um** lugar de estacionamento | 8. **um** papel |
| 9. **uma** cidade | 10. **um** teorema |
| 11. **um** cinema | 12. **uns** planetas |
| 13. **umas** fotos | 14. **um** dia |
| 15. **um** juíz | 16. **um** clima |
| 17. **um** mapa | 18. **uns** telefonemas |
| 19. **um** fim de semana | 20. **uma** imagem |
| 21. **uma** tribo | 22. **uma** moto |
| 23. **uma** internet rápida | 24. **uns** países |

*Exercício 2: Adjectivos / Exercise 2: Adjectives*

**2.1.** Adjectivos variáveis em género e número – Adjectives that are variable in both gender and number.

2.1.1. Os meus vizinhos são muito **barulhentos**.
2.1.2. Os lugares onde ele nos leva são **assustadores**.
2.1.3. Ela gosta de vestidos **feios**.
2.1.4. Eu gosto de ter casas **bonitas** à volta.
2.1.5. Cristiano Ronaldo é um jogador **rápido**.
2.1.6. O carro p**reto** é o meu preferido.
2.1.7. Eu hoje só quero uma cerveja **pequena**.
2.1.8. As flores **amarelas** são caras.
2.1.9. Os programas **chatos** de televisão não são educativos.
2.1.10. Os alimentos **congelados** são uma alternativa.
2.1.11. Ponha as flores **mortas** no lixo, se faz favor.

**2.2.** Adjectivos Variáveis em Número – Variable Adjectives in Number.

2.2.1. Uma casa **grande** tem mais espaço.
2.2.2. Ele tem uma coisa **interessante** para me mostrar.
2.2.3. Eu podia ver as pratas **brilhantes** da janela do quarto.
2.2.4. Eu acho que temos cerveja **suficiente** para todos.
2.2.5. Podemos ver que eles são um casal **feliz**.

**2.3.** Adjectivos Invariáveis – Invariable Adjectives.

2.3.1. Não quero comprar um relógio caro, mas tem de ser **amarelo-ouro**.
2.3.2. Quase todas as meninas gostam muito de roupa **cor-de-rosa**.
2.3.3. No outono a maioria das flores silvestres ficam **violeta**.
2.3.4. A mesa de bilhar é **verde-garrafa**.
2.3.5. Adoro ver o pôr do sol e o céu **cor-de-laranja**.

*Exercício 3: Advérbios / Exercise 3: Adverbs*

**3.1.** Filling in the missing adverbs and adjectives.

3.1.1. básico → **basicamente**
3.1.2. **rápido** → rapidamente
3.1.3. histórico → **historicamente**

3.1.4. **automático** → automaticamente
3.1.5. **calmo** → calmamente
3.1.6. raro → **raramente**
3.1.7. profundo → **profundamente**
3.1.8. **atencioso** → atenciosamente
3.1.9. imediato → **imediatamente**
3.1.10. breve → **brevemente**
3.1.11. **frequente** → frequentemente
3.1.12. natural → **naturalmente**
3.1.13. **honesto** → honestamente
3.1.14. **inocente** → inocentemente
3.1.15. normal → **normalmente**

**3.2.** Choosing the adverb that best fits each sentence.

3.2.1 Eu estou **bastante** feliz com os resultados do exame.
3.2.2 Nós trabalhámos **bem** a semana passada.
3.2.3. Eles não têm boas condições de trabalho **aqui**.
3.2.4. **Amanhã** tu precisas de ir ao dentista.
3.2.5. Nós **raramente** vemos os nossos vizinhos por aqui.
3.2.6. Apesar do tempo, você veio trabalhar **hoje**.
3.2.7. Eles conseguem melhores resultados a trabalhar **juntos**.

*Exercício 4: Diminutivos e Aumentativos / Exercise 4: Diminutives & Augmentatives*

**4.1.** Diminuitives.

4.1.1. O meu **gatinho** é muito calmo.
4.1.2. Eles têm uma **casinha** muito bonita.
4.1.3. Que **tempinho** gostoso nós temos hoje na praia.
4.1.4. Oh, que cachorro lindo. Ele é **novinho**, não é?
4.1.5. Este ano só tivemos problemas. Que **aninho** terrível.
4.1.6. Esta noite vou preparar um **jantarzinho** delicioso para as visitas.

**4.2.** Augmentatives.

4.2.1. Há um **carrão** à nossa porta.
4.2.2. O Ronaldo acabou de marcar um **golão**.
4.2.3. O nosso **chefão** é muito generoso.
4.2.4. Eu tenho um **sofazão** na minha sala.
4.2.5. Ele serviram um **jantarzão** na boda de casamento deles.

### Exercício 5: Conjunções / Exercise 5: Conjunctions

**5.1.** Filling in the correct conjunction.

5.1.1. Eu como frutas **e** legumes porque são muito bons para a minha saúde.
5.1.2. **Desde** que a ciência provou que fumar provoca cancro, não fumo mais.
5.1.3. Eu gosto do Vinho do Porto **mas** infelizmente hoje tenho que conduzir.
5.1.4. Eu acho **que** não vou poder ir à festa hoje.
5.1.5. Eu vou dar um chocolate ao Pedro **se** ele comer a comida toda.
5.1.6. Eu tenho de preparar o jantar **logo que** eu chegue a casa.
5.1.7. Vocês querem o café com **ou** sem açúcar?
5.1.8. A Índia tem mais habitantes **do que** Portugal.
5.1.9. Nós hoje não podemos sair **por causa da** chuva.
5.1.10. Ela vai preparar o jantar **enquanto** ele põe a mesa.

### Exercício 6: Preposições / Exercise 6: Prepositions

**6.1.** 'a' and 'para'.

6.1.1. Ela vai viver **para** Los Angeles.
6.1.2. Porquê não vamos **ao** cinema hoje?
6.1.3. Depois do trabalho eu vou **para** casa.
6.1.4. Eu preciso de ir **ao** supermercado comprar fruta.
6.1.5. O Manuel vai voltar **para** França na semana que vem.
6.1.6. Ela vai **a** casa buscar o guarda-chuva e já volta.
6.1.7. Eles querem ir **à** praia hoje.
6.1.8. Hoje à tarde elas vão **a** uma festa.
6.1.9. Eu quero ir viver **para** o México.
6.1.10. O pai dela vai **ao** Rio de Janeiro a negócios.

**6.2.** '**por**' and '**para**'.

6.2.1. Eu vou **para o** hotel agora. Estou cansado.
6.2.2. Eu vou visitar o Victor, mas tenho de ir **pelo** centro da cidade.
6.2.3. O trânsito **pela** ponte é intenso.
6.2.4. **Por** mim vocês podem avançar com a obra.
6.2.5. Quando eles viajam, eles vão sempre **pela** autoestrada.
6.2.6. Como se vai **para o** museu?
6.2.7. Eu gosto de passear **pelo** rio.
6.2.8. Preciso de passar **pelo** hotel.
6.2.9. Na viagem do Brasil à Tailândia, eles passam **por** Paris.
6.2.10. Hoje em dia as pessoas aceitam ser exploradas **pelos** governos.

**6.3.** '**em** and '**de**'.

6.3.1. A gente vai **de** avião.
6.3.2. Eu gosto de viajar **de** elético em Lisboa.
6.3.3. Eu sou **da** Irlanda.
6.3.4. Estou **no** autocarro agora.
6.3.5. Ela está **no** escritório às segundas e quartas feiras.
6.3.6. Eles vão **no** carro do Artur, e elas vão **de** táxi.
6.3.7. **No** domingo ele volta para casa.
6.3.8. Eles querem saber **de** onde elas são.
6.3.9. Eu tenho aulas **das** três às quatro horas.
6.3.10. Eles não querem trabalhar **de** segunda a sexta.

**6.4.** Locuções Prepositivas - Prepositional Phrases.

6.4.1. A bola **A** está **dentro da** caixa.
6.4.2. A bola **B** está **em cima da** caixa.
6.4.3. A bola **C** está **debaixo da** caixa.
6.4.4. A bola **D** está **por cima da** caixa.
6.4.5. A bola **E** está **atrás da** caixa.
6.4.6. A bola **F** está **entre** as caixas.
6.4.7. A bola **G** está a ir para **fora da** caixa.

### *Exercício 7: Infinitivo – Verbos Regulares / Exercise 7: Infinitive – Regular Verbs*

**7.1.** Verb meaning from Portuguese to English.

| | |
|---|---|
| 1. to be | 2. to be |
| 3. to do / to make | 4. to work |
| 5. to speak | 6. to organise |
| 7. to write | 8. to read |
| 9. to answer | 10. to have |
| 11. to leave / to go out / to exit / to get off | 12. to want |
| 13. to go | 14. to bring |
| 15. to prove / to try / to test | 16. to continue |
| 17. to grant / to assure / to guarantee | 18. to assist / to help |
| 19. to have / to be (there is / there are) | 20. to be able to / can |
| 21. to call (on the phone) / to connect | 22. to sleep |
| 23. to win / to earn | 24. to see / to watch |
| 25. to come / to come back | 26. to set free / to release |
| 27. to buy / to purchase | 28. to sell |
| 29. to involve | 30. to remember |

**7.2.** Verb meaning from English to Portuguese.

| | |
|---|---|
| 1. comer | 2. beber |
| 3. manifestar | 4. jantar |
| 5. adormecer | 6. ver / assistir |
| 7. querer | 8. conhecer |
| 9. dar | 10. dizer |
| 11. telefonar / chamar / ligar | 12. encontrar-se com / ir ter com |
| 13. cozinhar | 14. tomar o pequeno almoço (PT) tomar o café da manhã (BR) |
| 15. ir | 16. estudar |
| 17. descansar | 18. almoçar |
| 19. pôr / colocar | 20. escrever (no computador) |
| 21. ligar | 22. aquecer |
| 23. limpar | 24. arrumar |
| 25. memorizar | 26. preparar |
| 27. morrer | 28. regar |
| 29. reservar / fazer uma reserva | 30. sentar-se |

### *Exercício 8: Verbos Regulares / Exercise 8: Regular Verbs*

**8.1.** First conjugation regular verbs in the present indicative.

8.1.1. Em Portugal o comércio **começa** às nove horas da manhã.
8.1.2. Eu **apanho** o comboio das dez horas todos os dias.
8.1.3. A Paula só **trabalha** quatro horas por semana.
8.1.4. Nós raramente **almoçamos** em casa durante a semana.
8.1.5. Ela **toca** piano muito bem.
8.1.6. Eles **jogam** futebol todos os fins de semana.
8.1.7. O telefone nunca **toca** à noite porque eu desligo a ficha.
8.1.8. O senhor **paga** a conta?
8.1.9. Vocês **tomam** o café com ou sem açúcar?
8.1.10. O Ivo e a Inês **estudam** português.

**8.2.** Second conjugation regular verbs in the present indicative.

8.2.1. Ao almoço e ao jantar nós **bebemos** um copo de vinho.

8.2.2. Normalmente eu **resolvo** todos os problemas do meu departamento.

8.2.3. O John e a Joanna **aprendem** português na internet.

8.2.4. Eu já não **escrevo** cartas, eu envio e-mails.

8.2.5. A senhora, onde **vive**?

8.2.6. Eu **vivo** e trabalho em Maputo, em Moçambique.

8.2.7. Na tua cidade **chove** muito?

8.2.8. Eu **atendo** o telefone quando ele toca.

8.2.9. Nós **corremos** todas as manhãs durante 30 minutos.

8.2.10. Eu **respondo** aos meus e-mails logo que eles chegam.

**8.3.** Third conjugation regular verbs in the present indicative.

8.3.1 Ele **despe** o casaco quando chega a casa.

8.3.2. Eu **abro** a porta para si, minha senhora.

8.3.3. Eles **dividem** o bolo em fatias na festa.

8.3.4. Ao fim de semana nós **preferimos** ficar em casa.

8.3.5. O comboio **parte** às vinte horas e trinta minutos.

8.3.6. Elas não **conseguem** ter concentração com barulho de fundo.

8.3.7. A gente **serve** o jantar entre as 6.30h e as 10.00h da noite.

8.3.8. Normalmente tu **dormes** bem à noite?

8.3.9. Nós **subimos** a montanha com muito esforço.

8.3.10. Há dois aviões para Luanda. Um **parte** ás 11hrs e o outro às 17hrs.

*Exercício 9: Verbos com Preposições / Exercise 9: Verbs with Prepositions*

**9.1.** Combining verbs with prepositions.

9.1.1. Todas as noites eu **sonho com** um mundo mais humano e justo.

9.1.2. Ele é um escravo do trabalho. Ele sempre **sai do** escritório tarde.

9.1.3. Ela **gosta de** comer uma sobremesa depois do almoço.

9.1.4. Normalmente nós **começamos a** preparar o jantar às 18.00hrs.

9.1.5.  O clube **entra no** campeonato de futebol este ano.

9.1.6. Senhor Jonas, o senhor **vai ter com** a sua esposa ao café?

9.1.7. Ele vai **acabar por** desistir da ideia.

9.1.8. Eu **estou a pensar em** ir ao teatro logo à noite.

9.1.9. Nós **acabámos de** falar com o Diretor.

9.1.10. Eles conhecem-se e ela **apaixona-se por** ele imediatamente.

9.1.11. Eles **vêm ter com** a Maria aqui ao bar.

### *Exercício 10: Verbos Irregulares – Ser or Estar / Exercise 10: Irregular Verbs – Ser or Estar*

**10.1.** 'ser' or 'estar' in the present tense.

10.1.1. Onde **está** o dicionário?
10.1.2. **São** sete horas. O filme vai começar.
10.1.3. A Maria **é** do Canadá.
10.1.4. Tel Aviv **é** em Israel.
10.1.5. O café **está** muito quente.
10.1.6. O Carlos não pode ir tabalhar hoje. Ele **está** muito doente.
10.1.7. Amanhã **é** sexta-feira ou sábado?
10.1.8. Ela **é** loira e de olhos azuis.
10.1.9. Meu deus! Os pneus do carro **estão** carecas!
10.1.10. Este carro **é** cem por cento elétrico.
10.1.11. Os carros **estão** no estacionamento.
10.1.12. O Paulo **é** alto e forte.
10.1.13. Hoje o dia não **está** bonito.
10.1.14. O Alexios **é** grego.
10.1.15. Onde é que vocês **estão** agora?
10.1.16. A Maria e a Joana **são** simpáticas.
10.1.17. **Somos** nós que pagamos o jantar.
10.1.18. Eu e o Mário **somos** um casal feliz.
10.1.19. O senhor **está** sentado à mesa.
10.1.20. Eu **sou** o pai do Francisco.

### *Exercício 11: Verbos irregulares / Exercise 11: Irregular verbs*

**11.1.** Irregular verbs in the present indicative.

11.1.1. Eu **sou** o Carlos.
11.1.2. Eu **sou** casado.
11.1.3. Eu **tenho** 35 anos.
11.1.4. Eu e a minha mulher Joana **temos** dois filhos.
11.1.5. Agora, eu e a minha família **estamos** em Luanda, em Angola.
11.1.6. Normalmente aos fins de semana **vamos** viajar pelo país e conhecer outras cidades.
11.1.7. Os meus filhos **saem** com os amigos que conhecem da Internet.
11.1.8. Eles também **dizem** que é bom conhecer pessoas novas em diferentes partes do mundo.

11.1.9. Durante a semana eu **posso** ir a casa e almoçar com a minha família.

11.1.10. A empresa onde eu trabalho **dá** muitos benefícios aos funcionários.

11.1.11. Quando acabo de trabalhar, eu passo pela escola e **trago** os meus filhos para casa.

11.1.12. Quando chegamos a casa, os meus filhos **fazem** as tarefas da escola e depois brincam com os amigos e com o cachorro.

11.1.13. Sim, **há** um cachorro pequeno adotado por nós na nossa casa.

11.1.14. Normalmente, eu e a minha mulher **vimos** do trabalho cedo.

11.1.15. Quando chegamos a casa **pomos** o trabalho de parte e conversamos uns com os outros de coisas agradáveis.

11.1.16. Normalmente passamos tempo de qualidade juntos e **podemos** dar apoio uns aos outros.

11.1.17. Eu **saio** da rotina quando chego a casa.

11.1.18. Eu **vejo** alegria quando estou com a minha família.

### *Exercício 12: Presente Contínuo / Exercise 12: Present Continuous*

**12.1.** Filling in the present continuous of the given verbs.

12.1.1. Hoje está um tempo horrível e **está a chover / está chovendo** constantemente.

12.1.2. Eu **estou a tomar / estou tomando** um café agora.

12.1.3. Manuel, o telefone **está a tocar / está tocando**. Atenda por favor.

12.1.4. Eles **estão a ler / estão lendo** as notícias no jornal.

12.1.5. Nós **estamos a ver / estamos vendo** televisão.

12.1.6. Ó Maria e Joana, vocês **estão a fazer / estão fazendo** os exercícios?

12.1.7. As crianças **estão a brincar / estão brincando** no parque.

12.1.8. Eu não **estou a dizer / estou dizendo** que isso está errado. Só precisa de ser revisto.

12.1.9. Eles **estão a apanhar sol / estão apanhando sol**.

12.1.10. A água **está a ferver / está fervendo**.

### *Exercício 13: Pretérito Perfeito do Indicativo / Exercise 13: Preterite Indicative*

**13.1.** Mário's timetable.

*Na sexta-feira de manhã da semana passada, o Mário **acordou** às 8 horas.* Ele **levantou-se** às oito e quinze. **Tomou** o pequeno almoço / o café da manhã e depois **foi correr** às dez horas. Depois, **respondeu** aos e-mails. À tarde ele **marcou** duas reuniões, **leu** a correspondência e **escreveu** o relatório. À noite **jantou** com clientes, **dançou** e **foi dormir** tarde.

No sábado, o Mário **levantou-se** tarde e **almoçou** com a namorada (dele). À tarde **visitou** um amigo, **lavou** o carro e **lanchou**. À noite o Mário **encontrou-se** com os amigos no café. Finalmente **assistiu** a um concerto.

### *Exercício 14: Imperfeito do Indicativo / Exercise 14: Imperfect Indicative*

**14.1.** Filling in the imperfect indicative.

14.1.1. Antigamente eu **corria** 5 kms por dia.
14.1.2. Ele **levantava-se** sempre muito cedo.
14.1.3. Depois, **tomava** um duche bem quente antes de ir trabalhar.
14.1.4. Quando eu **era** mais jovem, eu saia mais do que agora.
14.1.5. Dantes, eu **apanhava** sempre o comboio das sete horas.
14.1.6. Em criança, eu **jogava** bem à bola.
14.1.7. Dantes eles **eram** médicos de medicina geral, agora são especialistas.
14.1.8. Nós **assistíamos** a todas as aulas sem exceção.
14.1.9. A casa **era** grande mas acolhedora.
14.1.10. Ela já **estava** lá quando eu cheguei.

### *Exercício 15: Pretérito Perfeito ou Imperfeito do Indicativo? / Exercise 15: Preterite or Imperfect Indicative?*

**15.1.** Filling in either the preterite or imperfect of the given verbs.

15.1.1. Antigamente as pessoas **tinham** uma vida mais modesta.
15.1.2. Quando nós **saímos** do cinema **chovia / estava a chover / estava chovendo**.
15.1.3. Quando eu **era** mais novo, eu **falava** com toda a gente.
15.1.4. Eu **lia / estava a ler / estava lendo** o meu livro quando a Ada e o John **bateram** à porta.
15.1.5. Eu não **pude** ir com vocês ao jantar. Eu **estava** doente.
15.1.6. Ontem, às onze horas da noite eu ainda **estava** no escritório.
15.1.7. Antes ele **usava** óculos, mas agora não. Agora ele vê bem.
15.1.8. A exposição **foi** boa, mas **estava** lá muita gente.
15.1.9. Eu **ia** visitar o Paulo, mas não sei se ele está em casa.
15.1.10. Eu **podia** conduzir mais depressa, mas é perigoso e ilegal.

## Exercício 16: Futuro do Indicativo / Exercise 16: Future Tense

**16.1.** Filling in the future indicative.

16.1.1. Eu não **subirei** os impostos.
16.1.2. Eu também **aumentarei** as pensões.
16.1.3. **Haverá** mais postos de trabalho.
16.1.4. Os medicamentos **serão** mais baratos.
16.1.5. A minha administração **contratará** mais médicos, e mais ambulâncias.
16.1.6. Os transportes públicos **estarão** mais baratos e acessíveis para todos.
16.1.7. Eu **acabarei** com a corrupção.
16.1.8. Eu não **deixarei** as grandes empresas controlar o país.
16.1.9. Com a minha eleição, os deputados não **terão** benefícios especiais.
16.1.10. Todos os cidadãos **serão** iguais perante a lei.

## Exercício 17: Condicional / Exercise 17: Conditional

**17.1.** The conditional.

17.1.1. Se eu não tivesse que trabalhar, eu **faria** uma viagem à volta do mundo.
17.1.2. Eu **levaria** a minha família comigo.
17.1.3. Eles **adorariam** descobrir outros países e outras culturas.
17.1.4. Nós **poderíamos** provar outras comidas também.
17.1.5. Nós **beberíamos** vinho e chá de várias origens.
17.1.6. E você, não **faria** o mesmo?
17.1.7. Você não **diria** a todos os seus amigos como é boa a aventura?
17.1.8. Você não lhes **pediria** para viajarem consigo?
17.1.9. No meu regresso, eu **traria** uma lembrança para todos os meus amigos também.
17.1.10. E depois de nós terminarmos a primeira viagem, **começaríamos** tudo de novo outra vez.

## Exercício 18: Particípio Passado / Exercise 18: Past Participle

**18.1.** Finding the past participle.

18.1.1. O filme foi **visto** por milhares de pessoas.
18.1.2. As flores que ela me deu estão **estragadas**.
18.1.3. A carta já foi **enviada**.
18.1.4. Quando eu cheguei à oficina, o meu carro já tinha sido **arranjado**.
18.1.5. As teorias científicas serão **apresentadas** na reunião.

18.1.6. Em tribunal provou-se que ele tinha **dito** a verdade.
18.1.7. Ele e eu temos **trabalhado** muito esta semana.
18.1.8. Quando ele chegou ao aeroporto, o avião já tinha **partido**.
18.1.9. Uma nova música foi **cantada** pelos artistas no concerto.
18.1.10. Ele não se interessa pelos prémios que tem **ganho**.

## *Exercício 19: Conjuntivo (Subjuntivo) / Exercise 19: Subjunctive*

**19.1.** Phrases used with the present subjunctive.

19.1.1. **Mesmo que** tu não gostes, não mostres má cara.
19.1.2. Eu não posso ir ao concerto **embora** goste da banda.
19.1.3. Ele vai falar com ele **mal** acabe de comer.
19.1.4. **Caso** você tenha tempo, podemos tomar um café juntos.
19.1.5. Vou mandar um e-mail à Dina **para que** que ela tenha toda a informação necessária.
19.1.6. Nós amanhã vamos à praia, **a não ser que** chova!
19.1.7. **Não acho que** ele venha à festa hoje. Ele está doente.
19.1.8. **Talvez** ele ganhe um prémio pelo seu trabalho notável.
19.1.9. **Oxalá** tudo corra bem na consulta com o médico.
19.1.10. **Espero que** que o sol brilhe amanhã.

**19.2.** Present subjunctive, regular and irregular.

19.2.1. Embora ela **seja** pobre, conseguiu comprar uma casa.
19.2.2. Caso vocês o **vejam**, digam-lhe que eu preciso de falar com ele.
19.2.3. Eu preciso de um advogado que me **ajude**.
19.2.4. É preciso que nós **organizemos** tudo antes de ela chegar.
19.2.5. Porquê é que ele quer que eu lhe **entregue** o relatório hoje?
19.2.6. Quer **faça** bom ou mau tempo, eu hoje vou correr 5 quilómetros.
19.2.7. Espero que eles **estejam** em casa hoje.
19.2.8. Compre os bilhetes para o concerto antes que **esgotem**.
19.2.9. Ela fala com toda a gente, embora não **conheça** ninguém.
19.2.10. É necessário que eu **saiba** a verdade agora.

**19.3.** Phrases to use with the future subjunctive.

19.3.1. Para **onde** ela for, ela avisa sempre os pais.
19.3.2. Vocês podem escrever o relatório **como** vocês quiserem.
19.3.3. Eu vou fazer o trabalho **conforme** as ordens que eu receber.

19.3.4. **Quando** chegares ao escritório, liga para o teu irmão.

19.3.5. **Enquanto** a lei proteger a corrupção, a situação do país nunca vai melhorar.

19.3.6. Eu posso preparar um café agora **se** o senhor quiser.

19.3.7. Sr. Ministro, **enquanto** o senhor jogar o nosso jogo, nunca terá problemas de dinheiro.

19.3.8. Nós vos avisaremos **logo que** chegarmos ao nosso destino.

19.3.9. **Se** chover nós ficamos em casa.

19.3.10. Vocês nunca devem fazer o vosso trabalho **como** ele vos disser. Vocês devem ser originais.

**19.4.** Future subjunctive, regular and irregular.

19.4.1. Quando eles **chegarem**, vai estar tudo pronto.

19.4.2. Onde quer que elas **vão** de férias, elas vão mandar um postal.

19.4.3. Quanto mais tu **trabalhares**, menos tempo tens para saber o que se passa no mundo.

19.4.4. Quanto menos bagagem nós **levarmos**, mais fácil será a viagem.

19.4.5. Se nós **corrermos** muito, podemos ganhar a corrida.

19.4.6. Se eles **abrirem** a janela, o ar fresco vai poder entrar.

19.4.7. Eles poderão organizar melhor a vida se **controlarem** o consumismo.

19.4.8. Quando você **terminar** o seu curso, poderá ajudar muita gente.

19.4.9. Ninguém vai perceber nada, se (vocês) não **prestarem** atenção.

19.4.10. É necessário nós estarmos atentos quando a verdadeira notícia **chegar**.

**19.5.** Imperfect subjunctive, regular and irregular.

19.5.1. Se eles **deixassem** avançar mais a tecnologia, teríamos uma vida melhor.

19.5.2. Se tu **comparasses** os jornais com a internet, terias outra visão do mundo.

19.5.3. Agradecia que o senhor me **desse** o seu nome e o seu número de contacto.

19.5.4. O patrão pediu-nos que **trouxéssemos** o carro hoje.

19.5.5. Gostava de comprar um carro que **fosse** completamente elétrico.

19.5.6. Estou a morrer de fome! E se **fôssemos** almoçar?

19.5.7. Se eu **tivesse** tempo, faria uma viagem ao mundo por um ano.

19.5.8. Se eu **pudesse** escolher viver noutro país, escolheria o Uruguai.

19.5.9. Se eu não **tivesse** possibilidade de ter uma casa, vivia numa caravana.

19.5.10. Eu praticava surf se **vivesse** perto do mar.

## *Exercício 20: Imperativo / Exercise 20: Imperative*

**20.1.** Instructing employees.

20.1.1. Carlos e Pedro **trabalhem** mais!

20.1.2. Américo, **mostre**-me o que já fez!

20.1.3. Maria, não **beba** enquanto trabalha!

20.1.4. António, por favor **faça** uma lista do material necessário.

20.1.5. Cristina, **mande**-me a informação por e-mail.

20.1.6. Não **fale** comigo agora! Estou muito nervoso!

20.1.7. João, **organize** os documentos para a reunião.

20.1.8. Ó Pedro, **dá** uma vista de olhos nisto.

20.1.9. Amigos **venham** comigo!

20.1.10. Pedro, não **compres** o carro mais caro.

## *Exercício 21: Infinitivo Pessoal / Exercise 21: Personal Infinitive*

**21.1.** Filling in the personal infinitive.

21.1.1. A Sofia ficou muito feliz ao **saber** que foi promovida.

21.1.2. Não preparem o jantar até eu **voltar**.

21.1.3. Sem nós **sabermos** falar português é difícil viver em Angola.

21.1.4. Apesar de eles **fazerem** barulho, os vizinhos não reclamam.

21.1.5. Não é muito provável amanhã **estar** bom tempo.

21.1.6. Temos que arrumar a casa depois da festa **terminar**.

21.1.7. Depois das pessoas **irem embora** podemos conversar.

21.1.8. Antes dos convidados **chegarem** temos de ter tudo pronto.

21.1.9. O José não vem trabalhar hoje por **estar** doente.

21.1.10. O Francisco e a Cláudia estão a estudar português para **viverem** no Brasil.

## *Exercício 22: Pretérito Mais-Que-Perfeito do Indicativo / Exercise 22: Past Pluperfect Indicative*

**22.1.** Filling in the pluperfect.

22.1.1. Quando nós chegámos à sala a reunião já **tinha começado**.

22.1.2. Ontem preparei um filme bom para vermos mas a Maria já o **tinha visto**.

22.1.3. O comboio já **tinha partido** quando eles chegaram à estação.

22.1.4. Elas **tinham acabado** de sair com o Pedro quando o táxi chegou.

22.1.5. Quando ele chegou ao escritório, a secretária já **tinha enviado** o e-mail.

22.1.6. Quando precisei de pagar o meu café, vi que me **tinha esquecido** do dinheiro.
22.1.7. O teste foi fácil porque eu **tinha estudado** bem a matéria.
22.1.8. Eu queria telefonar ao Zé, mas não sabia onde **tinha posto** o número dele.
22.1.9. Eu não comprei os bilhetes hoje porque eu já os **tinha comprado** antes.
22.1.10. A Maria já **tinha feito** o chá quando eles chegaram.

### Exercício 23: Pronomes / Exercise 23: Pronouns

**23.1.** Personal pronouns.

| | |
|---|---|
| 1. **nós** | 2. **mim** |
| 3. **ela** | 4. **elas** |
| 5. **eu** | 6. **tu** |
| 7. **o senhor** | 8. **eles** |
| 9. **ele** | 10. **a senhora** |
| 11. **a gente** | 12. **as senhoras** |
| 13. **os senhores** | |

**23.2.** Reflexive Pronouns.

23.2.1. Eu chamo-**me** António.
23.2.2. Nós reunimo-**nos** depois do almoço.
23.2.3. Ele lembra-**se** do seu tempo de escola.
23.2.4. A senhora chama-**se** Maria Castro?
23.2.5. Elas encontram-**se** sempre no restaurante.
23.2.6. No cinema, gosto de **me** sentar perto dos meus amigos.
23.2.7. Tu nunca **te** lembras do Rafael.
23.2.8. Eles atrasaram-**se** e perderam o princípio do filme.
23.2.9. Nós sentimo-**nos** bem.
23.2.10. Porquê o senhor **se** preocupa tanto?

**23.3.** Direct Object Pronouns.

23.3.1. Eu quero comprar este livro. Eu quero **comprá-lo** barato.
23.3.2. Ela leva o Manuel ao cinema. Ela **leva-o** de carro.
23.3.3. Eles trazem os livros no saco. Eles **trazem-nos** todos.
23.3.4. Tu tens que avisar o Paulo. Tens que **o avisar** hoje!

23.3.5. O senhor levou o carro para o escritório. O senhor **levou-o** cedo.

23.3.6. As senhoras querem água fresca, ou **querem-na** natural?

23.3.7. Eu não quero a salada simples. Eu **quero-a** com tomate e cebola.

23.3.8.  Eu entendo o Pedro, mas quando ele fala rápido eu não **o entendo**.

23.3.9. Na festa, nós bebemos vinho, mas nós não **o bebemos** todo.

23.3.10. Afinal comprei o carro. **Comprei-o** ontem.

23.3.11. Eu vou trazer o livro em breve. Eu vou **trazê-lo** até ao fim da semana.

23.3.12. Hoje as empresas comandam os governos. Elas **comandam-nos** todos.

23.3.13. Os progamas de TV controlam a mente. Eles **controlam-nos** a todos.

23.3.14. O Manuel quer comprar um barco. Ele **quer comprá-lo** novo.

**23.4.** Indirect Object Pronouns.

23.4.1. A Paula e o Ivo gostam do vinho. Eu vou dar-**lhes** mais vinho.

23.4.2. Ele quis a informação hoje. Eu enviei-**lhe** as informações imediatamente.

23.4.3. Eles querem conhecer a Joana. Vou apresentar-**lhes** a Joana na festa.

23.4.4. Eu tenho o meu carro avariado. Ele empresta-**me** o carro dele hoje.

23.4.5. Porque nós gostamos de livros, ele dá-**nos** um livro no nosso aniversário.

23.4.6. Quando tu precisas de dinheiro, eu dou-**te** algum dinheiro.

23.4.7. Dr. Fonseca, o seu quarto é lá em cima. Eu mostro-**lhe** o quarto.

23.4.8. A Tânia precisa de comer fruta. Maçãs fazem-**lhe** bem.

23.4.9. Sei que ela **lhe** escreveu uma carta porque eu vi ele ler a carta.

23.4.10. Eu preciso de uma caneta. Podes emprestar-**me** a tua?

**23.5.** Indefinite Pronouns – algum / alguma / alguns / algumas / alguma coisa / alguém.

23.5.1. David, você viu **alguma coisa** estranha no escritório hoje?

23.5.2. Eu vi **alguns** copos usados na mesa e **algumas** secretárias fora do lugar.

23.5.3. A Maria também viu **alguém** que não conhecia.

23.5.4. Claro! Quando eu entro no escritório, vejo **algum** pão, e doce por todo o lado!

23.5.5. O José também viu **alguma** água no chão.

23.5.6. Vamos ter **alguns** problemas para limpar tudo.

23.5.7. **Alguém** tem que nos ajudar.

**23.6.** Indefinite Pronouns – nenhum / nenhuma / nenhuns / nenhumas / nada / ninguém.

23.6.1. **Ninguém** sabe o que aconteceu ontem à noite.

23.6.2. Não há evidência de **nenhum** assalto.

23.6.3. As pessoas dos escritórios vizinhos não viram **nada** também.

23.6.4. Estranho! **Nenhum** documento desapareceu.

23.6.5. Bem, pelo menos não temos **nenhumas** consequências.

23.6.6. **Nenhuma** das instalações foi danificada.

23.6.7. No fundo, **nada** aconteceu.

**23.7.** Indefinite Pronouns – muito / muita / muitos / muitas / pouco / pouca / poucos / poucas.

23.7.1. **Muita** gente fala Português.

23.7.2. **Muitos** alunos que estudam e praticam frequentemente alcançam bons resultados.

23.7.3. O Jamie tem **muitas** amigas bonitas?

23.7.4. Não. Ele tem **poucas** amigas bonitas, mas elas são simpáticas.

23.7.5. Eu tenho **pouco** dinheiro para comprar um carro novo.

23.7.6. Ela quer fazer um bolo, mas tem **poucos** ingredientes.

23.7.7. Eles têm **pouco** tempo para terminar o trabalho.

23.7.8. **Pouca** gente sabe que a cultura só serve os interesses de certas entidades.

**23.8.** Indefinite Pronouns – todo (o) / toda (a) / todos (os) / todas (as) / tudo.

23.8.1. Eu conheço **todos os** países da América Latina.

23.8.2. Ela arrumou a casa **toda** para a festa.

23.8.3. Ela organizou **tudo**.

23.8.4. Quando eles lêem, eles reconhecem **todas as** palavras em português.

23.8.5. Nós gostamos de puzzles. É divertido juntar **todas as** peças.

23.8.6. **Todas as** línguas estão sujeitas a interpretação subjetiva.

23.8.7. Quando eu visitar o México, eu quero fotografar **tudo**.

**23.9.** Indefinite Pronouns – tanto / tanta / tantos / tantas.

23.9.1. Há **tantas** pessoas na miséria, enquanto que outras desperdiçam recursos.

23.9.2. Ela tem **tantos** amigos que às vezes se esquece do nome deles.

23.9.3. No Algarve há **tantos** turistas no Verão!

23.9.4. Ele tem **tanto** trabalho que não pode falar com ninguém agora.

23.9.5. Nas ruas de Lisboa há **tantos** carros que quase não há espaço para as pessoas.

23.9.6. Esta semana temos demasiado trabalho. Temos **tantas** reuniões!

23.9.7. Um tornado causa **tanta** destruição que ás vezes é impossivel calcular os danos.

**23.10.** Indefinite Pronouns – outro / outra / outros / outras.

23.10.1. Este carro já está velho. Eu preciso de comprar **outro**.
23.10.2. Umas vezes ela vai ao cimena, **outras** vezes ela vai ao teatro.
23.10.3. Nós não gostamos desta casa. Preferimos a **outra**.
23.10.4. Este dicionário é bom, mas o **outro** é muito melhor.
23.10.5. O senhor tem de apresentar este impresso, não o **outro**.
23.10.6. Eu queria **outra** cerveja, por favor.
23.10.7. Este sistema está corrupto. Precisamos de **outro** totalmente novo.

**23.11.** Write the opposites.

23.11.1. Nós **não** temos **nenhuma** sala vaga.
23.11.2. Ele bebe **pouca** cerveja.
23.11.3. Hoje nós tivemos **pouco** trabalho.
23.11.4. **Ninguém** telefonou.
23.11.5. **Pouca** gente admira Jacque Fresco.
23.11.6. **Ninguém** fez o exercício.

### *Exercício 24: Possessivos / Exercise 24: Possessives*

**24.1.** Possessive pronouns and adjectives.

24.1.1. Sr António, onde está **o seu** telefone?
24.1.2. **O meu** telefone está no meu bolso.
24.1.3. Eu vi o Sr António com o telefone **dele**.
24.1.4. Dona Maria, onde estão **as suas** filhas?
24.1.5. **As minhas** filhas estão na piscina.
24.1.6. Dona Ana, como estão **os seus** sogros?
24.1.7. **Os meus** sogros estão bem, obrigada.
24.1.8. A Maria já arranjou o carro **dela**?
24.1.9. O pai **dela** tem que pagar primeiro.
24.1.10. João e Pedro, como estão **os vossos** pais?
24.1.11. **Os nossos** pais estão bem, obrigado.
24.1.12. Esta bola é **vossa**?
24.1.13. Sim, essa bola é **nossa**, obrigado.
24.1.14. Este carro é **seu**, Sr Ivo?
24.1.15. Não. O carro é de um amigo **meu**.

## Exercício 25: Demonstrativos / Exercise 25: Demonstratives

**25.1.** Demonstratives: este, esta, estes, estas.

| | |
|---|---|
| 1. **este** livro | 2. **esta** casa |
| 3. **estas** guitarras | 4. **estas** mesas |
| 5. **estes** óculos | 6. **estas** cadeiras |
| 7. **estas** flores | 8. **estes** bolos |
| 9. **este** quadro | 10. **estas** mulheres |
| 11. **esta** cidade | 12. **estas** estradas |
| 13. **estes** homens | 14. **este** filme |
| 15. **esta** moto | 16. **este** dicionário |

**25.2.** Demonstratives: esse, essa, esses, essas.

| | |
|---|---|
| 1. **esse** livro | 2. **essa** casa |
| 3. **essas** guitarras | 4. **essas** mesas |
| 5. **esses** óculos | 6. **essas** cadeiras |
| 7. **essas** flores | 8. **esses** bolos |
| 9. **esse** quadro | 10. **essas** mulheres |
| 11. **essa** cidade | 12. **essas** estradas |
| 13. **esses** homens | 14. **esse** filme |
| 15. **essa** moto | 16. **esse** dicionário |

**25.3.** Demonstratives: aquele, aquela, aqueles, aquelas.

| | |
|---|---|
| 1. **aquele** livro | 2. **aquela** casa |
| 3. **aquelas** guitarras | 4. **aquelas** mesas |
| 5. **aqueles** óculos | 6. **aquelas** cadeiras |
| 7. **aquelas** flores | 8. **aqueles** bolos |
| 9. **aquele** quadro | 10. **aquelas** mulheres |
| 11. **aquela** cidade | 12. **aquelas** estradas |

13. **aqueles** homens                    14. **aquele** filme

15. **aquela** moto                       16. **aquele** dicionário

## Exercício 26: Negativas / Exercise 26: Negatives

**26.1.** Filling in the negative word.

26.1.1. Eu não consegui comer **nada**.
26.1.2. Eu nunca vi **nenhuma** série de TV em espanhol.
26.1.3. Nem eu **nem** ele gostámos do filme.
26.1.4. Nós não fomos a lado **nenhum**.
26.1.5. Na polícia ele **nunca** disse nada!
26.1.6. Eu **nunca** comeria carne ou peixe. Gosto demais dos animais.
26.1.7. **Ninguém** jamais se lembra das mentiras que ele nos disse.
26.1.8. Eu não me importo **de modo algum** levar o Tiago ao hospital.
26.1.9. Nós **nunca** trabalhámos com energias alternativas, mas gostávamos muito!
26.1.10. Eu não posso fechar a casa **sem** ele sair de casa.

## Exercício 27: Interrogativos / Exercise 27: Question words

**27.1.** Filling in the question word.

27.1.1. **Quando** é o concerto?
27.1.2. **De que côr** é o seu carro?
27.1.3. **Quem** é o diretor do jornal?
27.1.4. **Porquê** é que não pode vir à festa?
27.1.5. **De onde / Donde** é a Maria originalmente?
27.1.6. **Quantas** pessoas vão ao jantar?
27.1.7. **Qual** é o meu copo? Estão aqui tantos!
27.1.8. **Há quanto tempo** vocês vivem em Lisboa?
27.1.9. **A que horas** é a reunião?
27.1.10. **Para que** é que ele precisa disso?

## Exercício 28: Números Cardinais / Exercise 28: Cardinal Numbers

**28.1.** Filling in the numbers.

28.1.1. Quarenta mil, quatrocentos e quarenta e quatro, vírgula quarenta e quatro.
28.1.2. Vinte mil, duzentos e vinte e dois, vírgula vinte e dois.

28.1.3. Sessenta mil, seiscentos e sessenta e seis, vírgula sessenta e seis.

28.1.4. Cinquenta mil, quinhentos e cinquenta e cinco, vírgula cinquenta e cinco.

28.1.5. Setenta mil, setecentos e setenta e sete, vírgula setenta e sete.

28.1.6. Trinta mil, trezentos e trinta e três, vírgula trinta e três.

28.1.7. Noventa mil, novecentos e noventa e nove, vírgula noventa e nove.

28.1.8. Oitenta mil, oitocentos e oitenta e oito, vírgula oitenta e oito.

28.1.9. Cem mil e um, vírgula dez.

28.1.10. Quatro milhões, trezentos e setenta mil, quatrocentos e quarenta e quatro, vírgula quarenta e quatro.

# Glossary

**Adjective**

*A word that gives more information about a noun.*
e.g., brown, lovely, short, proven, soft, annoying.

**Adverb**

*A word that gives more information about a word other than a noun.*
e.g., quietly, then, slowly, deeply, there, most words which end with 'ly'.

**Articulation**

*The orchestrated movement and positioning of the mouth and vocal organs required to produce intelligible speech.*

**Augmentative**

*A word that is modified with either a prefix or a suffix to denote that it is bigger or better than normal. The opposite of diminuitive.*
e.g., megastar, supermarket, etc.

**Auxiliary**

*A type of verb which is used to 'help' a participle or the infinitive of another verb to form a compound tense.*
e.g., would, can, might.

**Cardinal**

*Standard numbering.*
e.g., 1, 2, 3 (See Ordinal).

**Compound**

*A grammatical feature which is made up of more than one word (for verbs, this means using an auxiliary).*
e.g., had been, would have gone, could do.

**Conditional**

*The name of a mood in which the tenses require a condition to be met for the action of the verb to occur.*

**Conjunction**

*A word that joins two thoughts or phrases together in a sentence.*
e.g., and, because, therefore, however.

**Conjugation**

*Lit. 'Joining Together'. In grammar, this word is used to refer to the act of joining different endings to the stem of a verb, or to differentiate the different endings of the infinitive forms of verbs.*
e.g., In Portuguese, 'ar' verbs are 'first conjugation', 'er' and 'or' verbs are 'second conjugation', and 'ir' verbs are 'third conjugation'.

**Continuous**

*A verb form that denotes an ongoing action, making use of the present participle.*
e.g., he is walking, she was skipping.

**Contraction**

*Where two words are merged into one, often with the loss of one or more letters.*
e.g., I'll, haven't, she'd, I've.

**Definite Article**

*The.*

**Diacritic; Diacritical Mark**

*An extra symbol that is placed above or below a letter to modify the pronunciation or clarify the meaning of a word.*

**Diminuitive**

*A word that is modified with either a prefix or a suffix to denote that it is smaller or cuter than normal. The opposite of augmentative.*
e.g., duckling, booklet.

**Diphthong**

*A pair of vowels which is pronounced as a single syllable.*

**Gerund**

*See Present Participle.*

| | |
|---|---|
| **Imperative** | *The name of a mood and its tense in which the verb is issued as a command or request.* |
| **Imperfect** | *A verb form that denotes that the verb's action is or was ongoing or that the completion or duration of the action is unspecified.* |
| **Imperfect Indicative** | *The tense which deals with actions that took place in the past, but were ongoing for a period of time and where the time of completion of the action is not specified.* e.g., I was running, we were thinking, they were going, he was walking. |
| **Impersonal** | *Not relating to a 'person' (in the grammatical sense – see 'person').* |
| **Impersonal Infinitive** | *The basic form of a verb from which all other forms and tenses are derived. Usually simply referred to as 'the infinitive'.* |
| **Indefinite Article** | *A, an, some.* |
| **Indicative** | *The name of a mood in which all of the tenses imply certainty of action.* |
| **Infinitive** | *The basic form of a verb from which all other forms and tenses are derived (also known as the impersonal infinitive). Also the name of a mood which contains the personal and impersonal infinitive tenses.* |
| **Irregular Verb** | *A verb which does not follow standard rules for conjugation.* |

**Mood**  
*The category to which one or more tenses belong. All tenses that are categorized according to the same mood have certain characteristics in common.*  
e.g. all tenses that belong to the 'subjunctive' mood, carry some degree of uncertainty.

**Noun**  
*The name of an object, concept, or entity.*  
e.g., (a) walk, house, microphone, concept, thinker, proposition, (an) attack.

**Noun Phrase**  
*A noun, along with one or more modifiying words, which could be represented by a single pronoun.*  
e.g., world champion, guiding principle, baseball cap.

**Ordinal**  
*Numbering according to order.*  
e.g., 1st; 2nd; 3rd (See Cardinal).

**Object**  
*The person or thing having the verb 'done' to/for/on them (whom).*

**Participle**  
*A word which is formed from a verb, but can be used as an adjective, or noun.*

**Past Participle**  
*A word formed from a verb which can be used as an adjective or in a compound verb tense to provide a description or describe a completed action – usually formed by adding the letters 'ed' to the stem of a verb in English.*

**Past Tense**  
*See Preterite Indicative.*

**Perfect**  
*A verb form that denotes that the verb action is in the past and has been completed.*

**Person**                    *In grammar, this word is used to denote the party or parties who perform the action denoted by a verb.*
i.e. first person = I/we
second person = you
third person = he/she/it/they.

**Preposition**               *A word or group of words which place a noun or noun phrase in space or time.*
e.g., in, at, on, in front of, with reference to.

**Present Indicative**        *The tense which deals with actions being performed at the present time – either directly or as a general rule.*
e.g., I run, we think, they go, he walks.

**Present Participle**        *A word formed from a verb which can be used as an adjective or in a compound verb tense to provide a current or ongoing description – always derived by adding the letters 'ing' to the stem of a verb in English. Also known as the 'gerund'.*

**Present Tense**             *See Present Indicative.*

**Preterite Indicative**      *The tense which deals with actions that were performed directly in the past.*
e.g., I ran, we thought, they went, he walked.

**Progressive**               *A verb form that denotes an ongoing action in progress and of limited duration or unfinished.*
e.g., I am being patient, he was making the cake.

**Pronoun**                   *A small word to replace a noun – usually to avoid repetition.*
e.g., you, him, them, it, she, thou.

**Proper Noun** — *An abstract name assignment.*
e.g., Fred, Emily, Paris, Brazil.

**Radical-Changing** — *A type of verb whose stem can change in spelling or pronunciation, depending on person, plurality, or tense.*

**Reflexive** — *Causing the subject and object to refer to the same individual.*

**Regular Verb** — *A verb which follows standard rules for conjugation.*

**Simple** — *A grammatical feature which is made up of a single word.*

**Stem** — *The part of the basic form of a verb which characterizes all of its forms, and usually does not change in spelling or pronunciation (see 'radical-changing').*

**Subject** — *The person or thing 'doing' the verb (who).*

**Subjunctive** — *The name of a mood in which all of the tenses carry some degree of uncertainty. Also known as the conjunctive.*

**Tense** — *The placement of a verb in time or circumstance.*

**Triphthong** — *A group of 3 vowels which are pronounced together as a single syllable.*

**Verb** — *A word denoting an action or process being carried out.*
e.g., to walk, to think, to love, to work, to go, to be.

# Index

## A

acute accent.................................................................15

adjective......................................................................53

adverb.........................................................................58

    interrogative.........................................................218

alphabet.....................................................................231

animals.......................................................................242

article...........................................................................41

augmentative..............................................................63

auxiliary verb...............................51, 77, **107,** 134, 173

## B

birds...........................................................................242

body (parts of)...........................................................236

## C

cedilla..........................................................................15

circumflex....................................................................15

colour........................................................................224

compound..................................................................173

    verb.....................................................................107

conditional............................................................93, **129**

conditional perfect..............................................129, **176**

conjugation.....................................................51, **81,** 245

conjunction..................................................................65

conjunctive................................................................144

consonant.....................................................................22

continuous..................................................................244

contraction...................................................................63

## D

dates..........................................................................233

## E

## F

## G

## H

# W

# '

Made in the USA
Coppell, TX
22 February 2021